MW00824367

The Professional ScrumMaster's Handbook

A collection of tips, tricks, and war stories to help
the professional ScrumMaster break the chains of
traditional organization and management

Stacia Viscardi

[PACKT] enterprise 88

PUBLISHING   professional expertise distilled

BIRMINGHAM - MUMBAI

The Professional ScrumMaster's Handbook

Copyright © 2013 Packt Publishing

All rights reserved. No part of this book may be reproduced, stored in a retrieval system, or transmitted in any form or by any means, without the prior written permission of the publisher, except in the case of brief quotations embedded in critical articles or reviews.

Every effort has been made in the preparation of this book to ensure the accuracy of the information presented. However, the information contained in this book is sold without warranty, either express or implied. Neither the author, nor Packt Publishing, and its dealers and distributors will be held liable for any damages caused or alleged to be caused directly or indirectly by this book.

Packt Publishing has endeavored to provide trademark information about all of the companies and products mentioned in this book by the appropriate use of capitals. However, Packt Publishing cannot guarantee the accuracy of this information.

First published: April 2013

Production Reference: 1120413

Published by Packt Publishing Ltd.
Livery Place
35 Livery Street
Birmingham B3 2PB, UK.

ISBN 978-1-84968-802-4

www.packtpub.com

Cover Image by Artie Ng (artherng@yahoo.com.au)

Credits

Author
Stacia Viscardi

Reviewers
Lee Devin

Steve Spearman

Acquisition Editor
Erol Staveley

Lead Technical Editor
Neeshma Ramakrishnan

Technical Editors
Jalasha D'costa

Ankita R. Meshram

Project Coordinator
Abhishek Kori

Proofreader
Jonathan Todd

Indexer
Monica Ajmera Mehta

Graphics
Aditi Gajjar

Production Coordinator
Prachali Bhiwandkar

Aditi Gajjar

Cover Work
Aditi Gajjar

Foreword

I've known Stacia Viscardi for many years now, since the very beginning of my connection with the Agile software world. In fact, Stacia introduced me to that world and has guided me from (alas!) a distance ever since. I have marveled at her knowledge, her skills, and (rare in her field) her sly and generous wit. She's plenty nerdy, Stacia, but unlike most of her colleagues, she makes wonderfully unexpected connections between this and that; connections that always illuminate all sides of this, all the innards of that. These surprises, little time bombs of unforeseen pleasure, make her writing exceptional in a field not known for wit or surprise.

Stacia doesn't browbeat you with erudition or intimidate you with exotica. She simply sets her imagination to work on connections she sees that you may not have. Or, if you have seen them, she shines her light on a different facet than the one you may find familiar. That light has qualities rare in the software biz. It's warm, that light. It invites you to join, to include, and to enjoy. It makes no pushy effort to impress you with its brilliance. It illuminates her subject, the processes that create that subject, and her idiosyncratic, persuasive take on it.

When you read this book, you'll find yourself in wonderful company. If you know Stacia's work, this book will confirm your admiration and gratitude. If this book is your introduction to her, brace yourself!

You're in for a treat!

Lee Devin
Consultant, AgileEvolution,
Senior Consultant, Innovation Practice Cutter Consortium

About the Author

Stacia Viscardi is an Agile coach, Certified Scrum Trainer, and organizational transformation expert, devoted to creating energized and excited teams that delight their customers and inspire others. With humble beginnings in Port Arthur, Texas, Stacia found her niche as a Manufacturing Project Manager in the early nineties; she landed in the technology world in 1999 and never looked back. In 2003 she became the sixty-second Certified ScrumMaster (there are now over 200,000!), and founded AgileEvolution in 2006. She has helped companies such as Cisco Systems, Martha Stewart Living, Primavera, DoubleClick, Google, Razorfish, MyPublisher, Washington Post, and many others find their way to agility. Co-author of the *Software Project Manager's Bridge to Agility*, Stacia has taught Agile in 17 countries and is active in the ScrumAlliance as a CST and trusted community advisor. When she is not doing Agile stuff, she is training for a marathon or other long race or spending cozy nights on the sofa with her husband Chris, and dogs Jax and Cobi.

A self-proclaimed process nerd, she loves helping teams and organizations discover the Scrum/XP/Lean mash-ups that enables focused, flexible, and fast delivery of products. She created the blog HelloScrum to share knowledge, tips, and tricks with Scrum practitioners, and co-founded KnowAgile, an Agile testing website.

Stacia has co-authored *The Software Project Manager's Bridge to Agility* with Michele Sliger (2008, Addison-Wesley).

Acknowledgment

Over the past decade, I have met thousands of people who are passionate about finding new and exciting ways to work, people whose hearts are in their work every day, where writing software and creating great products is not only the company's lifeblood but also their own. These people work extremely hard, put in many late nights, trudge through moments of trying frustration, and yet do it all over again to bring awesome technologies to the everyday person. I am humbled to have worked in their presence, and without them this book would not be possible. A million thanks!

Chris, you are the best husband a girl could ever want. I knew so many years ago that you were my one great true love in life. Thank you for being so supportive while my head was stuck in this book for the past year.

I am so grateful to my grandparents for their infinite supply of support and love, and to my parents for teaching me to be self-reliant, and for instilling a hard-nosed, never-quit work ethic. Barbara and Tony, thank you for loving me and treating me like family. Alicia, I couldn't imagine a greater sister — thank you for your support and love. And Aunt Maureen — my other mother — to the moon and back!

I'd like to thank Ken Schwaber for teaching me true Scrum. It is something much greater than I was capable of realizing so long ago; Lee Devin for being a great friend and for helping me find my edge and coming to the realization that no, I do not want to be an actor; Maria Thelin for her intelligence, friendship, and expert orienteering instruction; Dr. Rafael Landaeta for support and great ideas; Karen Delfau for taking a chance on me; and the CST and CSC community of brilliant and scandalous folks. I owe many martinis to Steve Spearman (Agile coach extraordinaire!) and Lee (Master Dramaturge), who worked those red pens through modifiers, tapeworms, and "izzes" and challenged me to take command of my ideas. Immense thanks to Abhishek, Neeshma, Erol, and many others at Packt who brought this book to life. I'm humbled by the loyalty of my dogs, Cobi and Jax, who sat by my side through many days and nights of typing, editing, and cursing. And finally, life wouldn't be worth living if not for running on the trails, where I can clear my head and think fresh, where God undeniably exists and always leads me to find myself.

About the Reviewers

Lee Devin taught theater while doing a PhD at Indiana University (1958-62), then at the University of Virginia (1962-66), Vassar College (1966-70), and Swarthmore College (1970-2002). He's an Equity actor and has played leading roles in productions from Shakespeare to Tennessee Williams. He has a residuals check from SAG in the amount of $0.01, to commemorate a brilliant movie career. With Rob Austin of the Copenhagen Business School he wrote *Artful Making; What Managers Need to Know about How Artists Work*, published in 2003. Stanford University Press published their next book, *The Soul of Design: Harnessing the Power of Plot to Create Extraordinary Products*, about the aesthetics of special things (gadgets that are better somehow than the sum of their parts would lead you to believe), in September of 2012. He and Rob have written numerous articles, including (with Erin Sullivan) *Ooops*, which appeared in the Wall Street Journal. Lee's a Senior Consultant in the Innovation practice at the Cutter Consortium, for whom he wrote *An Innovative Frame of Mind* and *Planning to Get Lucky*. He has taught many workshops at Agile meetings, Scrum gatherings, and software conferences. He has collaborated on various projects with Stacia Viscardi and Lyssa Adkins. He's also the Senior Dramaturg at the People's Light and Theatre and currently at work on writing projects that interfere with his trout fishing, and cause him to neglect his grandchildren.

I'd like to acknowledge the support, for my work on this book and many other projects, of Lyssa Adkins, Stacia Viscardi, and Robert D. Austin. And, in a class by herself, beloved wife, Abigail Adams.

Steve Spearman is an Agile coach and trainer. He has 30 years of experience in corporate software development settings including 20 years in a variety of leadership roles. Steve has been a software developer, architect, project manager, and a senior manager of teams encompassing all those areas. His enterprise experience includes Bell Laboratories, Lucent, Avaya, and Cisco Systems.

Steve is now providing Agile-focused training and coaching to companies ranging from late-stage startups to large corporations. Steve is associated with a number of leading firms, such as AgileEvolution, SwiftAscent, and TekSystems.

Steve has a BA in Psychology and a Masters in Computer Science. His certifications include: PMI-ACP, PMP, CSP, Certified Scrum Product Owner, Certified ScrumMaster, and SAFe Program Consultant.

www.PacktPub.com

Support files, eBooks, discount offers and more

You might want to visit www.PacktPub.com for support files and downloads related to your book.

Did you know that Packt offers eBook versions of every book published, with PDF and ePub files available? You can upgrade to the eBook version at www.PacktPub.com and as a print book customer, you are entitled to a discount on the eBook copy. Get in touch with us at service@packtpub.com for more details.

At www.PacktPub.com, you can also read a collection of free technical articles, sign up for a range of free newsletters and receive exclusive discounts and offers on Packt books and eBooks.

http://PacktLib.PacktPub.com

Do you need instant solutions to your IT questions? PacktLib is Packt's online digital book library. Here, you can access, read and search across Packt's entire library of books.

Why Subscribe?

- Fully searchable across every book published by Packt
- Copy and paste, print and bookmark content
- On demand and accessible via web browser

Free Access for Packt account holders

If you have an account with Packt at www.PacktPub.com, you can use this to access PacktLib today and view nine entirely free books. Simply use your login credentials for immediate access.

Instant Updates on New Packt Books

Get notified! Find out when new books are published by following @PacktEnterprise on Twitter, or the *Packt Enterprise* Facebook page.

Table of Contents

Preface   **1**

**Chapter 1: Scrum – A Brief Review of the Basics
(and a Few Interesting Tidbits)**   **7**

  The problem   **7**
  A brief history   **8**
  The underlying concepts of Scrum   **10**
    Complex adaptive systems   10
    The empirical process control barstool   14
    Scrum core values   15
    Scrum is inherently lean   17
  Scrum roles   **18**
    Scrum team   18
    Product owner   19
    ScrumMaster   19
  Brief review of the Scrum framework   **20**
    Sprint planning   20
    Daily scrum meeting   21
    Sprint review meeting   21
    Sprint retrospective   22
    Release planning (optional)   22
  Scrum artifacts   **22**
    The product backlog   23
    The sprint backlog   24
    The product increment   24
  Visible progress   **24**
    Release backlog and burndown   24
    Sprint burndown   25
  Dysfunctions or true constraints?   **26**

Is your team ready for Scrum?	**27**
Summary	**27**
Recommended reading	**28**
Chapter 2: Release Planning – Tuning Product Development	**29**
Start at the beginning – product backlog	**32**
Focus product backlogs on users and values	34
Engage the team early	36
Prioritization can be useful for other things	37
Release planning – when will you set your features free?	**39**
Timing of releases and release planning	39
Don't create the software big dig	40
Integrate early and often to mitigate risks	40
Make buffers visible	41
How to conduct a release planning event?	44
Do your homework!	45
Facilitating the release planning meeting	46
Release planning summary	54
Summary	**55**
Recommended reading	**56**
Chapter 3: Sprint Planning – Fine-tune the Sprint Commitment	**57**
Sprint planning basics	**57**
Preparing for sprint planning	**60**
High-octane stories	60
Help the product owner prepare for sprint planning	61
Physical space	62
Visualize the meeting	63
Scratchpad, script, and agenda	65
Running the sprint planning meeting	**67**
Part I – the What and the Why	67
Different types of stories	69
Part II – the How	70
Understanding capacity	70
Talk first, then identify sprint tasks	73
Anyone tasks, expert tasks, and pairing	74
Sprint buffering	76
It helps to see time	76
Team members should talk with each other	77
Don't over-facilitate	78
Sample sprint planning checklist	78
Commit!	80
Improving sprint planning	**81**
Summary	**81**
Recommended reading	**82**

Chapter 4: Sprint! Visible, Collaborative, and Meaningful Work **83**

How the Scrum team should work **84**

Working in a sprint **85**

Sprints shouldn't be just Sprints 85

Beware of the old mind-set creeping into the new paradigm 86

Estimating work **89**

The misunderstood daily scrum meeting **92**

Three questions 94

What did I do since yesterday's meeting? 94

What will I do by tomorrow's meeting? 96

What blocks me from being able to do my work? 96

Do we have to meet every day? 97

Who's allowed to attend the daily scrum? 98

Look ahead at the next sprint's product backlog items 99

It takes a village – communicating during the sprint 100

Individual influences to the work of the sprint **101**

Factor 1 – Openness 101

Factor 2 – Conscientiousness 102

Factor 3 – Extroversion, are you an innie or an outie? 103

Factor 4 – Agreeableness 104

Factor 5 – Neuroticism 104

What's 'Norm'al for one team is not for another **105**

A corporate culture and its impact on teamwork **106**

Team assumptions about management 107

Corporate mind-set opposes the Agile manifesto 107

Fear of empowerment 107

Employees feel like headcount 108

Summary **109**

Recommended reading **109**

Chapter 5: The End? Improving Product and Process One Bite at a Time **111**

Sprint review – inspecting and adapting the product **113**

Product owner acceptance 114

Prior to the sprint review 115

During the sprint review 117

Set the context 118

Give a visual 118

Keep your stories straight 119

Keep everyone focused 120

Does a Scrum team demo incomplete work? 120

See the whole 121

Possible outcomes of a sprint review 123
Don't surprise the product owner 124
Sprint reviews for continuous flow frameworks 124
Sprint review – a time for collaboration and trust 125
**Sprint retrospective – inspecting and adapting
processes and teamwork** **126**
SCRUM is not an acronym for Serious Crud
Required by Upper Management 127
Unearthing information for improvement 129
Set the safety 129
Recall sprint events 130
Ask – What worked well for us? What didn't work so well for us? 130
Who owns the improvement? 131
Prioritize and assign action items 132
Make REAL action items 132
Some different retrospective techniques 133
Change the scenery 134
Visualize the future 134
Team cave art 135
Retrospective yoga/meditation 136
Why should we care about reviews and retrospectives? **136**
Summary **139**
Recommended reading **139**
Chapter 6: The Criticality of Real-time Information **141**
Yesterday's news is old news **142**
Getting the message 143
Through the Scrum microscope **145**
1x magnification – product vision/initiatives 146
2x magnification – the product roadmap 147
4x magnification – the release plan 149
Release the burndown baseline 150
Baseline with updates 151
Team velocity chart 152
A Gantt chart in an Agile project 153
8x magnification – the product backlog 154
What does your user want? 154
16x magnification – the sprint 155
User stories in sprint planning 155
Acceptance criteria 156
Definition of Done 157
Sprint goals 157
Sprint reviews 158
32x magnification – tasks, daily scrums, and other information 158
Daily broadcasts 158
Daily scrums 158

Sprint backlogs	159
Sprint burndown chart	160
What burns down can also burn up	163
64x magnification – read all about it, in the team room!	164
Monitor this!	165
Scrum microscope summary	**165**
When physical taskboards and conversations aren't enough	**167**
Invite stakeholders to sprint reviews	168
Create and distribute reports	168
Waste and obstacle removal	**169**
Summary	**173**
Chapter 7: Scrum Values Expose Fear, Dysfunction, and Waste	**175**
Prepare for change aches and pains	**176**
The five core values of Scrum	**178**
Scrum value #1 – Courage	181
Free the spark	181
Scrum value #2 – Commitment	182
Commitment exposes fear of dedicated, cross-functional Scrum teams	184
What do we do about commitment issues?	190
Scrum value #3 – Openness	191
Secrecy and what to do about it	192
Openness exposes truth about capacity and demand	193
Openness exposes a need for slowing down in order to eventually speed up	196
Scrum value #4 – Focus	197
Lack of focus and personal control = missed commitments	198
Focus reveals waste	199
Focus reveals failure to understand small increments	199
Scrum value #5 – Respect	200
Power, position, and control and what to do about it	201
Summary	**202**
Recommended reading	**202**
Chapter 8: Everyday Leadership for the ScrumMaster and Team	**203**
Everyday leadership	**203**
First, what kind of personality do you have?	**205**
Learn to look into your reflection	206
Portrait of a leader	**209**
Selfless, confident, and accountable	209
Open to feedback	210
Builds trust	210

Leads with Theory Y	211
Honest	212
How to become a better ScrumMaster	**212**
Empower yourself and others!	213
Help others visualize the desired state	214
Influence others	216
Roll up your sleeves and servant-lead	218
Listen more than talk	218
Plant seeds	219
Choose to be happy, focus on the positive	220
Know your communication style	**221**
Loud or quiet?	221
Direct versus passive	222
Switzerland or Supreme Court judge	223
Other ScrumMaster characteristics	**224**
Procrastinator or proactive	224
Teacher	225
Student	225
Scrum buddy	226
Journal/walk up a hill	226
Which ScrumMaster persona are you?	**226**
Techie Taj	226
Bossy Betty	227
Clammed Up Carl	227
Thundering Thea	228
Officer Sophie	228
Summary	**229**
Recommended reading	**229**
Chapter 9: Shaping the Agile Organization	**231**
Will Agile cause a ripple, or a tsunami?	**232**
How does your organization measure up to the Scrum values?	234
What if the Scrum values score is low?	235
Culture change requires a multi-faceted approach	**236**
Illustrating the need for and direction of change	236
Pre-agility survey	237
Waste score	238
Old-fashioned interviews	239
The Agile organization chart and roles matrix	239
Traditional roles in an Agile organization	241
Scaling an Agile mind-set	241

Self-actualizing individuals create an Agile organization   **242**

Goals and metrics that motivate self-actualizing   243

Person has a say in it   243

Understanding what demotivates   244

Standardizing measurements   245

Frequent, multi-perspective feedback   246

CEO scorecard   247

Don't go it alone   **248**

Avoiding Scrum as a panacea   **249**

Why change? What blocks?   **250**

Immunity to change   **251**

Face it, Scrum might not be for your organization   **251**

Summary   **252**

Recommended reading   **252**

Chapter 10: Scrum – Large and Small   **253**

Scrum stops the resource shell game   **254**

Small Scrum   **255**

Big programs, small Scrum   256

When Scrum gets big—dysfunction or constraint?   **257**

Challenge 1: Fearful ScrumMasters   258

Challenge 2: Late integration   259

Challenge 3: Communication across multiple teams   260

Challenge 4: Big picture metrics   261

Customer happiness   264

Time to Market   264

Quality   264

Employee morale   264

Challenge 5: Not done – the root of all evil   265

Challenge 6: Too few product owners   267

Challenge 7: Scaling too much, too fast   268

Challenge 8: Wrong team structure   269

Challenge 9: Distributed teams   270

A real need for a project Grand Poobah   **271**

More tips for large Scrums   273

Agile DNA   **273**

Summary   **274**

Recommended reading   **275**

Chapter 11: Scrum and the Future   **277**

A leaner Agile Manifesto   **278**

Redefining the role of the organization   **279**

Self-managing teams – the inmates run the asylum!   280

Career paths   281

True visibility   282
Capacity, not projects   282
The CEO of Me   283
Customer collaboration via prioritized product backlog   283
Don't squeeze innovation out of the product backlog   284
Regular product reviews or demos   **289**
We are all ScrumMasters   **289**

Appendix A: The ScrumMaster's Responsibilities   **291**
The ScrumMaster's role   **291**
Core knowledge   292
Responsibilities   292
Running the sprint   293
Assisting the product owner   294
Creating a high-performing Scrum team   294
Making progress visible   295
Supporting and living the Scrum core values   296
Educating others   296
Improving personal skills and characteristics   297

Appendix B: ScrumMaster's Workshop   **299**
**Chapter 1: Scrum – A Brief Review of the Basics
(and a Few Interesting Tidbits)**   **299**
Chapter 2: Release Planning – Tuning Product Development   **300**
Chapter 3: Sprint Planning – Fine-tune the Sprint Commitment   **301**
Chapter 4: Sprint! Valuable, Collaborative, and Meaningful Work   **302**
**Chapter 5: The End? Improving Product and
Process One Bite at a Time**   **303**
Chapter 6: The Criticality of Real-time Information   **304**
Chapter 7: Scrum Values Expose Fear, Dysfunction, and Waste   **305**
Chapter 8: Everyday Leadership for the ScrumMaster and Team   **307**
Chapter 9: Shaping the Agile Organization   **308**
Chapter 10: Scrum – Large and Small   **308**

Index   **309**

Preface

Technical projects are like an old horse I had when I was a kid; they'll flip you when you least expect it! Yet the element of surprise is actually a surety in our technical world. Agile methods, with their focus on helping teams deliver quality features and products quickly and flexibly, have drawn me in as a way to help tame the bucking horse, the element of surprise in technical projects, and Scrum, in particular, as a gateway to discover which day-to-day processes and working styles fit best for a particular team in a particular setting.

A ScrumMaster, like a good rider, must know when to go easy on the horse, when to use the spur, when to pull the reins, and when to just hang up the bridle and put the saddle away for the day. There are nearly a quarter million CSMs now, and many more to follow. While this is great news and represents a steady interest in Agile methods, we are in the soup. There is rampant misuse and misunderstanding of Scrum, which diminishes and possibly eliminates the amazing possibilities that people discover by using it correctly. I've observed too many examples of good Scrum gone bad—times in which tough, courageous, persistent ScrumMasters could have really made a difference, but didn't; times when product owners could have been a bit more involved; times when teams hid poor quality and shouldn't have. Additionally, with the advent of several newer methods, the terms Iteration Manager and Agile Master are floating around and representing an increasingly watered-down, dangerous version of what the true ScrumMaster was meant to do. That sucks, and makes me sad—and spurs me to action. I don't want the original vision for ScrumMaster to become lost in the methodology/certification wagon train; I want people to reach their full potential and believe that Scrum is one way to facilitate that.

Scrum is a simple process and it will not fail; you'll become extremely knowledgeable about this by the end of the book. Yet it becomes the butt of the failure because it's just too hard sometimes for people to accept responsibility. In other words, the horse bucked, so it's easiest to just blame the horse! But maybe it was a rock in the hoof, or a burr under the saddle—maybe there was another explanation or reason for the undesirable behavior. A good ScrumMaster pokes and prods to find the real source for organizational saddle burrs—and works diligently to pluck them out to make things more comfortable.

My utopia is a world in which everyone in technology has the ScrumMaster mind-set—whether they are team members, the named role of ScrumMaster, a line manager, or an executive. That's probably not realistic, at least for now, so luckily we have this very special role called the ScrumMaster to help others along. A professional ScrumMaster willingly accepts the role, realizes that he/she must help create an eager trial-and-error mind-set within the team and beyond, keep bad habits in check, and let the best working patterns and styles emerge. This is an extremely challenging, uphill both ways, in the snow, knee-deep journey. Sharp ScrumMastering is so much more than running a daily Scrum meeting with a team; using Scrum the right way can help a company do the right things and do them quickly (which is the definition of Agile, after all).

Scrum is not something to transition TO; rather, it is something to transition THROUGH. Through to what, exactly? Well, you will discover the answer when you do it. Some teams realize that they like to throw in some Extreme Programming practices, others find Kanban concepts to really help them out. Over time, you want to help the team and organization create a process that works for them, and not the other way around. As you become more aware of the wonderful ideas from other Agile/Lean methods, you'll realize that what you call it—the names of methods or frameworks—don't matter nearly as much as results. Keep your eye on helping your team deliver in a fast, focused, yet flexible manner, and you're well on your way. Scrum can help you get a nice running start.

I want you to become the Olympic-dressage-rider-on-a-Friesian kind of ScrumMaster, not atop-a-Shetland-pony-being-led-around-a ring version (henceforth known as a ScrumPuppet). You should know that you have more power than you probably give yourself credit for. One person—you—can make a difference, and creating just one successful Scrum team can change your organization. If you choose to accept this mission, get ready for the ride of your life.

What this book covers

Chapter 1, Scrum – A Brief Review of the Basics (and a Few Interesting Tidbits), provides you with the history, philosophies, and practices of Scrum. If you're new to Scrum, you must read this chapter; and if you're experienced, read it anyway. This chapter contains the underlying reasons why this Scrum thing works. This and subsequent chapters also have a *Recommended Reading* section with some of my favorite websites and books for you to check out.

Chapter 2, Release Planning – Tuning Product Development, will help you help your product owner prepare the product backlog for various planning uses, while we focus on release planning specifically at this point. This chapter provides you with preparation and facilitation tips to have you up and running a release planning session in no time.

Chapter 3, Sprint Planning – Fine-tune the Sprint Commitment, suggests ways for you to envision, prepare, and facilitate sprint planning meetings, but more importantly, how to set your team up for success in a sprint.

Chapter 4, Sprint! Visible, Collaborative, and Meaningful Work, gets into the heart of the sprint—what happens day to day, how team members should work together, and how you can clear the path for team productivity. And what about that pesky daily Scrum? Yep, we get into that too!

Chapter 5, The End? Improving Product and Process One Bite at a Time, suggests that what you consider the end of a sprint is really only a pause that sets up the beginning of the next. Learn how sprint reviews and retrospectives help teams build trust with business stakeholders, and learn how retrospectives build a team.

Chapter 6, The Criticality of Real-time Information, presents ideas for giving visibility to your team's work so that the product owner and other business stakeholders can make smart decisions. You'll learn how to help the right people look through the lenses of the Scrum microscope so that they may make smart and timely decisions.

Chapter 7, Scrum Values Expose Fear, Dysfunction, and Waste, walks you through the five core values of Scrum and the top five responses of reluctant teams and organizations.

Chapter 8, Everyday Leadership for the ScrumMaster and Team, gives ideas and tips for you to hone your personal skills in order to make your team as strong as it can be. This is preparation for *Chapter 9, Shaping the Agile Organization*.

Chapter 9, Shaping the Agile Organization, expands on *Chapter 8, Everyday Leadership for the ScrumMaster and Team*, by turning your attention to the organization outside the team. We'll explore motivation for knowledge workers, HR carrots and sticks, Agile organizational structures, and the like.

Chapter 10, Scrum – Large and Small, gives you some ideas for scaling the Scrum framework to accommodate larger multi-team programs. We'll also delve a little into distributed teams.

Chapter 11, Scrum and the Future, will take you on a journey to the future world of knowledge work, what organizations will look like, and how, if done with serious professionalism, ScrumMasters can make that happen sooner rather than later.

Appendix A, ScrumMaster's Responsibilities, provides a run-down of ScrumMaster responsibilities and duties. You can use this list as a quick way to stock your Impediment Backlog.

Appendix B, ScrumMaster's Workshop, is full of thought-provoking questions, scenarios, and exercises—broken out by chapter—for you to work through and think about while reading the book. This appendix is also available online for download at http://www.packtpub.com/sites/default/files/downloads/AppendixB_ scrum_master_workshop.pdf.

I created a companion website, www.helloscrum.com, to provide you with more ideas, tips, and tricks to help you along your way.

 A few images used in this book have been purchased from iStockPhoto.

What you need for this book

This is not a technical book with code snippets and scripts and such. But you still need to bring some things to the table while reading it: courage, open-mindedness, honesty, and a willingness to take a hard look at yourself and your organization with the goal of identifying room for improvement. Please leave the vanity at home.

Who this book is for

This book is primarily for practicing ScrumMasters, who need help and new ideas to bring their teams and organizations to the next level.

Conventions

In this book, you will find a number of styles of text that distinguish between different kinds of information. Here are some examples of these styles and an explanation of their meaning.

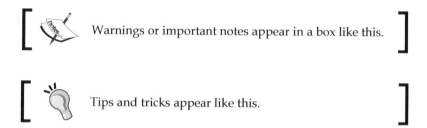

Warnings or important notes appear in a box like this.

Tips and tricks appear like this.

Reader feedback

Feedback from our readers is always welcome. Let us know what you think about this book—what you liked or may have disliked. Reader feedback is important for us to develop titles that you really get the most out of.

To send us general feedback, simply send an e-mail to feedback@packtpub.com, and mention the book title via the subject of your message.

If there is a topic that you have expertise in and you are interested in either writing or contributing to a book, see our author guide on www.packtpub.com/authors.

Customer support

Now that you are the proud owner of a Packt book, we have a number of things to help you to get the most from your purchase.

Errata

Although we have taken every care to ensure the accuracy of our content, mistakes do happen. If you find a mistake in one of our books—maybe a mistake in the text or the code—we would be grateful if you would report this to us. By doing so, you can save other readers from frustration and help us improve subsequent versions of this book. If you find any errata, please report them by visiting http://www.packtpub.com/submit-errata, selecting your book, clicking on the **errata submission form** link, and entering the details of your errata. Once your errata are verified, your submission will be accepted and the errata will be uploaded on our website, or added to any list of existing errata, under the Errata section of that title. Any existing errata can be viewed by selecting your title from http://www.packtpub.com/support.

Piracy

Piracy of copyright material on the Internet is an ongoing problem across all media. At Packt, we take the protection of our copyright and licenses very seriously. If you come across any illegal copies of our works, in any form, on the Internet, please provide us with the location address or website name immediately so that we can pursue a remedy.

Please contact us at copyright@packtpub.com with a link to the suspected pirated material.

We appreciate your help in protecting our authors, and our ability to bring you valuable content.

Questions

You can contact us at questions@packtpub.com if you are having a problem with any aspect of the book, and we will do our best to address it.

1

Scrum – A Brief Review of the Basics (and a Few Interesting Tidbits)

The purpose of this chapter is to review the history, basics, philosophy, benefits, and a few interesting tidbits about Scrum. A well-balanced, effective **ScrumMaster** understands both the principles and the practices of Scrum. I have discovered over the years that people often realize the true nature of the ScrumMaster; unfortunately, the role is consistently misperceived and downplayed as a mere "iteration manager" or "Agile project manager". Along with your reading of the referenced source materials, this chapter will provide you with the foundational information necessary to navigate the murky waters of organizational change—the real task of the ScrumMaster.

The problem

In order to stay in business, the typical for-profit company must meet its consumer demand with an adequate supply of valuable services or products. The primary role of the ScrumMaster is to bring visibility to the development team's true capacity, so that the organization may balance that against its consumer demands. Unlike a manufacturing line in which the management measures units delivered per day, Agile software development is measured in terms of customer happiness based on the features or feature set delivered by the team. In this day of viral **YouTube** videos, tweets, and other such media, companies must stay focused on delivering today's most important demands quickly, while maintaining a flexible response to rapidly changing competitive and consumer landscapes.

A few decades ago, the waterfall response was, in fact, adequate because new markets weren't being created every day, the Internet did not exist as we know it today, and it took much longer for people to spread their messages and ideas around the world. The viral **Gangnam Style** or recent **Harlem Shake** are testaments to just how quickly words (and funky dances) can travel. There is simply no time to play around these days.

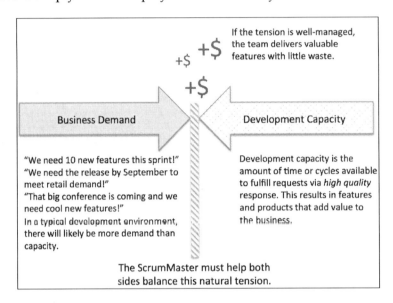

I've attempted to illustrate the opposing forces of supply and demand in the figure above. The business continuously demands new features and products from the technical team, whether it's the CEO with a new mandate or a product manager in need of a cool new feature. A professional ScrumMaster can help the business see when the balance is tipped too far in one direction; and most importantly how to best use its capacity to respond to demand with speed and quality. There is no perfect long-term solution; rather the ScrumMaster must help the organization find balance as the landscape on both sides constantly changes.

A brief history

In the past two decades, companies have increasingly relied on **Agile** methods to keep up with growing demand and changing markets; today, about half of all companies that use Agile use Scrum. Over the years, we have observed Scrum's adoption at companies new to these ideas, as well as renewed/continued interest even in experienced Scrum/Agile organizations. We have also noticed a trend that companies have adopted subsequent processes — **Extreme Programming**, **Lean**, **Kanban**, and others — usually after initiating Scrum first.

Jeff Sutherland first used Scrum at Easel Corporation in 1993, and subsequently used it at companies such as VMARK, Individual, and IDX Systems throughout the 90s. Ken Schwaber, who worked with Jeff at Individual, 'formalized' Scrum at the OOPSLA Conference in 1995. At the turn of the millennium, Jeff famously applied Scrum at Patient Keeper and Ken helped scale Scrum at Primavera Systems, the latter whose case study was made popular by an online whitepaper and several anonymous mentions in Ken's second book, *Agile Project Management with Scrum*.

However, these early applications in the mid to late 90s weren't the first rumblings of Scrum. In 1986, Harvard Business Review published an article by Hirotaka Takeuchi and Ikujiro Nonaka entitled *The New Product Development Game*, in which the authors wrote that development organizations must extend their focus beyond scope, time, and cost to find ways to increase speed and flexibility of product delivery in order to win in the new competitive landscape. Instead of the relay race, "…a holistic or 'rugby' approach – where a team tries to go the distance as a unit, passing the ball back and forth – may better serve today's competitive requirements." This article was the first mention of Scrum as a new paradigm for product development—a thought framework for quick, flexible, and competitive product development. It's important for ScrumMasters to remember that Scrum practices—a set of work steps, outputs, and artifacts—are nothing without the underlying mind-set and concepts toward product development that Takeuchi and Nonaka set out to describe: built-in instability, self-organizing project teams, overlapping development phases, multi-learning, subtle control, and transfer of learning.

The concepts behind Scrum go even further back in time. In the 1950s, a management consultant by the name of W. Edwards Deming created the **Plan-Do-Check-Act (PDCA)** cycle as a framework for continuous improvement. PDCA, also known as the Deming or Shewhart cycle, had an early influence on Toyota's lean approach to manufacturing. These ideas map one-to-one to that of a Scrum's sprint, and even to a sprint's daily scrum, as indicated in the following figure and later in the book, but Deming didn't know he was doing Scrum. Or more appropriately, perhaps, is that today's Scrum teams don't readily realize that they're applying the Deming cycle!

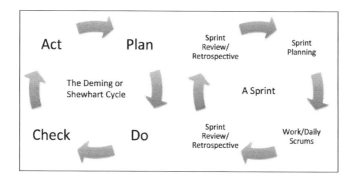

Scrum's foundation is even older than Deming. Go back 1,000 years to when Alhazen, a Muslim scientist and mathematician, ran experiments with reflection, refraction, lenses, and mirrors, thus deriving some of the principles of optics (captured in his book, *The Book of Optics*). Alhazen is considered by some to be the father of the scientific method (`http://www.wikipedia.org/wiki/Scientific_method`), a process through which a scientist creates a hypothesis or asks a question, runs an experiment, discovers results or gains knowledge, analyzes the findings, and possibly modifies the hypothesis (or decides to run a subsequent experiment). This empirical, or evidence-based, process is one in which a person will use knowledge gained from one experiment to draw conclusions or influence the next experiment, like the process by which Alhazen discovered the basics of human eyesight.

Finally, if we go a bit further back in history, you could imagine that even a primitive tribe's hunting session looked a lot like a Scrum sprint: everyone gathered together, grunted about where to stalk the prey, gathered up their hunting tools, killed dinner, and then talked about the hunting experience, which improved the plan for next time. We see evidence of these primitive retrospectives in cave drawings around the world. Scrum a most natural way of working that relies on the collaboration and close work of people to achieve an outcome. It's been this way for at least 11,000 years. We'll explore in later chapters why, even though it reflects a natural approach toward work, Scrum is so challenging.

The underlying concepts of Scrum

There are three categories of concepts that provide the foundation for Scrum. The first set of ideas resides in management approach for complex and chaotic situations, the second is a set of core values, and the third is a deep-seated focus on delivering product in a lean fashion. You should gain a thorough understanding of these concepts, not for passing a certification exam, but for explaining to others in the organization why and how Scrum is different than waterfall.

Complex adaptive systems

Complex adaptive systems are made up of varied interdependent elements whose relationships change as a result of experience. Complex systems adapt; as one variable emerges, others are affected. A simple example from biology is the Staph bacteria; in the 1940s, more than 99 percent of Staph bacteria were sensitive to penicillin. Today, Staph is resistant to penicillin; due to the introduction and exposure to the antibiotic, the bacteria evolved to survive.

In our world, requirements, technology, and people are intertwined; a change in one means a change in the other. When I was a kid, I loved to go to the movie theater to, and sometimes I would go just to play video games at the adjoining arcade (**Ms. Pac-Man**, **Frogger**, **Pole Position**, and **Asteroids**). My family couldn't afford a home system such as an **Atari** (and, having played at the arcade, I much preferred the arcade to an Atari home system anyway). Well, all that changed when Nintendo launched its **Nintendo Entertainment System** (**NES**). The kids next door got the system as a Christmas gift that year and next thing you know, we were over at their house many times per week after school playing Super Mario Brothers. Then along came the handhelds, Super NES, PlayStation, Sega to name a few, and now mobile phones and interactive play are all the rage. The advances in 16-bit and 32-bit consoles initially improved the user's experience at home with better graphics, competitive pressure resulted in more innovative home products from which a user could choose, and new technologies have allowed gaming companies to extend offerings into new arenas and find new markets. The technology, user needs and requirements, and developers in the gaming industry are all intertwined. A change in one necessitates a change in the others. Little did I realize, at that time, Mario and Luigi's importance to technology—much greater than just saving the princess!

Here's the deal: today's users change their minds about needs and desires minute to minute, developers continuously release new technologies and better versions of the old, and stakeholders and customers are never shy about saying how they feel about existing features. This emergence, that is, the evolution of new knowledge, needs, and desires about requirements and technologies during the course of a project, contributes to one heck of a complex situation. Complex projects cannot be adequately managed in a traditional approach, where all tasks are defined up front and then delegated to workers. In situations where the exact answer is not known, and must be discovered, an empirical process or evidence-based process is the best approach to use. (Take a look at the article *A Leader's Framework for Decision Making*, by *David J. Snowden* and *Mary E. Boone*, at *Harvard Business Review*). But it's more than just applying the right tool or technique to the matter; complex systems involve complex human interactions. While a complex project requires a process that allows for emergence, it also requires a leadership style that facilitates humans getting along together.

The following figure is the famous **Stacey Matrix**, adopted from Dr. Ralph Stacey, Professor of Management at the Business School of the University of Hertfordshire, who has spent many years exploring how the complexity sciences can be leveraged to understand organizations. You may remember hearing about his work during your ScrumMaster training. The Stacey Matrix looks at certainty and agreement, which correlate to technology and requirements, respectively, in our world. The farther from certainty and agreement a situation is, the more complex or even chaotic the situation; on the other hand, a simple situation is one with agreement and knowledge. Think about an easy project from your career. The requirements for the new feature were very clear and straightforward, and you wrote all the existing code a few weeks ago. It was easy for you to provide a time estimate since you figured that surprises weren't likely. This is a simple situation, rare in the software world. A complex scenario, on the other hand, is one in which you may not have been very familiar with the code, the customer often changed her mind, and the vendor team never met its deadlines. In this case, it was impossible for you to estimate beyond the tip of your nose as surprises (mostly bad) were guaranteed.

You'll notice that I overlaid the Scrum roles and control points onto the Stacey Matrix. ScrumMasters know that they do not control complex projects by acting as task masters and telling everyone what to do every day, rather, control is acquired by allowing a team to self manage through a series of sprints (or time-boxes) and by requiring the product owner to force rank the product backlog. Each role in Scrum has a specific and important set of responsibilities, each steeped in the idea of controlling chaos (in fact, Ken Schwaber's original Scrum website is called www. controlchaos.com). Many people ask me if there is a role called project manager in Scrum and the answer is a resounding no! The reason is that by giving control to only one person over what gets done, how it gets done, and why it gets done results in chaos and other bad effects. Three main responsibilities divided among three main roles creates checks and balances in our complex project systems; these three main Scrum roles, coupled with a simple process framework, control chaos. Each sprint, by focusing on a narrow selection of product backlog, an empowered team devises the appropriate technical solution bit by bit, thus bringing the project closer to the simple range sprint after sprint. If these controls are not protected, it is all too easy for the scale to unfavorably tip. Scrum is a very simple concept and extremely powerful once implemented (and yet rather difficult to do). You, my dear ScrumMaster, must keep that sprint to the simpler side of things by thwarting interruptions and helping the product owner keep the product backlog in order.

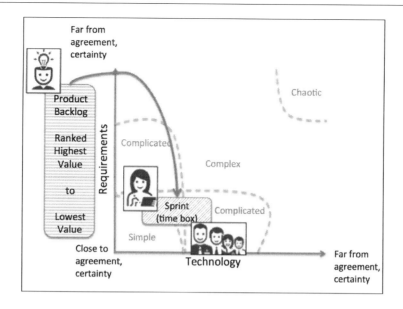

Even though Dr. Stacey's matrix and Snowden and Boone's article provide us with nice frameworks of thought to choose the right process for the situation, please do not oversimplify this information! Dr. Stacey didn't publish the matrix beyond the second edition of his book, and he's now up to six editions! What happened? Dr. Stacey stopped publishing the matrix because people oversimplified it, thinking that one can just choose a tool or technique depending on the classification of their project. Dr. Stacey warns us that it's not that simple, that, "what happens is the result of the interplay between the intentions and strategies of all involved and no one can control this interplay, hence the fundamental uncertainty and unpredictability of human life." This is another way of saying that Scrum doesn't fix the problems, people do; Scrum only exposes where the challenges lie. People must solve the problems exposed by Scrum and should craft different solutions for different scenarios. This book attempts to explore how the ScrumMaster may facilitate some of those challenges both inside and outside of the team.

Knowledge is the outcome of experience. In a traditional approach to managing projects, all the decisions are made at the beginning of the project. This has always been interesting to me because a person has the most knowledge about a project at the end of the project! Scrum puts urgency on teams so that they deliver value quickly; in doing so, knowledge about requirements and technology increases rapidly and team dynamics begin to emerge and stabilize. The sooner a team gets started, the better. When a team has knowledge its members can make better, well-informed decisions. Scrum teams delay decisions around lower-value requirements for a later point in time, as requirements in their fast-paced technology worlds are bound to change anyway.

The empirical process control barstool

There are four legs supporting the Scrum barstool that make it unique and effective in complex situations: prioritized product backlog, dedicated cross-functional team, time-boxes, and inspection and adaptation. These four entities form the necessary boundaries that allow us to call Scrum an empirical process. When a barstool loses a leg, it is imbalanced (ever try sitting on one?); even if one leg is slightly shorter than the others, the barstool is wobbly and annoying. The same idea applies with the Scrum concepts: when the team become lax on one or more boundaries, the project gets loosey-goosey; the experiment gets shaky as it loses its control points. For example, if for some reason the ScrumMaster allows interruptions during a sprint, the team runs the risk of not finishing anything by the sprint's end. Everyone must stop and start again—we call this chaos. Likewise, if the product owner does not rank features in the product backlog, and no thought is given to priority, the team may or may not deliver the right features to customers. A simple violation of these guiding principles can cause major downstream effects. If a team adheres to these four principles of Scrum, it will likely attain a higher degree of stability and knowledge.

Ken Schwaber and Jeff Sutherland designed these four "legs", or principles, of Scrum to enable empirical process control for software development projects (although the techniques are useful in just about any type of project). Scrum is an evidence-based way of progressing through a project or initiative. Without designated points in time around which people can provide feedback on features, like in waterfall projects, the team, management, and customers really have no idea what is being developed. Try to recount a status meeting for a traditionally managed project. What was that meeting like for you? I can say that, for me, it was often daunting. I would present a status report with a bunch of red, green, and yellow dots on it, some numbers and percentages of 'phase complete', and sometimes a list of risks. I can honestly say that as a traditional project manager, if I didn't truly know the status, I'd just put a yellow dot on the dashboard, reckoning I'd figure it out later. Or, even worse, I'd stay at work very late for a few nights ahead of the status meeting attempting to make the Gantt chart look something like reality. Scrum, with its emphasis on potentially shippable product increments each and every sprint leaves nowhere to hide. Sprint reviews replace status meetings; and the status is real—that is, the team shows real features that work! That is exciting and tangible! It's evidence, and we can work with evidence! Instead of a bunch of guesswork about what we think is the status of the project, in Scrum we can actually see, touch, and feel the status of the project by attending a **sprint Review** and interacting with the software or system as it exists at that point in time.

I recently watched a television program that featured George Cleverley and Company, a famous London shoemaker. Founded in 1958, Cleverley makes some of the most expensive handmade shoes in the world, shodding some of the world's most discriminating tootsies. In order to make such a beautiful product of unprecedented quality, the shoemakers must work very closely with the customer to understand their desires and requirements. After crafting precise shoe-lasts (forms around which the shoe is built) made from several measurements of a customer's foot (bunions and corns included), the shoemaker must then work with the customer's choices regarding various leathers, soles, dyes, laces, thistles, welts, and stitching in order to make the shoe that the wearer has envisioned and will love. It takes months for a customer's shoes to be finished, and at least three thousand U.S. dollars, but for 58 years customers have gladly paid and anxiously waited for the call that their shoes are ready. George Cleverley and Company involves its customers in the design and creation; there's simply no other way to build the perfect shoe. In reading about the craftsmanship, attention to detail, and customer satisfaction — the hallmarks of the Cleverley brand — I realized that the process in which Cleverley shoes are built is very Scrum-like: an iterative creation process where the customer is an essential part of the desired outcome. Even though the product backlog in this process is relatively fixed — that is, the order of the steps in shoemaking is fixed, the customer must be involved every step of the way.

Scrum core values

In addition to the basics in complex adaptive systems theory, Scrum also has at its center five core values: **commitment**, **focus**, **openness**, **respect**, and **courage.** (Take a look at *Agile Software Development with Scrum*, by *Ken Schwaber, Prentice Hall*.) We will explore these in more detail in *Chapter 8, Everyday Leadership for the ScrumMaster*.

Teams commit to their goals for the sprint, product owners commit to ordering the product backlog, and ScrumMasters commit to removing obstacles along the way in order to steady the flow of product development. The Scrum team should do whatever is necessary in order to meet their goals, and it's important that they are empowered to do so.

Additionally, for a team to be able to complete its work, its members must be allowed to focus. The ScrumMaster does not allow changes in the sprint's commitment so that the team may keep its focus. When a team gives its full attention to the problem, its work is much more productive, predictable, and fulfilling.

As Scrum uses empirical process control to make progress through a project, it is essential that the results and experience of an experiment (that is, a sprint) are visible. For example, the sprint review provides visibility into how the product's features and capabilities have emerged, and the sprint retrospective engages the team members to discuss their personal and team successes and challenges experienced during the sprint. Once visibility exists, inspection and adaptation can occur. Again, evidence (information) is the heart of an empirical process; thus, openness is one of the five core values.

Respect is something that all humans should have for each other, but unfortunately it does not always exist. In order to be its best, a team's members need to respect for each other and, the knowledge that each brings to the table, experiences, working styles, and personalities, just to name a few. Respect doesn't come for free; it is earned. Scrum team members should be dedicated, cross-functional, empowered, and self-organizing—any team that is not provided this environment or structure will have a tough time achieving mutual trust and respect. We will discuss in subsequent chapters how a ScrumMaster can model (and thus create) trust and respect within the team.

It takes buckets of courage for a ScrumMaster to apply Scrum the way it was intended. Even though Scrum is very simple in design, people end up over-engineering its intended plainness. I often see management at various companies bring in Scrum as a way to do more with less (not always the case!), and they don't at the very least realize or acknowledge that the use of Scrum puts pressure on organizations to change. One of the primary responsibilities of the ScrumMaster is to help the organization identify its weaknesses so that it may improve. This takes courage. Sometimes, a team has to push back on the product owner when asked to take on too much during a sprint. It takes courage to say no to that sort of pressure. A product owner must have courage when communicating with other stakeholders about the reality of a project. These are just a few examples that require courage in order to not break the boundaries of empirical process or introduce more waste into the product or process.

An interesting tidbit: the Scrum core values sound a lot like the U.S. Army's seven values of loyalty, duty, respect, selfless service, honor, integrity, and personal courage. We might not find that too surprising as the grandfathers of Scrum have military backgrounds: Jeff Sutherland was a Top Gun fighter pilot in the U.S. Air Force, and Ken Schwaber attended the U.S. Merchant Marine Academy.

Scrum is inherently lean

Lean software development is the result of the translation of lean manufacturing into the software and systems development space. Whether it falls underneath the Agile umbrella is hotly debated in the community, yet it really doesn't matter when it's all said and done. This is because the seven principles of lean are inherently reflected in Agile methods, but perhaps in different ways and with different lexicons or naming conventions.

The first principle of Lean is to eliminate waste. From unclear requirements, unused documentation, hand-offs, wait time, and so forth, lean practitioners seek to reduce or eliminate altogether these wastes from the process. The Scrum framework echoes this lean sentiment by providing the retrospective so that a team may discover and fix anything that's not working well. You'll often hear teams discussing subjects such as wasteful documentation, overbearing and/or manual processes, too many defects, and other such issues in the retrospective.

Lean thinking also stresses that everyone on the team gets the chance to learn. Scrum mirrors this by requiring that every sprint ends with a potentially shippable product increment. This quality threshold requires that team members code, integrate, and perform tests, of various sorts in order to learn what is defective, while the product owner learns about the emerging product. Additionally, members of a team work very closely together, which means that they often learn a little about the others' domain.

In any project, people know the most about the project at the end of the project. Scrum teams would rather make well-informed decisions; therefore, they do not make decisions about every requirement up front. This is a manifestation of the fourth value of Lean: decide as late as possible.

Lean says deliver fast; in Scrum we deliver at most every 30 days, while many teams deliver even faster than that. Lean says empower the team, and so does Scrum. Lean says that integrity should be built into the system; Scrum answers this by requiring a team to define done with a customer. Finally, Lean guides us to see the whole—how the entire value stream, or chain of events leading to customer value, operates. Any bottlenecks should be removed immediately, and teams should be staffed so that they can complete finished product increments. Scrum reflects this by guiding us to create dedicated, cross-functional teams that conduct retrospectives. Such retrospectives help us unearth bottlenecks (or obstacles as called in Scrum) so that they can be eliminated.

Scrum roles

This section serves as a very light introduction to the three roles in Scrum: **Scrum team**, **Product owner**, and **ScrumMaster**. While the book focuses predominantly on the ScrumMaster role, we will touch upon the other roles in more detail due to the natural interconnectedness of all three. As you probably already know, people get very anxious about roles and responsibilities; we'll go into more detail about Scrum (and non-Scrum) roles in *Chapter 9, Shaping the Agile Organization*.

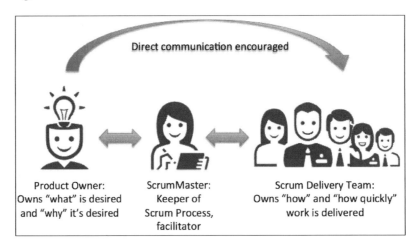

Scrum team

The Scrum team includes the product owner, ScrumMaster, and the team members, whereas the Scrum delivery team is a subset made up of only the technical team members. The entire Scrum team huddles around a problem (a requirement from an ordered list known as the Product Backlog) and innovates solutions. Scrum teams should be five to nine team members, dedicated to the life of the project (and perhaps beyond), cross-functional, empowered, and self-organizing. Scrum teams plan, estimate, and commit to their work, rather than a manager performing these functions for them. The end goal of the team is to deliver a potentially shippable product increment that meets an agreed-upon Definition of Done each and every sprint. The George Cleverly shoe craftsmen would be considered Scrum delivery team members while the craftsmen, customer, and shoe design consultant together would comprise the overall Scrum team (it takes everyone's participation to make the right shoe).

Product owner

The product owner is responsible for the product's success. In other words, while the team is responsible for delivering a quality solution, the product owner is responsible for knowing his market and user needs well enough to guide the team toward a marketable release sprint after sprint. There are different types of product owners in different types of projects, but regardless of the technical situation or the desired outcome, there should be one (and only one) product owner who makes final decisions about the direction of the product and the order in which features should be developed. The product backlog, or list of items to be completed by the Scrum team, is ordered by the product owner so as to reflect his most valuable requests or changes for the product in development. The product owner, since he is representing the "what" and "why" of the system, should be available to the team to have regular dialogs about the requirements in the product backlog; additionally, the product owner must make the product vision clear to everyone on the team and regularly maintain the product backlog in keeping with the product vision. The product owner always keeps the next set of product backlog items in a ready state so that the team always has work in the queue for the next sprint. The George Cleverley shoe customer is the 'purest' product owner a team can get—the actual person paying for the product!

ScrumMaster

The ScrumMaster safeguards the process. He/she understands the reasons behind and for an empirical process, and does his or her best to keep product development flowing as smoothly as possible. This "servant leader" (take a look at *Servant Leadership, by Robert K. Greenleaf, Paulist PR*) protects team members from interruptions in order to keep them focused on their sprint commitments, as well as helps the product owner get the product backlog in order if he or she does not understand how to do so. Additionally, ScrumMasters facilitate all Scrum meetings, ensuring that everyone on the team understands the goals and that they share a commitment together as a true team and not just as a collection of individuals. ScrumMasters remove obstacles that prevent a steady flow of high-value features; many times, the obstacles are organizational in nature.

Think of the ScrumMaster as the Switzerland of the Scrum process—remaining neutral, helping both business stakeholders and development, interacting at the right times to create the most important and most valuable features first.

Brief review of the Scrum framework

Scrum is simple; it consists of six time boxes (one of which is optional), three roles, and three 'official' artifacts.

A sprint, the first of the six time boxes, is an iteration defined by a fixed start and end date; it is kicked off by sprint planning and concluded by the sprint review and retrospective. The team meets daily, in a daily scrum meeting, to make their work visible to each other and synchronize based on what they've learned.

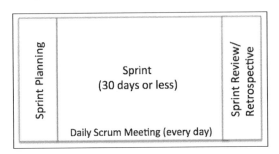

Sprint planning

During sprint planning, the second time-boxed event, the product owner and the team discuss the highest priority items in the product backlog and brainstorm a plan to implement those items. The set of chosen product backlog items and their subsequent tasks collectively is referred to as the team's **sprint backlog**.

The sprint planning meeting is time-boxed to eight hours for a 30-day sprint, reduced proportionally for shorter sprints (for a two-week sprint, for example, one may reduce that time to a maximum of four hours). The meeting is comprised of two parts. The first segment of the meeting is driven by the product owner who presents the most important product backlog items — along with any helpful drawings, models, and mockups, for example — and clarifies questions from the development team about what he/she wants and why he/she wants it. The second segment of the meeting is driven by the Scrum delivery team who work together to brainstorm approaches and eventually agree on a plan. It's at the start of this second segment that the sprint actually begins.

Of course, teams are always searching for ways to make planning faster and more efficient. You will likely see sprint planning take less time over a number of sprints for a team whose members have remained consistent.

The result of sprint planning is a sprint backlog that is comprised of selected product backlog items for the sprint, along with the correlating tasks identified by the team in the second segment of sprint planning. We'll discuss many details and ideas for effective sprint planning meetings in *Chapter 3, Sprint Planning – Fine-tune the Sprint Commitment*

Daily scrum meeting

In the daily scrum meeting, the third time box of Scrum, team members make their progress visible so that they can inspect and adapt toward meeting their goals, sort of like a mini-Deming (PDCA) cycle every day! The meeting is held at the same time and in the same place, decided upon by the team. Even though a team makes its best attempt at planning for a sprint, things can change in flight. Tom finishes a task late, Beth finishes early, Ashish is stuck. In this 15-minute meeting, team members discuss what they did since yesterday's meeting, what they plan to do by tomorrow's meeting, and to mention any obstacles that may be in their way. The role of the ScrumMaster in the daily scrum is to facilitate, keep the conversation from delving into problem solving, and record any obstacles that team members feel they cannot fix for themselves. The ScrumMaster will attempt to remove said obstacles after the meeting. The daily scrum meeting represents inspection and adaptation at a daily level. The Scrum delivery team members, product owner, and ScrumMaster are participants in the meeting. Anyone else is welcome to attend but only as observers.

Sprint review meeting

The sprint review, the fourth time-boxed event of Scrum, provides the opportunity for stakeholders to give feedback about the emerging product in a collaborative setting. In this meeting, the team, product owner, ScrumMaster, and any interested stakeholders meet to review the features and talk about how the product is shaping up, which features may need to change, and perhaps discuss new ideas to add to the product backlog. It is common for a ScrumMaster to summarize the events of the sprint, any major obstacles that the team ran into, decisions that were made in-flight with the product owner's help, and so on, and of course the team should always demo what they've accomplished by the sprint's end. This meeting is time-boxed to four hours (for a 30-day sprint).

Sprint retrospective

During the final sprint meeting—the sprint retrospective—team members discuss the events of the sprint, identify what worked well for them, what didn't work so well, and take on action items for any changes that they'd like to make for the next sprint. The ScrumMaster will take on any actions that the team does not feel it can handle; likely broader organizational issues. The ScrumMaster reports progress to the team regarding these obstacles in subsequent sprints. This meeting is time-boxed to three hours. We will dive into more details about sprint reviews and retrospectives in *Chapter 5, The End? Improving Product and Process One Bite at a Time.*

Release planning (optional)

The final time box in Scrum is release planning, an optional event, in which Scrum teams plan for long-term initiatives comprised of multiple sprints' worth of work. The product owner and team discuss product backlog items, dependencies, risks, schedule, and capacity, among other topics, in this meeting to settle on a forecast for upcoming work. Since the product backlog can be infinite, release planning helps the team and product owner understand what may be possible given a release deadline. This subset of the product backlog is called the release backlog and is a valuable output of the release planning meeting. Release planning should be time-boxed but the time required depends upon the scale of the program, the number of teams, team distribution, and how well the product backlog is prepared. Release planning meetings are often held at the beginning of the project, and teams will meet with their product owners throughout the project to re-plan based on emergent knowledge. It is not unheard of, however, for teams to postpone planning a release until they have a few sprints of work under their belts, as the experience and knowledge they gain in a few sprints results in greater confidence in a longer-term release plan (more details in *Chapter 2, Release Planning – Tuning Product Development*). Either approach is acceptable and depends upon the needs of the organization.

Ken Schwaber once said to me, "I don't know why people make this such a long, drawn-out event. It isn't really that hard." And with that, we completed our release planning in 15 minutes.

Scrum artifacts

Scrum only has a small set of artifacts: the product backlog, sprint backlog, and the product increment. We will briefly review these artifacts here and dive much deeper into them in subsequent chapters.

The product backlog

The product backlog is the product owner's 'wish list'. Anything and everything that they (and other stakeholders) think they might want in the product goes in this list. It could be infinite as there are always new ideas about how to extend a product's features. The product owner maintains the product backlog, although other stakeholders (including the team) should have visibility of and the ability to suggest new items for the list.

The product owner prioritizes the product backlog, listing the most important or most valuable items first. That is, there aren't 10 critical items at the top of the backlog with equal value; rather, there are 10 critical items that are ranked according to their priority or urgency, and they appear at the top of the product backlog, one after another. This is because items at the top are next in the queue to be implemented. Once a team selects items for a sprint (or iteration), those items and their priorities are locked; however, priorities and details for any not-started work may change at any time. Through this mechanism, teams are able to focus on this sprint's work while the product owner retains maximum flexibility in ordering the next sprint's work.

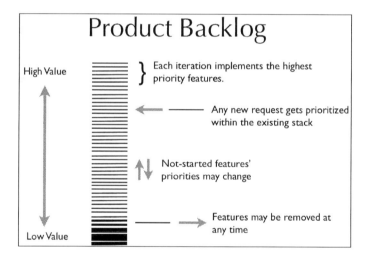

Product owners have many ways of evaluating and thus prioritizing their lists. They may also attribute product backlog items with additional information such as improves brand recognition, allows scaling, infrastructure, contracts greater than 10,000 dollars, and so forth. Attributes are unique to a particular company and a particular product and help the product owner to keep the list in the proper order.

The sprint backlog

Owned by the team, the sprint backlog reflects the product backlog items that the team committed to in sprint planning, as well as the subsequent tasks and reminders. Team members update it every day to reflect how many hours remain on his or her tasks; team members may also remove tasks, add tasks, or change tasks as the sprint is underway.

The product increment

The product increment is a set of features, user stories, or other deliverables completed by the team in the sprint. The product increment should be potentially shippable—that is, of high enough quality to give to users. The product owner is responsible for accepting the product increment during each sprint, according to the agreed-upon Definition of Done and acceptance criteria for each sprint deliverable. Without a product increment, the product owner and other stakeholders have no way to inspect and adapt the product.

Visible progress

A team must keep its progress visible at all times. It will create many additional artifacts in order to ensure visibility. Some common visibility tools are the release and sprint burndown charts.

Release backlog and burndown

A subset of the product backlog that has been identified for a particular release is called the release backlog. Even though release backlog can be defined up front, the product owner may remove items, exchange items, or negotiate scope depth for some items as he/she considers scope, time, and cost throughout the duration of the project. Therefore, the release backlog should be updated throughout the project. *Chapter 2, Release Planning – Tuning Product Development*, provides more detailed information about product backlogs, release burndowns, and backlogs.

The release burndown chart displays how much work remains in the release backlog at the end of each sprint. This provides the product owner with important information so that he/she may make well-informed decisions about scope, cost, and time. In the following diagram, you can see that the amount of work remaining at the end of each sprint is more than the work planned:

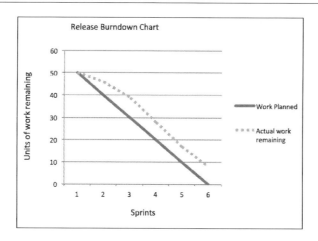

Sprint burndown

During a particular sprint, if everyone on the team updates the sprint backlog with the number of remaining hours per task every day, then the team can see if they will be able to burn down the number of task hours by the end of the sprint. In the following figure, you can see that the team did not complete all the tasks it had identified in sprint planning; approximately 50 hours remain.

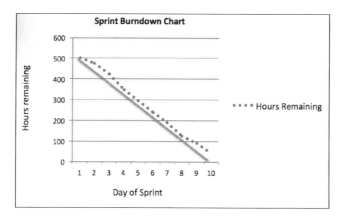

This burndown concept is very important because, once set, the sprint end date does not change. Coupled with a daily Scrum, the sprint backlog and burn down chart can help teams visualize when they might be getting off track and turn the conversation to focus on what to do about a given situation. The sprint burndown "burns down" hours over days of the sprint, while the release burndown looks at units of work (often referred to as points) for a release, or number of sprints. *Chapter 3, Sprint Planning – Fine-Tune the Sprint Commitment* and *Chapter 5, The End? Improving Product and Process One Bite at a Time*, provide more details about burndowns and backlogs.

Dysfunctions or true constraints?

Scrum is based on the lean concept of turning an idea into a feature as efficiently as possible. The Scrum framework is designed to surface obstacles that get in the way of delivering value. The game rules of Scrum are in place to protect the team from chaos so that they may finish their commitments for the customer by the end of a given sprint.

Because of the short cycle time and the relentless pursuit of identifying obstacles, there seems to be a never-ending list of challenges that the ScrumMaster needs to fix. The team surfaces—on a daily basis—any interruptions or impediments to their work. The product owner and other stakeholders inspect the product in the sprint review, which frequently leads to adaptations in product backlog and thus the evolution of the product. Finally, the retrospective provides time for the team to focus on process improvements so that the experience is smoother in the future. In conclusion, there are three built-in mechanisms in the Scrum framework for discovering obstacles. As they say in Texas, "If you go hunting for trouble, you'll sure find it." Scrum can feel very challenging because of what it brings to the surface.

So how do we handle these tough challenges as ScrumMasters? We have to ask ourselves: is this issue/challenge/hardship a constraint within our organization or is it a dysfunction? An example of a true constraint would be a document that must be written for U.S. **Food and Drug Administration (FDA)** compliance. The team mentioned it in retrospective because they think it's wasteful, but the product won't make it to market if it doesn't achieve FDA compliance. Therefore, it's a true constraint that must be worked around.

On the other hand, let's say that a team member mentions in the retrospective that he is being pulled away from the team to work on another project for a different manager. Is this a constraint? Maybe. But perhaps it's a dysfunction. Why? Well, Scrum says that team members are dedicated so that they can focus on and finish the functionality they've committed to implement. When a team member gets pulled onto another initiative, this makes for an unhappy developer who now must multitask and probably feels inadequate because the workload is too much to bear. It is likely that he or she won't finish either of the teams, commitments. Without finishing features, it's impossible to inspect and adapt, which breaks the benefit of empirical process control. This scenario is simply not acceptable; team members are not to be pulled from their teams. In this case, the ScrumMaster should alert the product owner that the developer's commitments are now in jeopardy. The situation may have to be escalated to managers to put a stop to this behavior. Eventually, team members must learn to say no, but that is not likely to happen in the beginning.

Is your team ready for Scrum?

While you're probably not going to have a perfect team in a perfect environment as you start or continue your Scrum practices, I've provided a short checklist to help you identify the most important elements to help you as you begin:

- Do you have a team whose members are dedicated to the project? Do the members represent a cross-section of skills and talents — everything necessary to build features for the customer?

- Do you have a product owner? If not, can you find someone to play this role so that the team can get started working on the most important items?

- Does the product owner have a product vision and a product backlog? (See *Chapter 5, The End? Improving Product and Process One Bite at a Time*, for more details)

- Can you establish — at maximum — a 30-day sprint? Shorter if possible?

- Can you get participation from business stakeholders in the sprint review? (Not a requirement, but sure to drive urgency and visibility to your team).

- Do you feel courageous enough to communicate obstacles as they arise?

- Can you help the team create and maintain the sprint backlog? (See *Chapter 2, Release Planning – Tuning Product Development*, for more details)

- Can you commit to protecting the team from interruptions, no matter the interrupter?

Summary

The professional ScrumMaster must understand the principles and the practices of Scrum — the historical perspective, foundational concepts, and the mechanics of meetings, artifacts, and roles. This knowledge will help you as you face mismatches of expectations, beliefs, and knowledge about Scrum and its intent. Applying Scrum will expose innumerable challenges, unique to the organization and team in which it's been applied. Categorizing a challenge as a constraint or a dysfunction is at the heart of the ScrumMaster role. As you continue reading, you'll discover why this is so difficult and why a ScrumMaster needs courage.

Recommended reading

- Nonaka, I. and Takeuchi, H. (1986), *The New Product Development Game*, Harvard Business Review

- Royce, Winston (1970), *Managing the Development of Large Software Systems*

- Schwaber, Ken (1 February 2004), *Agile Project Management with Scrum*, Microsoft Press

- Schwaber, Ken; Beedle, Mike (18 February 2002), *Agile Software Development with Scrum*, Prentice Hall

- Schwaber, Ken (2007), *The Enterprise and Scrum*, Microsoft Press

- Snowden, David and Boone, Mary (2007), *A Leader's Framework for Decision Making*, Harvard Business Review

- Stacey, Ralph D (2012), *The Tools and Techniques of Leadership and Management: Meeting the Challenge of Complexity*, Routledge

- Stacey, Ralph D (1996), *Strategic Management and Organizational Dynamics, Second Edition*, Routledge

- *Jeff Sutherland's Scrum Handbook* at http://jeffsutherland.com/scrumhandbook.pdf

- Stacia Viscardi's Scrum website at www.helloscrum.com

2

Release Planning – Tuning Product Development

People in traditional projects attempt to define and then control scope during the project, while Agile teams approach the problem differently: figure out enough to get started, embrace changes, and then proceed as the way opens. Agile teams, by definition, try to respond to changing market or user needs as soon as those needs are discovered, yet business requires them to plan ahead from time to time. Agile teams know that they cannot predict a project's outcome, so they use pragmatic planning approaches to tune their development efforts to the latest and greatest needs. This is somewhat like what your local meteorologist does every night on the six o'clock news—his next-day forecast is usually spot on, but the seventh day is always off! Unfortunately, no team (or weatherman) can predict the future, which is why I keep a backup umbrella in my car.

The traditional project metrics of *all planned scope, on budget*, and *by the deadline* don't work for complex technical projects. Here's a quick example out of thousands: if the project team changes direction because a customer's needs change halfway through the project, is this a failure? Agile teams would say certainly not, and that it's actually a success to respond to changing needs, but I've actually heard the counterargument that if the team members would have spent more time in requirements gathering, they would have been able to predict all the customer's needs up front rather than encounter a surprise downstream (as if someone can simply throw out the cast net and drag all the requirements in with the fishes!). This traditional project management logic says that we fail when we don't achieve the holy trinity of scope, time, and cost. Unfortunately, there are still many organizations, managers, and teams that have this embedded mind-set; this can disrupt the best Agile planning attempts.

I'd give anything to have the ability to see the future of a project, and I'm sure most of you reading this book would as well. Why do you think this is? Humans love to have the perfect plan, and we want the security of knowing what will happen next. We feel safe and secure when we have a tidy Gantt chart, risk logs, and resource plans. It feels good to think about the problem for a long time until we're sure that we have the perfect solution. We're problem solvers, after all, so isn't this what we're supposed to do? Plans make us feel secure. That is, until they change.

If the real world didn't exist, my advice to you and your team would be to plan your projects barely enough to deliver value early and spend more of your time adapting to the realities that unfold as a result of delivery. I'd also recommend that you help your teams resist the temptation of estimating tasks to the nth level and to committing to anything more than a week's worth of work; and please, thwart any attempt by your organization to put you or your colleagues on more than one task or project at a time! Stage a revolt if you must!

Since you live in the real world, and you're not likely to stage a revolt, I have to give advice that's a bit more useful than "go ahead, break all the rules." First, think differently about planning. Consider that, in your current work environment, you are most likely asked to plan projects because the business requires it. Constraints such as budgets, deadlines, and resources (human or not) are finite entities that a ScrumMaster must work with or around in a project. Or are they? Agile gives us the opportunity to pause to think that budgets, deadlines, and people assigned to the project can change based on the adaptations that the organization needs to make in order to win. Be aware that there is a growing trend of modern organizations moving away from the traditional mind-set of projects, and I fully attribute this to the Agile movement. This movement from "crystal-balling" to "continuous adaptation" is a real, modern business adaptation. *Mary Poppendieck*, author of *Lean Software Development: An Agile Toolkit*, says that successful companies don't create a plan and execute it; rather, they create capacity and respond to reality as it unfolds. Scrum provides two activities for understanding capacity and planning: release planning for long-term and sprint planning for short-term. Both utilize the product backlog as an input. This chapter will teach you how to use release planning techniques, but in parallel, also think of Scrum as your quiet revolt; use its philosophies and tools to change the way your organization thinks about projects and value(s).

As we discussed in the first chapter, the Scrum framework is the Deming Cycle incarnate: plan-do-check-act. (*Wash. Rinse. Repeat.*) The reasons for doing so are as clear as a sunny day: knowledge about requirements, technology, and personal interactions emerge throughout the lifecycle of a project. Owing to this emergence, it makes sense to plan with just enough detail for the timeframe and expected outcome. In other words, long-term plans are coarse in their level of planning and estimation, while near-term plans are very detailed. The following figure illustrates the idea of narrowing the view and focus for the time horizon; roadmaps, which we'll discuss in *Chapter 6, The Criticality of Real-time Information*, have wide swaths of possibilities—the roadmap's range is long-term (years, in some cases). Release plans are usually one to three months (although they can be longer) into the future and the possibilities aren't so robust; in fact, release plans are just as much about what a team won't do, as what they will try to do. Finally, you can see that the sprint really nails it down; a team commits to a specific amount of work for a near-term goal (one to four week cycles, more in *Chapter 3, Sprint Planning – Fine-tune the Sprint Commitment*).

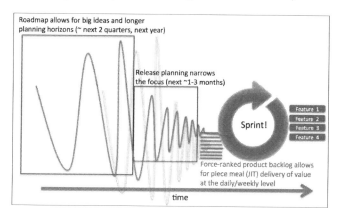

I used to play violin. Every day before I could practice, I had to tune my instrument. Tuning is physically done by first using the wooden pegs by the scroll, matching the pitch with that of a piano or a tuning fork. I'd get as close to the standard pitch as I could for the A string and then use the fine tuners near the chin rest to make it perfect. From a perfectly tuned A string, it was easy to tune the other strings because when tuned, the sound waves synchronize and notes would blend into a beautiful synthesis of sound. If you've ever watched an orchestra, I'm sure you've noticed the string players tuning their instruments several times throughout. This is because the circumstances of the concert change while the concert is in play—the wood of the violin expands from the heat of the player's body and fingers, strings loosen, and bow hair relaxes through intense pizzicato and crescendo; or perhaps the musician noticed that his instrument was just a bit off while playing the previous piece. Musicians see tuning as part of the concert, part of playing the piece or movement. While getting the instrument back on pitch, the musician is also getting his mind in tune as well.

A release plan is similar to the tuning fork; it represents the direction, goal, or outcomes to which teams should align. Sprint planning is like fine-tuning; turning the little metal fine-tuners at the bottom of the violin bridge in order to get perfect pitch; planning for exactly what we can commit to for one, two, or four weeks of time. I wouldn't fine-tune my violin today and think that I could play in an orchestra five months from now without re-tuning. I have to re-tune to account for changes in the instrument. So while I dislike the word *plan* because it has the connotations of finality, exactness, deadlines, and fixedness, I like the concept of *tuning* product development to the needs of users and customers by use of adaptive planning techniques such as release and sprint planning. And just as tuning is part of playing the piece or movement, think of release planning and sprint planning as part of *doing* the project.

To make it even more interesting, there are non-standard tuning techniques, called *scordatura*, evident in French composer Camille Saint-Saens' Danse Macabre, where the violin's E string is tuned down to E flat (`http://en.wikipedia.org/wiki/Violin#Tuning`). Likewise, there are different methods and styles of planning releases and sprints. The simple answer is to keep planning simple and efficient; think of planning sessions as times for tuning product development in accordance with the stakeholders' needs. Since those needs are certain to change, tuning will be a continuous process much like you observe in the string section at the concert. This chapter focuses on the long-term release plan, while *Chapter 3, Sprint Planning – Fine-tune the Sprint Commitment*, is all about the short-term sprint plan. It is your responsibility as ScrumMaster to find the best tuning techniques for your team and organization. Carry on, ScrumMaestro.

Start at the beginning – product backlog

A product backlog is an ordered list of features or work to be implemented in a product. It could be infinite in length; that is, there could always be new requirements for a product. The product owner is an actual customer or an internal representation thereof (think of an iPad product owner representing many millions of users), maintains, updates, administers, and ranks the product backlog. Based on market research, a product vision statement, industry analytics, technical innovations, or simply ideas to test, the product backlog represents the product owner's most valuable ideas and features for a product.

Once the team has selected, planned, and committed product backlog items to a sprint, the product owner cannot make any changes to those items. However, the product owner is given free reign to change the priority, requirements, and even remove any product backlog item that hasn't been committed and planned in a sprint. This simple game rule drives the product owner into a routine behavior of just-in-time preparedness: the product owner must rank and prepare detail for the most important product backlog items for the next sprint planning meeting. Likewise, the product owner should prioritize and prepare a set of features desired for a release in anticipation of that release's planning discussion.

Product backlogs are very useful for managing change because work that hasn't started can easily be re-ordered (tuned) to the market needs at any given point in time. If the team needs to react to an emergency competitor situation, the product owner can defer any not-started items to make way for the features to meet the competitive demand in the very next sprint. Since we know that market needs will change, it's in the product owner's best interest to put more planning effort and detail into the most important items the team will need to implement next. In the following figure, the product backlog is depicted as the basis for both long and short-term planning. The product backlog facilitates both levels of planning; that is, product backlog can be quickly and easily re-ordered for long-term forecasting, while in sprint planning, the highest priority backlog items will be planned with utmost detail (tasks, hours, owners, and so forth) because they are ready to be implemented at that time. The leanest implementation of a product backlog is to pull the top item from the backlog, finish it, release to production, followed by the next item, and so on, with no planning other than for one item at a time. This scenario is actually a reality for some companies, as we'll discuss in *Chapter 11, Scrum and the Future*. However, most teams at most companies engage in both long-term and short-term planning activities and use the product backlog as the main input.

Product Backlog

Supports long-term planning by:	Supports short-term planning by:
- Enabling release planning and commitment - Communicates big picture - Helps business understand forecasted deliveries against business opportunities	- Powering the sprint - Enabling sprint commitment - Facilitates task creation, estimation, team ownership - Helps team understand value of sprint deliverables

Focus product backlogs on users and values

Product backlogs should be written for and releases should be planned around the product or features, not the components of a system. "The user can view a list of products on the main page" is a user-facing product backlog item, while "update the CSS to persist product header fonts" is not. Looking at a plan from the product perspective in user language helps the product owner bind release plans to market rhythms. In many cases, an even higher level of planning called a product roadmap will precede a release plan (see *Chapter 6, The Criticality of Real-time Information*, for more about roadmaps). Product backlogs, roadmaps, and release plans enable product owners and teams to *see the whole*; a lean concept that reminds us to step back and look at the big picture from time to time, not just the day-to-day details. In the following example, which product backlog do you think the product owner would have an easier time explaining to other business stakeholders? From which do you think it would be easier for the product owner to understand status? Which better enables the product owner to *see the whole*?

Product Backlog A		Product Backlog B	
Rank	Description	Rank	Description
1	The user should br able to login securely	1	Install latest Apache version
2	The user can search for products to buy	2	Write Javascript getters and setters for product ID
3	The user can add items to a shopping bag	3	Refactor pricing engine
4	The user can pay and select shipping options	4	Update CSS to reflect new background color
5	The user can rate the product and service	5	Update backend to support different image sizes
6	The user can recommend products to friends		

Product Backlog A is expressed as the best. Visualizing plans in terms of user value allows the product owner to move things around, de-prioritize scope, and negotiate the depth of feature delivery. Additionally, tracking status this way, along the lines of user value, helps him immediately realize when he may have a product increment for release (in this case probably after item number **4** has been implemented). He could also do this for **Product Backlog B**, but because the items are expressed as lower-level technical to-dos, the product owner would likely have to call a meeting or two to understand how all of these items map back to units of value that can be delivered. In fact, the items in **Product Backlog B** are better suited as sprint backlog items, tracked day-to-day by the team, that all together enable features to be implemented. We will explore this in greater detail in *Chapter 3, Sprint Planning – Fine-tune the Sprint Commitment* and *Chapter 6, The Criticality of Real-time Information*. As a ScrumMaster, you must ensure that your product owner and team understand the importance of expressing and tracking product backlog items as user value.

You may hear people refer to product backlog items by different names; legacy Scrum calls them generic **product backlog items** (PBIs), while teams may refer to them as features, user stories, and/or requirements in daily practice. Keep in mind that it really doesn't matter what they're called as long as they are written in a language that everyone understands. Since the product backlog enables both long and short-term planning discussions, we should try to use user or business language whenever possible

Product backlogs should have, at minimum, three columns of information: rank/order, a description, and an estimate (or cost). However, I have seen and worked with all varieties of backlogs, even one that spanned 17 columns and was accessed by as many as nine people at once (this was a huge program with seven teams, multiple area product owner proxies, one product owner, and several ScrumMasters). Many product owners choose to maintain their product backlogs in low-tech ways: on sticky notes (posted on the wall along with important information like a product vision statement), wireframes, page mockups, and so on.

Remember, the product backlog is both a planning and a communication tool at which many different people with different skills and responsibilities will look!

Rank	ID	Parent ID	Name	Estimate	Description
1.0	US37		Built-in charts and reports	5	Implement remaining charts and reports currently in legacy product. See document docv2.0_xyz for a list
2.0	US47		Implement performance monitoring	3	
3.0	US43		EPIC: real-time alerts for VMWare		(Was 40 points)
4.0	US44	US43	Detect and log VMWare real-time alerts	13	Admin will be alerted if metric meets any of the defined alert conditions
5.0	US44	US43	Administer VMWare real-time alerts	20	As an administrator I would like to configure the real-time alerts in the VMWare setup tool so that I can specify my conditions.

Rank	ID	Parent ID	Name	Estimate	Description
9.5	US41		Control user permissions		As an admin, I want to be able to control what my users can view, modify, create, or delete, so that critical information remains secure.
10.0	US10		Epic: generate, publish, and distribute reports	20	
11.0	US11		EPIC: real-time data visibility	13	
12.0	US24		EPIC: role-based views and access rights	20	

Engage the team early

Make sure that the product owner engages the development team early in product backlog planning. Each team member has his or her own skills, experiences, and ways of thinking about the product. Given an opportunity to brainstorm with the product owner and the rest of the team, team members can express new and innovative ideas, things that the product owner couldn't have thought of by himself. Some technical teams have been able to greatly influence the product's direction given a chance to participate in product backlog brainstorming very early in the product's development!

Paper prototyping is one of my favorite tools to help teams brainstorm products and product backlogs. In a paper prototyping session, the product owner and team work together to mock up the user interface, underlying components, and model system interactions—using paper! This is an excellent way to collaborate and get a feel for how the user will use the system; additionally, it provides a mechanism for the team and product owner to see if they missed any critical user stories, as well as facilitates the creation of some early acceptance criteria. Of course, a team can use paper prototyping for any type of system; modeling component interactions this way helps the team think through and gain a common understanding of the system's architecture. I use UXPin's (http://uxpin.com/web-kit.html) web and mobile paper prototyping kits in the classroom and coaching sessions; every team who has tried them loves them! The paper prototyping session brings value to a team in the form of product envisioning, collaboration, teamwork, shared understanding, and the creation of product backlog items.

I've stumbled across many sad mistranslations of Agile in the field; one is that only the product owner can add items to a product backlog. Please consider a better practice: anybody should be able to add an item to the product backlog. A product will certainly benefit if the product owner allows contributions of ideas by others, but keep in mind that in order to prevent a chaotic and stressful situation, the product owner is solely in charge of prioritizing—or more accurately, ordering—the items. Could you imagine how crazy life would be if 10 people were contributing to the backlog and fighting about priority every day?

Prioritization can be useful for other things

The following screenshot is an example of a project portfolio backlog created in Excel in December of 2012. The purpose of this list was to collect, in one place, all the 2013 project ideas from various product owners and prioritize them based on corporate objectives. The list is very high level and represents a mash-up of product launches, performance optimizations, and technical infrastructure projects. You may also notice that there are different requestors for each of the items (**Dev, PO, QA**). I like this example because it shows that the backlog concept is not only useful for prioritizing features within one product or release but also useful to plan a portfolio of projects based on organizational strategy. This list required several meetings with various product owners and department heads to work through, but it was the first time that they put all of their work into one list and ranked it, making all the work visible. There were some very tense moments during these meetings as some product owners realized that their ideas might not get much budget in the early part of 2013.

The CEO acted as *uber-product owner* in this meeting and ultimately decided where the money would go. I liked the organization and simplicity of this list; note how the product management team divided the backlog into months of work (December, January, and so on) in a spreadsheet. It's easy to group rows under month headings (or whatever headings you like) in order to collapse/expand parts of the backlog; it was really easy in the prioritization meetings for the ScrumMaster to click around to expand/collapse certain months in order to focus everyone's view. This view eventually acted as a landing page from which product owners could drill down into specific product backlogs; notice the link for the **New Product Blog** item—the product owner could click on the link in order to go to the specific product backlog of features contained in a separate worksheet for only that project. This allowed the group to drill down to supporting detail and quickly click back to the landing page to support different levels of conversation in the prioritization meetings. Google Sheets works really well for product backlog organization and enables real-time collaboration with many users at once. There are many Agile tools on the market that help product owners maintain their product and project portfolio backlogs (see www. userstories.com for a list of tools and ratings).

Product Backlog Item	Requestor	Dev Est	Prep work for 12/3 Release Planning
December Candidates			
January Candidates			
Enterprise messaging	Dev	$75,000 savings	Identify user stories and high-level estimate
Launch Product 1	PO - Bob		
- gap analysis/what's left to do			provide list of stories identified as needed for release
- new cover			
- work with supplier to understand impact			
Launch Product 2	PO - Callie		
- Cool gadget			Identify stories & acceptance criteria
- Neat social media feature			Identify stories & acceptance criteria
- other surprise			Identify stories & acceptance criteria
Decrease load time (<2 seconds) of pages	PO - Jack		
Launch Product 3	PO - Callie		Need supporting stories and acceptance criteria
New Product Blog	PO - Callie		User stories in Worksheet
Access user data from other sources	Dev		Prioritize sources & provide acceptance criteria
Research for Launch Product 4	Dev		Provide questions to be answered
Test automation	QA		
Optimize Client Applications	Dev		IDENTIFY top 10-20 Jira issues in each application/ongoing work
System Maintenance (ongoing)	Dev		
February Candidates			
March Candidates			

Release planning – when will you set your features free?

So now we have a product backlog. What next? Well, if you're not required to forecast a set of functionality for a future point in time, then the team should simply start working by pulling items from the top of the backlog to implement. When an organization requires a team to forecast a set of scope for a set period of time, they will, however need to do release planning.

Timing of releases and release planning

Releases themselves should occur at a point in time designated by the product owner when he has evaluated the return on investment and determined that a set of features should be made available to customers or users. The product owner, likely, will have an idea of release timeframes before any work has begun (I needed it yesterday!). There is a frequency at which customers or users would like to see new features, and it is the product owner's responsibility to determine this cadence. For example, in the map application on my new iPhone, I welcome new features and versions anytime they're available! On the other hand, I would not like it if brand new, different iPhones were available with brand new operating systems and user interfaces every month (I think device releases such as these are already a bit too frequent, but the market seems to have proven otherwise, at least for now).

It is necessary that the product owner is able to communicate release plans to other groups within the business; for example, marketing and sales groups in many companies need to communicate about the release ahead of time in order to generate buzz and interest, and it's critical from a business perspective to give those groups a heads-up about what's coming. Most organizations begin selling functionality before it's even finished—signing contracts based upon promises—and as much as I loathe the concept of fixed-scope/fixed-time contracts, there should be at least some indication of when features will land! I'd estimate that release planning happens before the project starts in about 80 percent of cases, and the rest of the time the team either does not do any release planning at all, or release planning occurs after a number of sprints through which the team has discovered its velocity. Regardless of when or how it's created, the product owner and team should revisit the release plan throughout the duration of the project as circumstances will change. It is your responsibility as the ScrumMaster to ensure that this happens.

Don't create the software big dig

You might be familiar with Boston's Central Artery/Tunnel project (aka *The Big Dig*). The initial project estimate was 2.5 billion dollars with an originally estimated completion year of 1998; estimates increased to 14 billion dollars by 2006, and while considered *done* by some in 2006, there remains to this day a need to replace 25,000 deteriorating light fixtures, to the tune of an additional 54 million dollars. According to Virginia Greiman of Boston University, "no single catastrophic event or small number of contracts caused costs to escalate. The critical cause was a lack of experience and knowledge about dealing with the complexity and uncertainty" (of giant projects). (`http://www.nasa.gov/offices/oce/appel/ask/issues/39/39s_ big_dig.html`). The people who designed the project were part of a different company than the people who built the structures, and there was not a policy of early and frequent engagement and communication among these thousands of people. The ultimate cost of the Big Dig, sadly, was the loss of life: a woman was crushed in her car and died a few years ago because the glue used to hold the roof in place was insufficient for long-term bonding. There was so much uncertainty and complexity at the beginning of this project that it was foolish for any contractor to bid a defined amount, and foolish for the Massachusetts Turnpike Authority to accept such. However, we live in a world in which low bids and sketchy promises often do win the contract, unfortunately.

There are numerous lessons from Boston's Big Dig that apply to release planning

Integrate early and often to mitigate risks

Encourage team members (and multiple teams if you're on a larger program) to integrate early and often, and to account for these activities in the release plan. Many developers put off merging their work because they don't want to deal with the problems that integration surfaces. As ScrumMaster, you must remind team members that a sprint's features aren't done until one person's code works with everyone else's code and that all test cases pass. It may be difficult for the team to reach this level of *done* in early sprints for many valid reasons—antiquated build practices, old tools, and so on—but you must help the team develop the ability to ultimately integrate on a continuous basis. Falling short of this will impede the ability of the organization to respond to customers' most pressing needs. You must ensure that your team discuss and address issues such as integration, testing, and a general *Definition of Done* in release planning initially, and revisit these goals throughout the project. For more ideas, check out Henrik Kniberg's article on version control for Agile teams (`http://www.infoq.com/articles/agile-version-control`).

Make buffers visible

As ScrumMaster you should encourage your team to communicate realistic estimates and add buffers for when uncertainty is particularly high. This means that the team should pad estimates for the unknown; for example, if your team must leverage a third-party technology in a few sprints from now, the team should buffer those estimates to reflect the unknowns of the integration effort in the release plan. The team could choose to give a low estimate, tell the product owner what he wants to hear, and make him happy in the short term; the trouble is that the team might have to go back to the customer with tail between legs to ask for more money or more time, which I don't advocate as a sustainable practice. Worst case, the team might try to pull off a miracle, resulting in cut corners and quality issues that will only come back to haunt them (or some other poor team) in the future. Teams should pad estimates to compensate for uncertainty and regularly communicate their concerns and fears to the ScrumMaster and product owner. It's always better for the team to have buffered a little too much; in that case, they can just pull another few stories into the release. I'd rather have this situation than my team having to cut stories from a release!

Buffering for uncertainty simply means not planning each sprint to 100 percent maximum capacity. Let's say that our team initially feels that it can accomplish 20 points per sprint, but after a bit more discussion, the team realizes that they should buffer about 25 percent of their capacity for ramp up (they're all new to the project) and maintenance of the existing production version. A 25 percent buffer means that the release commitment would now be 15 points — not 20 — per sprint. Makes sense, right? Well, I've met many people who have had extremely negative gut reactions to this concept. I've heard comments such as, "We can't lie to our customer!" or "Management wants to see 100 percent utilization, we can't plan for and only show 75 percent!" Actually, wouldn't teams be lying to the customer if they dismissed the ramp-up time and production support activities that they know they are responsible for and instead stuffed each sprint in release planning to 100 percent? After two or three sprints of working and realizing that they had overcommitted in the first place, they've only managed to delay this inevitable touchy conversation! You see, release planning should be a meaningful discussion between the team and product owner about what's realistic; sometimes this means making some tough decisions and trade-offs. Every product owner I've met says that they'd rather know the concerns and risks as soon as possible so that they have time to make the appropriate decisions. Buffering helps teams create plans that are realistic and sets them up with a better chance of meeting their commitments to the product owner.

Keep in mind that your job as ScrumMaster is to make buffers visible; in fact, since the customer or product owner attends your release planning meeting, he would understand the reasons behind the buffer because he was engaged in an intelligent dialogue about it with the team. Most people recognize buffering as good risk mitigation practice.

If our team finishes the 15 points of work by the first half of the sprint, they should pull the next items from the top of the product backlog to fill up the remainder of the sprint. (They would need to hold a mini-planning session to figure out how much to pull—see *Chapter 3, Sprint Planning – Fine-tune the Sprint Commitment.*) Let's say they pulled eight additional points of work and were able to complete the eight points in addition to the 15 they originally committed. As a result the team has an observed velocity of 23—a number they can use to re-forecast the release with increased confidence.

The more uncertain the team and product owner are, the more they should buffer. The following screenshot shows an example of buffering for work that is not feature implementation:

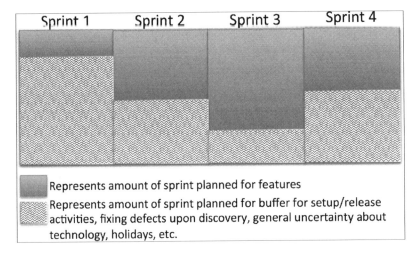

Represents amount of sprint planned for features

Represents amount of sprint planned for buffer for setup/release activities, fixing defects upon discovery, general uncertainty about technology, holidays, etc.

Some teams apply a buffer by leaving empty an entire sprint or two at the end, as shown in the following screenshot:

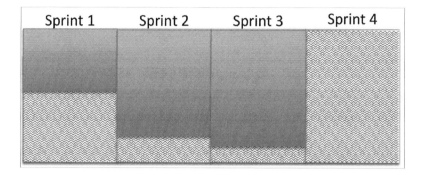

Release planning is like tuning to the standard pitch. Release plans will be *off*. And maybe *off* is acceptable to customers, maybe it's not—we'll discover that through playing (sprinting). We want to partner with customers to build the right features to an acceptable level of quality in an acceptable amount of time while making uncertainty and estimated costs visible so that the customer is not surprised. Likewise, we shouldn't expect our customers to know everything about what they want today, because they simply cannot. Remember that a Scrum team should partner with the product owner (from the Agile Manifesto: "customer collaboration over contract negotiation"). In any partner relationship, both parties should operate with full transparency.

Release planning isn't a mandatory event. The legacy Scrum documents don't even mention it; only recently has the Scrum framework been extended to recognize release planning as a bona fide (yet optional) Scrum meeting. You may need to question if your team needs release planning in the first place. If you have the ability to push to production at any time and have a product owner who's flexible about dates and scope, then your team might be able to skip this meeting.

Release planning opens up a dialog and an acknowledgement that planning is not a prediction—rather, a forecast—and that some features may need to be traded-off or de-scoped. It can often feel that release planning is not just about a team figuring out what will be in the release but also making tough cuts for features that won't be in the release.

In the following figure, there are three areas: a solutions space (features/user stories/ PBIs), timeframes, and business problems that need solutions. The role of the product owner (the guy in the middle there) is to pick the right set of features to solve the current (and projected) business problems within a timely manner (a sprint, a release next year). The difficulty is that the problem and solutions spaces are dynamic. There are always problems to solve—some we know as regularly recurring events (user conference), and yet there are true emergencies from time to time (responding to competitor x, production issue, and so on). The good news is that the product backlog is stocked with many ideas from which the product owner may choose in order to formulate the best possible response. The goal of this game is to line up items in the backlog to the right timeframe in order to satisfy the business need, sort of like when you play a slot machine: if three cherries line up in the middle, you've won. The difference in the technology slot machine is that things just don't ever quite line up perfectly, no matter how hard you try, because of all the interdependencies: a change in one necessitates a change in another. Since the problem and solutions spaces change all the time (and timeframes/deadlines can too, for that matter), planning should be viewed as an ongoing dialog between team and product owner that takes into account the latest changes in these spaces in order to formulate a new best response each time, lining up the cherries as closely as possible.

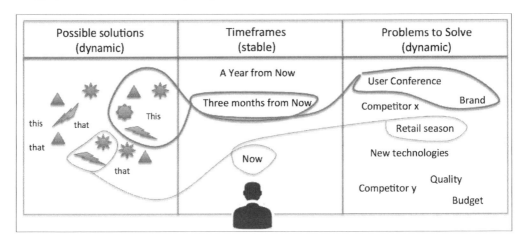

How to conduct a release planning event?

So your product owner and team have brainstormed a product backlog with features, and everyone is ready to get started. The product owner is ready to pull the lever on the technology slot machine. How do you engage everyone in an effective release planning conversation?

Do your homework!

Do a little homework before release planning; see if you can get answers to the following questions in order to help your release planning event run smoothly and efficiently. Some of these questions may not apply, but this list is a good representative set for most situations:

- When can everyone meet, ideally face to face? If your team is collocated, then you're already set! If you have a distributed team, then release planning is definitely one time, in addition to sprint planning, when you'd like to have everyone meet face to face. Try to make it happen. If your team is distributed, try to get the budget to fly people to a common location. If people can't meet face to face, then decide upon a technology combination to best facilitate and accommodate this less-than-desired state (see *Chapter 10, Scrum, Large and Small*, for more about adaptations for distributed Scrum teams).

- Is the meeting space equipped with a whiteboard, dry erase markers, flip charts, permanent markers, and plentiful sticky notes?

- What's the desired release date? You can probably get this from the product owner. It's usually *yesterday*.

- Does the product owner have a product vision statement and information about users, market, customers, personas, and so on? It's helpful for the team to understand the big picture, the overall problem they're trying to solve, or how they will delight their customers. When development team members see the whole, they very often come up with innovative ideas.

- How many sprints will the release need? Will sprints be one, two, three, or four weeks in length? Does management dictate the length of a sprint? Is that acceptable to the product owner? Should you challenge it?

- Who will define closure for the release? For each sprint within the release? (See the next section.)

- Is your team staffed to handle the Definition of Done? If not, what workarounds can they implement?

- Is there an existing production process or protocol that the team must follow? (Get machines, setup development environments, testing frameworks, and so on.)

- Is there a release process understood before going to production? What is it, if so, and how does that impact your release plan?

- Does the team have a known velocity? If not, you will have to facilitate a capacity planning exercise in the release planning meeting.

- How will the team raise impediments during the release? What's the escalation path?

- Where will the product backlog be housed? Can the product owner commit to making it visible to the team, at least?

- Does the team understand the Scrum framework?

- Do we know where we will keep our sprint backlogs and burndowns? Other project information?

- Should we invite any other stakeholders?

- What risks are currently present in the release? Do we know of any impediments that we have today? Will any team members be away for large chunks of time?

> I once worked with a team that had an offsite meeting planned in Aruba for mid-November (unfortunately, I was not invited). We were release planning in September for the fourth quarter (October-December). Aruba in November meant that the team shouldn't take on as much functionality during sprints that span that timeframe. It sounds like common sense, but you'd be surprised at the number of teams that don't think of it and overcommit themselves on Day 1.

Even though you may get some answers ahead of time by doing your homework, you must review this information with the team in order to unearth any additional concerns, questions, and possibly disagreement. For example, you and the product owner may have identified three risks before release planning; you'd still want to ask the team if they can think of any additional risks. They usually will.

Facilitating the release planning meeting

Your role as ScrumMaster in the release planning meeting is to serve as guide, time-keeper, organizer, and facilitator. Unlike a project manager, you do not make the decisions about scope, time, and cost; in Scrum, that responsibility belongs to the product owner. The release planning meeting is the time for the product owner to present the problems that he is trying to solve and the timeframes that would be most beneficial, and work with the team to figure out the best response.

Participants

The primary participants in release planning are the ScrumMaster, the product owner, and the delivery team members. Other stakeholders may wish to attend. For example, the support representative who had requested some fixes to customer issues wants to attend release planning so that he/she can provide the team with additional context about those issues.

Since he/she is the first line of communication to the customer, he/she is a vested stakeholder and needs to be present. It is important to remember, however, that even though other stakeholders might attend, the product owner still owns the order and depth to which product backlog items are implemented. The ScrumMaster and product owner should work together to identify and invite any appropriate stakeholders ahead of time.

Agenda

The release planning conversation should be just that—a conversation. It should not be a presentation of a plan from product owner to team; rather, the spirit of the meeting is that team members and the product owner share a vision and together create a plan. In order to get the best, most focused discussions, and ensure that you have the results you need, you'll need a well-crafted agenda.

A sample release planning agenda is as follows; please tailor it to meet your needs and remember to keep it as light as possible:

Items
Short introduction by ScrumMaster welcoming all attendees, reviewing purpose, agenda, and time-boxes for the meeting. Reiterate the use of Parking Lot, Action Items, Risks, and Decisions flip charts in order to stay on track for the meeting.
Review the roles and responsibilities for release planning.
ScrumMaster – facilitator and scribe.
Product owner – clarifies user stories and makes decisions about priority, core value, and so on.
Delivery team members – provide estimates and advise product owner about technical issues and risks; decompose user stories with product owner.
Product owner reviews the product vision and business goals for the release and conducts a high-level walkthrough of the highest priority user stories. Team members should ask questions to clarify understanding.
BREAK
ScrumMaster presents the high-level release schedule that includes sprint start/end dates, drops, and other important dates. Team members should account for any known PTO, vacation, holiday, other time away from the release as known. This can be designated by team members writing on the calendar (if collocated and using flip charts) or by the ScrumMaster entering this info into an electronic calendar for all to see.

Items

ScrumMaster should do a quick review of the team members' allocations to the release. It is ideal if the team is 100 percent dedicated to the effort, but sometimes this is not possible. Find out the percentage of dedication to the effort and include a risk on the risk log, the capacity for the sprints will probably be overestimated (due to switch-tasking cost). ScrumMaster also writes an Action Item to attempt a resolution so that team members are dedicated (also logs this in his Impediment Backlog).

Review the Definition of Done and refine it if necessary. This will most likely be defined at the release level so that all teams consistently present product increments to the same standard. Ensure that every team member realizes what the the Definition of Done truly means.

Understand velocity. Does the team have a velocity (amount of work it has historically completed in a sprint or sprints) as an input to the release planning meeting? If so, record that number and move on to the next step. If no velocity exists, use one of the following two methods to estimate the velocity:

- **"Gut" method**: Ask team members if they feel they can complete the first priority story during the first sprint. Keep going down the list until they feel they have enough work. Resist the behavior of putting 'expert to task'.

- **"Value of 1" method**: Find a story that equals a "1" is small in size. Task out this story into work tasks, and estimate each task. For example, a small user story with the value of one point equals 10 hours of work for our team. If our team have 100 total team hours available in a sprint, then that means we can take on roughly 10 points of work. WARNING: Please keep team members from delving into assigning persons to tasks or from figuring out all tasks for the sprint (this is meant to be rough estimation, not precise, and tasking out is for sprint planning, NOT release planning!)

BREAK

Team members place stories into sprints. Some stories may need to be decomposed with the guidance of the product owner if necessary. If a story must be decomposed, the team must estimate the smaller pieces. Remember the **INVEST** acronym when decomposing user stories: **Independent**, **Negotiable**, **Valuable**, **Estimatable**, **Small**, and **Testable** (see Bill Wake's article at `http://www.xp123.com`).

Have all team members 'walk the wall' and voice any concerns or risks. Add risks to the Risk board and discuss Concerns. Add any unresolved concerns to the Parking Lot for follow-up after the meeting.

Ask the team if they feel that they can commit to the release forecast. Resolve any issues that are obstacles to commitment.

It is imperative that the product owner attends and participates (that is, not on a 'crackberry') during the release planning discussion. In this day and age, there's simply no excuse. If you can't get his time, raise an impediment right away! It's called: "Cannot start project due to risk of delivering the wrong features! Need a product owner, stat!" And dig in your heels until you get what you need. Otherwise, the technical team is blindfolded, shooting arrows at a target with toddlers all around it. This is a big risk and probably not a pretty scene. It is up to you, the ScrumMaster, to raise impediments like this. And be courageous about it. Terminate a sprint if you have to. Call attention to it. Quantify the risks; put it in dollar signs!

I recently worked with a team whose product had been in development for three years (and never once released!). The CEO was the product owner, but he was only able to attend every third or fourth demo. When he would attend, he would change everything. As a result, the product stayed in development and developers stayed grumpy; worst of all, the product remained in the incubator. What if the CEO could have invested in a product owner who could have found a way to get something to market in a year? The company could have recognized return on investment much earlier!

The physical space

It is critical for good meeting outcomes that you set up the appropriate physical space for release planning. You should aim for a space that allows team members to face each other, trade ideas, and easily capture those ideas throughout the meeting. You want them to have everything they need at their fingertips—the energy of a meeting completely crashes when someone has to run down the hall to find a white board marker or eraser! Don't let this happen to your team.

In setting up the space, think about the purpose of the meeting and the expected outcome. In which topics of conversation do you think the team will most likely engage? How can you set the room up to efficiently capture these ideas? The following figure shows some common release planning questions and statements:

Teams talk about scope, estimates, and deadlines in release planning, and they are also usually pretty vocal about risks and concerns. That means that you need to have tools to help you capture this stuff without interrupting discussions, all the while keeping the information available for the team to work with throughout the meeting. If your team is collocated (or if at least 80 percent of them are), plan to use flip charts and sticky notes. I usually arrive 30 minutes prior to the meeting to prepare the space, following this mental checklist:

- Make sure that there are enough chairs for everyone and that are they facing each other (a U-shaped conference room table is not ideal for this meeting).

- Put out Sharpie pens and sticky notes on the table—enough for everyone.

- Put flip charts on the walls to capture information and radiate any guiding information such as the **Definition of Done**, **agenda**, and **ground rules** (see the following figure for an example).

- Bring a notebook to capture notes and reminders during the meeting.

- If the product backlog has been captured electronically, I will have spent the afternoon the day before writing these onto sticky notes for use and manipulation by the team during the meeting.

- Review your agenda and look for opportunities for group activities.

- Open windows if possible, for natural light. Ensure that the room is at a good temperature.

- If there are a couple of remote team members, send out Skype or a similar invitation; recruit a volunteer (not a team member) to come to the meeting with a camera phone in order to stream planning artifacts and work products to the remote team members.

Definition of Done

It is imperative that the team define and agree upon the state of acceptable 'doneness' for sprints and the release during the release planning meeting. In other words, is the customer willing to accept a lower level of quality because the product is first-to-market? Or is the system life-critical and therefore absolutely no trade-offs in quality are allowed? Reaching a common Definition of Done for the release and for each sprint is imperative to set expectations and in keeping with the mind-set of *build quality in*. It also prevents lots of confusion during the sprint.

An example Definition of Done for a release is *product features work; that is, no show-stopping defects (severity 1, 2, or 3). Page load times are less than one second. All integration tests are automated so issues are more readily and quickly found in the future.* We'll discuss the sprint Definition of Done in the next section, and see *Chapter 10, Scrum, Large and Small,* for a nested Definition of Done concept.

Release planning output

After release planning, the ScrumMaster and product owner should decide on who will communicate the release plan, including sprint start/end dates, functionality milestones, other drops/milestones, changes in milestones, and impacts to dependencies, risks, concerns, action items, and so on. This information can be reported from a tool (if necessary) once it's been entered after the release planning event, or simply put into an Excel spreadsheet for easy consumption. Some ScrumMasters simply take a photograph of the flip chart and communicate it that way!

Here's a very simple release plan:

Write a book (release date December 15, 2012) *I'm late, by the way

Sprint 1 = chapter 1

Sprint 2 = write chapter 2, edit chapter 1

Sprint 3 = write chapter 3, edit chapter 2

...

Release sprint = final edits, graphics

Release = publish and party!

All book jokes aside, following is a visual concept of a release plan:

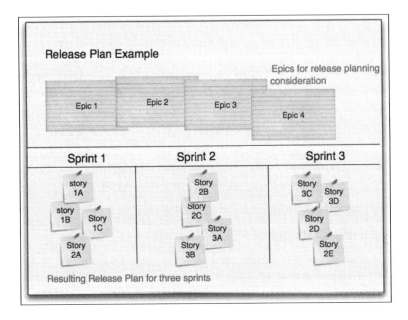

Another way of thinking of a release plan is as a **cut line** in the product backlog; the team have forecasted everything above the cut line for the release, anything below the line as not in the release.

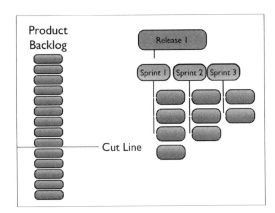

The following image is a real release plan from a real team using flip charts and sticky notes:

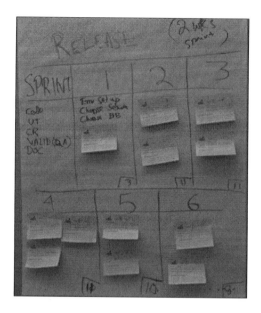

Following is a product backlog that the ScrumMaster extended in order to easily show the status of items. You can see the rank, item description, and estimate — the bare minimum columns for a product backlog, plus the added *planned sprint* and *actual sprint* to record when the feature had been planned to finish versus when it really was finished. The highlighted fields for **Tool Review Page**, **Social Media**, and **Google Analytics** show that there was a domino effect of stories planned that slipped into the following sprint. I tallied up both estimated and actual velocities to the right, which could be used to generate a release burndown chart (see *Chapter 6, The Criticality of Real-time Information*).

Rank	Item	Estimate	Planned Sprint	Actual Sprint	
1	Buy domain and secure hosting	1	1	1	
2	Create site map	5	1	1	Sprint 1 estimate = 14 points
3	Get artwork	3	1	1	Sprint 1 actual velocity = 9 points
4	ScrumMaster page	5	1	2	
5	Product owner page	5	2	2	Sprint 2 estimate = 21 points
5.5	Team page	5	2	2	Sprint 2 actual velocity = 15 points
6	Tool review page	3	2	3	
7	Q&A page	8	2	3	
8	Rate your trainer page	8	3	3	Sprint 3 estimate = 21 points
9	Find a scrum mentor	5	3	3	Sprint 3 actual velocity = 24 points
10	Social media	5	3		
11	Google analytics	3	3		
12	Newsletter	3	4		

Finally, here's a release planning timeline that shows the highest level epics (or chunks of functionality) along with approximate delivery timelines. This can be helpful for executive communication situations in which too much detail can hinder the message.

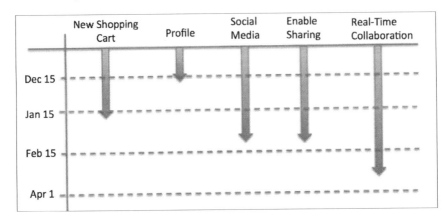

Release planning summary

The traditional mentality of predictive fixed-time/fixed-scope planning is an unspoken impediment every single day. You must fight this impediment every step of the way in the way you conduct, facilitate, and communicate the results of planning. In a meeting with stakeholders from sales and support, you should say, "Here's our forecast, based on what we know today". In a status meeting with executives, say the exact same thing. Every sprint, keep the plan completely transparent and set (and reset) the expectations. DO NOT CAVE INTO existing corporate pressures! Nothing will change if you do so. It is a decision on your part and a responsibility you take on when you put those three letters after your name: John Doe, CSM.

You can't pour two yards of ale in a yard glass. Well, you can, but some ale will spill to the ground. And that's a sad thing, indeed. Likewise, the team will only be able to deliver a certain number of features in a release, with its given resources, team members, product owner (and subsequent level of engagement), and other constraints. It may only be a yard of features, while the customer wants two up front. Do we promise two anyway? What happens to quality, then?

Please don't misunderstand me: a team is surely committed to doing whatever they can to deliver what the customer needs, but the team should also be up front and readily acknowledge that a release plan is the best guess based on what its members collectively know at that point in time. Since knowledge about requirements, technology, and human interactions increases through time, why would we commit and feign crystal ball levels of prediction ability? For example, if a new technology came about that could help our customer's product scale for half of the estimated cost, why would we continue with the original technology choice? Wouldn't our customer have appreciated the opportunity to choose the new technology and spend the savings on another feature (or release early)? A release plan is merely the revisited result of an ongoing dialog between the product owner (customer) and the development team. The most important part of the release plan are the discussions between the product owner and team regarding needs, uncertainty, approaches, and trade-offs.

Summary

Release planning is not a crystal ball into which someone can look and predict the outcome of a project. Rather, release planning provides a way for the team and product owner to tune committed work to users' and customers' needs without planning for too much detail too soon. The team and product owner must revisit the release plan periodically during the release and work together to deliver features that delight customers.

In *Chapter 3, Sprint Planning – Fine-tune the Sprint Commitment*, we will discuss how the team works with the product owner to create a good short-term plan for one sprint.

Recommended reading

- Cohn, Mike (2009), *User Stories Applied*, Pearson Education
- Pichler, Roman (2010), *Agile Product Management with Scrum*, Pearson Education
- Reis, Eric (2011), *Lean Startup*, Crown Business
- Website of Carolyn Snyder, author of Paper Prototyping: http://www.paperprototyping.com/
- UXPin (paper prototyping kits): www.uxpin.com
- Tabaka, Jean (2006), *Collaboration Explained*, Pearson Education

3

Sprint Planning – Fine-tune the Sprint Commitment

If release planning is the tuning fork, then sprint planning is the fine-tuning that a musician does before and during play. Since an instrument's tune is affected by its age and damage throughout the years, external factors such as the weather, and by the musician and his playing style, tuning is the way the musician brings the instrument back to the desired sound, matching usually an external source such as a tuning fork or digital tuner. In our Agile concerto, sprint planning is like fine-tuning the deliverables in the product backlog to the overarching pitch—or goals—set forth in the release plan. Just as instruments will get out of tune, so will a plan. But an Agile plan will never get too far out of sync since the product owner maintains a product backlog with the latest priorities and engages with the team in sprint planning. Sprinting allows the team and customer to readjust, or tune short-term deliverables to meet the longer-term release goals sprint after sprint.

Sprint planning basics

Sprint planning is, simply, the time when a team plans its sprint; it happens on the first day of the sprint. **Legacy Scrum** tells us that we have up to eight hours to plan for a 30-day sprint. In the past five years, many teams have moved to two-week sprints, and sprints of one or three weeks are also common. In any case, when the sprint length is shorter than one month, it's logical that the team should reduce the amount of time spent in sprint planning. A two-week sprint, for example, should not require a team to spend more than four hours of sprint planning (and can usually be completed in just a couple of hours). I worked with a team a couple of years ago that planned its three-week sprints in 15 minutes. And they consistently completed 85 to 95 percent of their commitments. More planning doesn't necessarily mean better planning!

Weight Watchers is very similar to Scrum. When a person begins the Weight Watchers program, he/she initially weighs in so that there is a baseline for assessing improvement. The person identifies his/her target goal and works in weekly increments to lose weight and improve health. Weight Watchers is known for its weekly weigh-in, which is similar to a Scrum team's sprint review, and for its weekly meeting, in which dieters talk about how the previous week went for them and to plan for the upcoming week. Weigh-ins force visibility and accountability of results, and although a dieter may request a "No Weigh-in" pass, it's probably not productive to do so each week. If a dieter's progress isn't visible, it's impossible to know if he is making steps in the right direction, doing the right things; therefore, it's impossible to adapt. Without visibility there is no urgency. Weight Watchers encourages its members to attend the weekly meetings to learn from others, envision the week ahead, devise a strategy for the week, build excitement, and make a commitment. The spirit of a Scrum's sprint planning meeting should be exactly like this: envision, get excited, and commit. Unfortunately, this spirit gets crushed in the real world by mechanics — that is, agendas, rules, outputs, backlogs, and numbers that really are just a means to an end. As ScrumMaster, you should change the mechanics and tools as needed – heck, do away with them altogether sometimes! You'll be surprised to see how your meetings change when you focus on the *feeling* that you're trying to create, and not so much on the measurable stuff. Change it up; don't be afraid to experiment.

Over the past decade, many team members have told me that they loathe sprint planning; I consider this the ScrumMaster's fault. Your responsibility as ScrumMaster is to make this meeting a meaningful and interesting part of the team members' experience. If your idea of running a sprint planning meeting is to project a spreadsheet on the wall while developers sleep at the table, drooling from their mouths, stop it now. If you have created tasks for team members, stop it now! If you have suggested to team members how long their tasks should take, please stop it now! A ScrumMaster should create an engaging environment in which team members may contribute. During sprint planning, they should discuss important design and coding approaches, figure out test cases, and create their own sprint plan. Don't waste technical professionals' time by having them watch you type tasks into a spreadsheet or other tools during this meeting. Nor should they have their tasks dictated to them, or their estimates handed to them by you or a team lead. They are plenty capable of doing this stuff themselves.

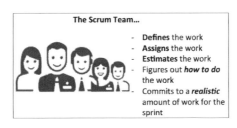

The Scrum Team...
- **Defines** the work
- **Assigns** the work
- **Estimates** the work
- Figures out ***how to do*** the work
- Commits to a ***realistic*** amount of work for the sprint

And finally, by all means, the team should not be pressured to commit to seven stories when they feel that only three may be done competently. Sprint planning is intended to be an active, thoughtful discussion among team members to share a vision and plan for the sprint, ultimately so that they may arrive at a commitment that reflects a realistic, professional quality deliverable.

Let's say that one day I have to see a doctor because I'm having heart trouble. After a few tests, the doctor calls me to his office, shuts the door, and has a very serious look on his face. "Stacia," he says, "you need open heart surgery. This surgery won't be easy because you have several complications. I'm thinking that you're going to be out for four or five hours; you'll wake up with a very long scar along your sternum, and it'll take you six to eight weeks to recover. And, by the way, this surgery isn't cheap. It's going to be in the $100k range." I have a blank stare on my face. I'm troubled as I imagine such a grisly and invasive surgery. I look up at the doctor and I say to him, "Doc, I respect you as a professional and all. But I need to be up and about within two days of surgery, I don't want a long scar. Oh, and I only have one thousand dollars to spend on this. Think you can help me out?" Of course, the doctor sends me on my way and slams the door behind me. The doctor would never agree to such terms; he's a professional and wants to do a quality job. Why, then, when pressured, does our software developer relent on her estimates? "Two weeks?!" her manager exclaims. "Why, you should be able to do that in two days!" And the developer looks at her manager, nods her head, and says, "Ok, two days it is." What do you think happens as a result of this compromise?

The clock officially starts ticking for a sprint during sprint planning when the product owner and the team get together to discuss what they will commit to for the sprint. During this meeting, the product owner explains the highest value items in the product backlog, and the team tells the product owner what they feel they can realistically commit to. Check out an excerpt from *Agile Project Management with Scrum*, Microsoft Press:

> *Sprint planning meetings cannot last longer than eight hours — that is, they are time-boxed to avoid too much hand-wringing about what is possible. The goal is to get to work, not to think about working.*

Many ScrumMasters, I've found, mistranslate this eight-hour time box as, "I need to fill up an eight-hour meeting with all sorts of planning activities." No! Nothing could be further from the truth! It seems that the more time a team has to plan, the more anxious they can get about the work, so plan with a "just enough" mind-set, and then hop to it!

Just like the Scrum framework provides a light framework in which work will happen, think of your sprint planning agenda as a light framework in which team members interact. You have a well-constructed agenda if the team does the talking and is interactive 80 percent of the time, or more. If that doesn't describe your meetings, please read on.

Preparing for sprint planning

If you're new at facilitating meetings, preparation, especially in the beginning, is extensive and burdensome. It will be, simply, trial and error until you figure out what works best for you and your team, in your unique environment. You should be your own worst critic; make observations and notes about what is and isn't working during your meetings, and ask the team members for their feedback as well. Meeting results are directly proportional to your preparation and your overall facilitation experience.

High-octane stories

The product backlog powers sprint planning. Just as engines run more efficiently with high-octane fuel, teams can plan more efficiently with well-prepared product backlog items.

I've found Bill Wake's INVEST acronym to be the best readiness litmus test for PBIs coming into sprint planning. **INVEST** stands for Independent, Negotiable, Valuable, Estimatable, Small, and Testable:

- **Independent**: Stories' boundaries are explicit so that the team can implement stories in any order. For example, a team can first implement the user login story, followed by a user preference one. They are independent pieces of functionality.

- **Negotiable**: A story is not a contract. The PBI provides a good idea about what the product owner wants, and why he/she wants it, but the details will be filled in by further discussions between the product owner and the team. For example, as the team and product owner discuss the user login story in sprint planning, the product owner might say that it's not critical that the team implement the "forgotten password" case in this sprint. He would then create a separate story for that functionality and put it back in the product backlog for a later time.

- **Valuable**: A story's description should help the team understand why it's important to the user.

- **Estimable**: The delivery team should be able to estimate the story. Estimating helps the product owner prioritize it and it gives an indication of size. This is important because…

- **Small**: … the story should be small when it comes in to sprint planning. A small story means that its scope is understood and the boundaries are clear. If a story is small, it can be completed and tested within the sprint time box. "Implement social media" is a large story (probable an epic!), whereas "enable Facebook Likes on our home page" is a small PBI.

- **Testable**: The team should have an idea of how to test that the story was properly implemented. "Like buttons should display on our page – 90x20 pixels. Decide on XFBML or iFrame – if XFBML, users can add comments; if iFrame, then they can only like the page", and so on.

Furthermore, INVEST is a great acronym because it reminds us that the product owner makes an investment in each sprint and wants to see a return on that investment in the sprint review; therefore, it's important for a team to discuss how PBIs will be demonstrated at the sprint review so that the ROI is evident.

Messy product backlog items will cause your team, like an engine with bad quality fuel, to sputter, knock, and falter. A well-prepared product backlog is like high quality gasoline for your team, so work with the product owner to help him/her prepare the product backlog and subsequently set the team up for success. Additionally, remind your team that it is rare that a product owner creates a perfect PBI or user story (and that's really not the point anyway); rather, he/she will do his/her best to create good enough user stories that he/she and the team will subsequently discuss in order to get to a level of good understanding. When the product owner involves the team early in the product backlog preparation, as we discussed in *Chapter 2, Release Planning – Tuning Product Development*, they share an understanding of the problem that later helps them with the story writing and implementation.

Help the product owner prepare for sprint planning

Contact your product owner a few days prior to sprint planning to ensure that:

- He/she is available for planning.

- Very large features (sometimes called **epics**) are broken down into bite-size chunks (sometimes called **user stories**).

- The product backlog reflects the latest priorities (not only feature to feature, but depth of any one particular feature).

- The product owner has made an attempt to identify the acceptance criteria, or conditions of satisfaction for the sprint's candidate stories. Additionally, the product owner may have diagrams, wireframes, mockups or other supporting visuals, or documents to support his/her explanation of the product backlog items in sprint planning. The old adage "a picture is worth a thousand words" is spot on!

- You understand how you may best assist the product owner before, during, and after the meeting. For example, does he/she have a set of wireframes that they plan to walk through that you could print and put on the wall during the meeting? Would the product owner like for you to take notes during the meeting? It's always a good idea to ask your product owner, "How may I support you?".

Physical space

Just like you did for release planning, make sure that the room has ample space and supplies such as sticky notes, whiteboard, markers, and yes, walls—at least in the first few meetings (then move it to the park!). Do you need to purchase materials beforehand? Do you have a digital camera or a camera built in to your phone so that you can just snap a picture of the plan after the meeting, instead of typing it as you go? Can you take five minutes prior to the meeting to put up a calendar of the sprint or make a handout that includes important milestones? Even something as simple as setting up a round table so that team members may face each other can greatly improve the amount and quality of collaboration during sprint planning.

 Unlike a traditional manager who might control the planning or even come up with the plan by themselves, the ScrumMaster creates the best possible space in which the *team* creates and commits to the plan.

I like to post an empty sprint task board, a calendar, the Definition of Done, and the standard meeting tools (agenda, purpose, concerns, parking lot) on the wall prior to sprint planning. This is ready to go when team members come to the meeting; if I don't have access to the meeting space beforehand, I'll prepare the flip charts before the meeting so that I can just quickly stick them to the wall when I arrive.

Visualize the meeting

As I'm preparing the agenda a few days prior to the meeting, I'll just sit down with a pen and paper and picture the meeting in my head. I'll imagine the team gathering right before the meeting starts, chatting, and laughing, and I'll envision how I'll interact with them, and how events might transpire.

ScrumMaster envisions the meeting in order to create a good agenda.

The following is an example of my visualization exercise for a sprint planning meeting; thinking of the meeting in such a way helps me solidify the agenda as well as identify things to do to better prepare for the meeting. Keep in mind that you can use this visualization technique for any meeting!

- What will I do when I first arrive at the meeting? Set up the space, organize my materials, start the online meeting, dial into the conference call, straighten the chairs, put sticky notes out for people to use, erase the whiteboards…

   My actions: Write the meeting purpose, agenda, and parking lot flip charts and post them on the walls before the meeting starts.

   Make sure that the meeting invitation contains the meeting URL and conference call information. Test it out and make sure it works.

   Buy sticky notes before work tomorrow.

- What will the beginning look like? Team members arrive, get seated, chat a bit, and check their phones. I'm at the front of the room having a few side chats myself.

   My actions: Bring in coffee and donuts tomorrow.

- What happens next? On time, get everyone's attention, ask people to put down their cell phones and close their laptop lids. I reiterate the purpose of the meeting and walk them through the agenda. I discuss the meeting's time box and breaks (bathroom, lunch, and so on as applicable).

  My Actions: Order lunch and find out where the facilities are so I can tell the team.

- Then what happens? The product owner reads through the product backlog to help the team understand what needs this sprint (and why he/she needs it). The team will ask questions and discuss.

  My Actions: I will offer to scribe the acceptance criteria for each story so the team can stay focused on the discussion.

  Take a look at the product backlog and make sure it's ready for the meeting.

  Set up a quick meeting with the product owner to discuss his/her part in this meeting and help him/her prepare.

- Then what? The team creates a plan for the sprint. They need to understand capacity, so I should have them do a capacity exercise. Then, they will take each story, one by one, and figure out the best approach. They will capture this work somehow and then present the plan and the commitment. They should feel a sense of confidence and give consensus to the plan.

  My Actions: Create a capacity worksheet for the meeting; send it beforehand.

  Suggest that the team breaks out into teamlets to "divide and conquer" detailed planning.

  Give them flip charts and have them create their own task board (show example).

  Use a consensus "fist of five" exercise to understand the team's confidence level.

Your imagination can be a wonderful tool to help you think through your meetings and uncover additional ways to prepare. Set aside some quality time in which to do so. Write this down on a scratchpad, which will in turn help you create your script and agenda.

Scratchpad, script, and agenda

The scratchpad is just a place to gather your ideas and get a rough sketch of how things will happen. Ultimately, the ideas on the scratchpad need to be transformed into an agenda for the team; additionally, I like to create what I call a script, which is simply an augmented agenda with reminders, notes, pictures, things to try, and so on, during the meeting. The script is for the facilitator (you), while the agenda is for the entire team. The ScrumMaster's script is critical so that he/she doesn't forget or miss team members' names, dial-in passcodes, URLs for mockups, and so on during the meeting (ahem, this has *never* happened to me!). There's nothing worse for the team's psyche and focus in a meeting than a ScrumMaster disrupting the flow by fumbling around for information, charger cables, projector remote, or scurrying around because he/she forgot to dial in the remote team members at the beginning of the meeting!

The script also reminds the ScrumMaster when the team should have certain conversations; for example, if in the last retrospective the team mentioned that it wasn't clear who was working on what, I would write a note on my script to remind the team members during task planning to figure out how to fix the problem for this sprint. The following diagram shows how a scratchpad evolves into essentially two agendas: the agenda that the team will follow during the meeting, and the same agenda with overlaid comments, reminders, and prompts that you will use in parallel.

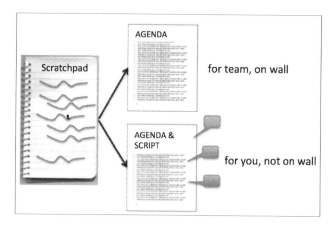

The following is a sample of what I typically create before facilitating a team's meeting—my scratchpad, if you will, that helps me envision and then script out the meeting. This particular scratchpad and script was for a two-day event with a few teams: the first day was the sprint review, retrospective, and product backlog prep (which I was not facilitating), followed by release planning and sprint planning on the second day for which I was the facilitator.

The first thing that you should notice is that my personal scratchpad is quite messy! It's for me, so that's okay. You can see that I was envisioning today and tomorrow. Under the heading "Tomorrow", you can see that I had considered all the prep work for the room: benchmark stories on wall, create sticky notes…. Under the "Script" section, notice that I created reminders for myself about lessons learned from previous sprints, as well as information from one-off conversations that I wanted to bring to the entire team. I added the handwritten notes under "Team Feedback" based on discussions I heard previously in the team's retrospective. I wanted to take the opportunity in release planning to remind them of roles and responsibilities:

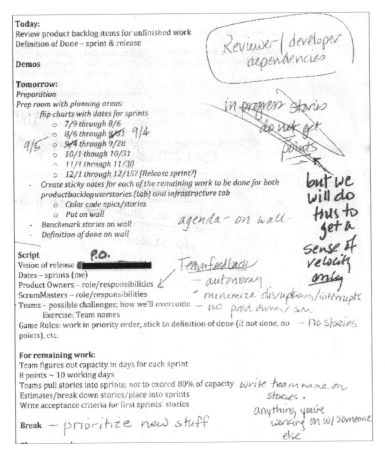

Also, you'll notice in my handwritten notes that I originally didn't want the team to assign story points to work in progress, but scratched this out as I later changed my mind because the team needed to get a sense of velocity. A scratchpad is just that—a place to scribble ideas, reminders and notes in order to formulate a meeting plan, or agenda.

Once I went through the envisioning and scratchpad exercise, I created a nice, organized agenda that I copied to a flip chart the morning of the second day, and retained my script to help guide me through the meeting.

I know it seems like a lot of work. It is. But the more you prepare and practice (and inspect and adapt!), the easier it becomes. What may take you initially four hours to prepare now will only take you fifteen minutes at some point in the future. When you prepare your meeting with such thought and detail, team members can tell that you value their time, energy, and engagement. By preparing such a meeting, you will make it easy for the team members to discuss how to have a successful sprint, and they *will* appreciate your preparation. Meetings that aren't bogged down—that stay on course, and flow from one topic to the next with crisp agendas and a sense of productivity—are collaborative, energized sessions. Create meetings that your team members won't loathe!

Running the sprint planning meeting

Sprint planning has two parts: in the first part the product owner describes the stories he/she wants, why he/she wants them, and how they provide value or solve a problem. The product owner also answers clarifying questions from the team. During the second part of the sprint planning meeting, the development team members discuss the approach, tasks, ownership of tasks, and other tactics for meeting their commitments.

Part I – the What and the Why

Start with the end in mind. The goal of each sprint is for the team to deliver a potentially shippable product increment—features that work, features that the customer can put their hands on. The purpose of sprint planning is to figure out how to do that.

The product owner drives the first part of sprint planning by giving detail about the most important items from the product backlog. As the product owner reviews and explains the stories, the team asks questions to clarify the product owner's needs. You can further encourage this discussion by asking prompting questions such as the following:

- Are there any additional questions?

- Is anyone unclear as to how the feature should behave?

- Can someone volunteer to explain what he or she's heard to make sure we're hearing it correctly?

- What issues or concerns do you have with this feature?

- Are there any missing acceptance criteria?

- Are there any additional suggestions for how the user might use the functionality?

It's not that the product owner won't ever be around during the sprint to answer questions, it's just that the team can better plan the sprint if they have a good understanding of stories—that's the point after all! If the team misses some important acceptance criteria, they may not adequately identify all the work tasks, which could mean that they greatly underestimate the work. Worse than that is the mismatch of expectations; the product owner may be greatly disappointed in the sprint review because he/she was expecting one thing and the team delivered another. Throughout sprint planning, make sure that the product owner addresses the team members directly and vice versa; you are only there to *facilitate and not impede* the conversation. If you suspect that people really don't understand the stories, use some of the prompter questions to rev up the conversation. You must, after all, attempt to create the circumstances for a successful sprint, and good planning discussions are a part of that.

It is imperative to define "done" or revisit the existing Definition of Done for each sprint. The conversation about the definition is critical so that the product owner and team share a common understanding. You can kick off this discussion by asking a simple question: "How will we know we're done?" If in every sprint a team attempts to attain the highest quality level possible (aka "potentially shippable product increment"), then that means there is very little to do to go from staging to production. Defining done helps the team understand and identify *all the work* (not just programming!) that must be done in the sprint; work like testing and sometimes documentation. Maintaining a thorough level of "doneness" means that the team can quickly deploy the functionality to the market when needed, which is very agile indeed.

The following is a real-world sprint Definition of Done:

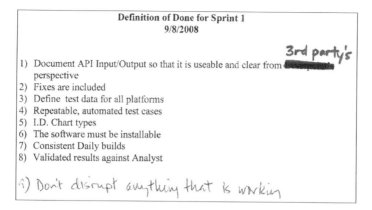

Different types of stories

Try as we might, not every story may result in a working functionality at the end of the sprint. Sometimes a team needs to conduct research or create a proof of concept for a feature; or perhaps a team needs to do a quick hack in order to test out a vendor's API. It's important that the team and product owner discuss these stories to first understand and agree upon why only a piece of the value will be delivered. In other words, Scrum strongly pushes teams to deliver potentially shippable pieces of functionality, not a proof of concept or research. So we should treat these different stories as anomalies and be prepared to explain or rationalize why they'll have a different end state than a normal story that results in working functionality. Secondly, even though these stories aren't the normal kind, the team and the product owner should still discuss and define acceptance criteria for them, even though the end result won't be the same as a real story. For example, if the team strongly suggests that they need to do some research for the Sell Stock epic, they should write down the questions that they need to answer (figure out how to set stock price thresholds, learn more about buy high/sell low), define a time box for the research (eight hours), and identify the output of the research.

Another example is perhaps the team wants to implement Selenium in order to automate tests, so they write a story called "As a team, we want to implement Selenium so that our testing can keep up with the rate of feature development." This is not a real user story; in other words, no end user would ever request this from a development team; most end users don't know a thing about Selenium! While the value of the team's request for Selenium may not be immediately apparent to the product owner, the team can certainly explain how test automation gives early visibility into problems and will ultimately help them move faster. In most cases, a product owner will agree that the story is important and will get the value, thus giving his/her blessing for the investment in this story in the sprint. Remember that the product backlog is a starting point for discussion and while usually expressed in stories that represent user value, other types of work may certainly pop up. As ScrumMaster, a red flag should go up for you when you see a story that does not result in user or customer value; it is important that you challenge the team to rewrite it so that it does end up in value delivery. If this is not possible, consider it an anomaly and help the team identify the end state so that the product owner is not surprised or disappointed. In other words, set expectations that anything in the product backlog that does not result in user or business value should very much be the exception and not the rule.

Part II – the How

In Part II of sprint planning, team members work together to understand their capacity, the approach to building the features, their subsequent work tasks, estimates, and task owners—ultimately resulting in a detailed plan and a team commitment to the sprint's work.

Understanding capacity

Team members need to know how much of their time they truly have to work on the product backlog in the sprint and can figure this out by calculating their rough capacity.

Prior to the meeting, I like to send a capacity worksheet (see the following example) so that my team members have a chance to think about their available time for the sprint. The capacity worksheet is informal, a way to get people thinking about any commitments or other work that may pull them away from the Scrum team's commitments. Each team member can complete the worksheet prior to and bring it along to the meeting; that way, when we jump into capacity planning, everyone is prepared (which might save some time). The team probably won't need this after a few sprints as they'll be accustomed to thinking through their available time.

Capacity Planning Worksheet for Nitin		Sprint 4 Feb 14-28
My total number of hours available for this sprint is	54	(9 working days * 6 hours per day)
I have ___ hours of vacation planned during this sprint	12	Number of vacation days * 6
I have ___ hours dedicated to work outside this team this sprint	0	Number of days * 6 (or apply a percentage of hours, e.g. "50% of my time is for production support")
I have ___ hours of training during this sprint	6	Number of days * 6
Other	2	(dentist appointment Feb 21)
Total Remaining Hours	34	= 54 – 12 – 0 – 6 – 2
Nitin should ensure that his task hours in sprint planning don't exceed ~ 34		

As you can see in the example above, Nitin worked through his capacity worksheet prior to sprint planning. He thought about his upcoming work and personal activities and reflected them in his worksheet: he'll be out two days for vacation and has a dentist appointment on February 21. Nitin deducted a total of 20 hours from his available sprint hours in order to reflect his personal commitments as well as time for a training course he'll take offsite during the sprint. He brings his worksheet with him to the meeting, along with any questions or ideas that he identified when reviewing the product backlog.

When people are assigned to more than one team, they have sprint tasks for two teams, two sets of meetings (planning, dailies, and so on), context switching, and interruption time unfortunately not accounted for. This situation causes many distractions to a person's focus, an over-allocation of that person's time, and is just generally a wasteful way of staffing work. Scrum team members are supposed to be dedicated to the team for the life of the project; if this is not your team's reality, you should make a note of this for investigation and follow up by adding it to your impediment backlog (see *Chapter 5, The End? Improving Product and Process One Bite at a Time*, for more details).

During the meeting, write the team members' names on the wall and ask them to provide the number of days or hours they're available to this team and this sprint. If they haven't done so already in their capacity worksheet, they must now consider any vacation days, training, commitments to other teams, and so on. At this point, I usually ask the team, "What other activities will pull you away from this sprint's work?" Write their responses on the board as they're talking. Many times, one team member will remind another of time away from the office. You'll overhear conversations such as, "Hey Addison, don't you have a tech brown bag session to give this week? That's gonna take you some time to prepare and present. Might want to figure that in." This very example is why the ScrumMaster shouldn't come to the meeting with team members' hours already written down; sometimes team members think of things during the meeting by talking with others. The capacity planning worksheet is a great thought prompter and preparation tool for team members, but still plan on having a discussion about it.

The following example depicts something like what you would write on the planning wall. You can see the entire team's availability: Tony is on a Florida vacation for half the sprint, and Barbara has commitments to another team as she is transitioning fulltime to this team. Both Suresh and Chris are available 100 percent of their time:

Sprint 4 Feb 14-28	9 working days @ 6 hours/day
Name	Hours available
Suresh	54
Nitin	34
Barbara	20
Tony	15
Addison	20
Chris	54
Total	197
Team-wide buffer of 25% (new team, learning curve, risky story)	~ 150 total team hours available

Also consider the workday. Do team members calculate capacity based on a workday assumption of eight productive hours? Or is six hours more realistic? Remember that you must support working at a sustainable pace, so this might be a discussion worth having with your team. I coach my teams to start with the assumption that they'll have six productive hours a day to devote to the team (reflected in both the previous worksheets) and then begin subtracting from there. For an interesting read on this subject, check out Evan Robinson's *Why Crunch Modes Doesn't Work: Six Lessons* at `http://www.igda.org/why-crunch-modes-doesnt-work-six-lessons`.

Talk first, then identify sprint tasks

Once team members have an understanding of their capacity, they'll discuss all the work that needs to be completed in order for them to implement the product backlog items. What does this activity look and feel like during the meeting? Well, team members take one story, discuss it, make sure they all share the same design approach, challenge each other, argue a little, and finally agree to a solution. The backend developer says, "I have to create a new table and field for this story and update the XML tags." The frontend developer says, "Well, I need to update the CSS code so that the background image is consistent for all pages." The designer adds, "I need to make sure our production image is ready for that story; otherwise, we'll need to use a placeholder image." The tester also adds, "I wrote some test cases in the last sprint for this story and will automate them this sprint." Each person talks about the work from his or her own perspective while the others listen to see if that might impact their approach toward their own work. They may go back and forth on some of that work a bit before they can settle on the tasks.

Each team member should have a stack of sticky notes and a fine-tip marker, writes his or her tasks, along with hourly estimates, on the sticky note, and places it on the sprint planning task board. Traditional Scrum encourages team members to break down the work into tasks that range from four to sixteen hours of team member effort. During the sprint planning meeting, the ScrumMaster should keep a running total of task hours as the team plans its tasks and periodically compare this to the team's capacity to ensure that the team has not overcommitted itself. Once the total task hours get close to the team's capacity, the team should stop pulling stories from the backlog and begin solidifying the sprint commitment. Traditional Scrum asks that team members put all the tasks and their associated hours and owners into a spreadsheet, sum up the tasks, and start burning down hours.

The following example depicts this traditional approach:

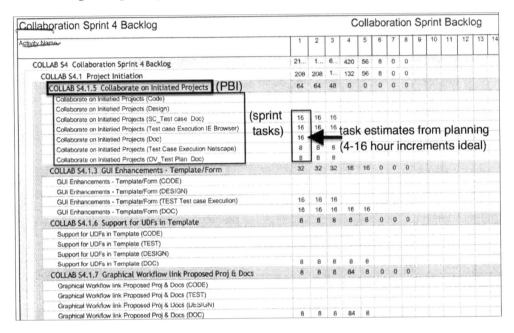

Anyone tasks, expert tasks, and pairing

I take it one step further than the traditional Scrum approach. After the team members have thought through the work and have placed all of their tasks on the wall, I'll give them each red dot stickers. I'll ask them to look at the tasks and put a red dot on those tasks that they know that one and only one person is capable of doing (circled in the following diagram). I call these **expert tasks**. Expert tasks are dangerous because they represent current bottlenecks in our team. If Addison, for example, is the only person who knows XML and SQL, and all of the stories for that sprint require intense XML and database work, Addison might be overloaded. If Addison is overloaded, that means there is the risk that she won't finish all the backend work. If she doesn't finish the backend work for the feature, then the feature cannot be considered done at the end of the sprint. If the feature isn't finished then it's considered a waste as the customer can't give feedback on it or use it. So the point of identifying expert tasks is two-fold: first, we do this to make sure the expert isn't overcommitted with work for the sprint. Secondly, we want to identify expert tasks as they present great opportunities for team members to cross-train. Many teams invoke a game rule that as soon as they identify an expert task, a team member will volunteer to pair with the expert so that the knowledge is shared and someone else begins to pick up that set of skills. This cross-training takes time, but after three or four sprints of this your team may notice that the number of expert tasks identified in sprint planning is now a much smaller and a more manageable number:

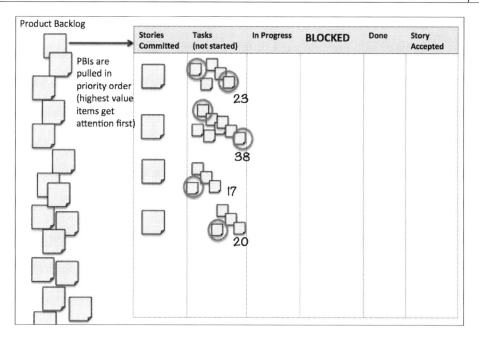

Any task that isn't identified as an expert task is an **anyone task**—that is, anyone on the team is able to work on it, even if it falls outside of his/her main expertise. Anyone tasks are not assigned to any one person; the idea is that any team member can pick up an anyone task when available during the sprint. The rule is that the total number of anyone task hours should not exceed the rest of the team capacity. This practice greatly cuts down on time spent in planning. Expert and anyone tasks are techniques that aren't mentioned in the default Scrum literature; they're just helpful practices I've picked up along the way that help in many situations. Keep inspecting and adapting your meeting techniques and you are likely to come up with some great practices of your own.

The typical task board has columns for tasks that haven't started, tasks that are in progress, and tasks that have been completed; team members move task sticky notes across columns during the sprint to represent a task's status. Just as there are different ways to tune a violin, so are there different ways to run sprint planning meetings and task boards.

Sprint buffering

You may have noticed in the earlier team capacity worksheet figure that I took off a flat 25 percent for new team, learning curve, and risky stories, bringing the team's available hours to only 150 or so. This team was new to Scrum, and it's been my experience that most new Scrum teams overcommit to their first sprints. Therefore, after I explain buffers and the gotchas that most new teams run into, my teams agree that it's a good idea to buffer extra time for the unknown. Just the fact that they're a new team will mean that they'll have to pause from time to time in order to figure out how to work together. It will be rocky in the beginning. Buffer accordingly. You may be thinking, "Gosh, she's just buffering away all the team's time. When do they actually get any work done?" And that is a good point! One of the things I love most about Scrum is that a team's capabilities will be visible each and every day of the sprint (see *Chapter 4, Sprint! Visible, Collaborative, and Meaningful Work,* for more). If they happened to have over-buffered, everyone will see this—the team can just pull in more stories in the sprint to fill up the extra space. Over time, the team will develop a good sense for the appropriate amount of buffer. Until then, help them err on the side of under-commitment.

It helps to see time

Calendars can be very helpful. In the following calendar example, the team members (Alain, Pete, Vilas, and all) put their features on the date of their anticipated delivery so that they could visualize the flow of features through the sprint. In addition, they added some milestones such as the vendor's technology update and a user conference build of the system that they needed to consider and work with during the sprint. A calendar helps the team see the whole (that lean concept again!) and can drive some interesting discussion about how the team orders its work. I usually put a blank calendar on the wall for use during sprint planning. Sometimes the team doesn't use it, but it's there in case the team needs help visualizing the time box:

Sprint 4 - September/October 2003

Monday	Tuesday	Wednesday	Thursday	Friday	S
15	16	17	18	19	
SEPTEMBER **SPRINT 4** **PLANNING**				Bhaskar - overallocated resources feature	
22	23	24	25	26	
Alain - security backend for stats Steve - notebooks for projects	Alain - stats on personal profile Steve-view attendees Vilas-calendar view	Bhaskar - resource requests	Alain-schedule,index Performance for portal Vilas-communication center	Schema change cut- off	
29	30	1	2	3	
		OCTOBER Alain - Risks portal Vilas - review communication center	Alain-project portal Alain-schedule, index performance review Pete-User invitation **SPRINT HEALTH CHECK**	bhaskar-milestone project portal bhaskar-critcal activities portal **OFFICIAL VENDOR** **UPGRADE 3.1**	
6	7	8	9	10	
Alain - risks portal review Vilas - News portal	Alain-project health portal Pete-invite user review **USER CONFERENCE** **BUILD**				
13	14	15	16	17	
SPRINT 4 REVIEW					

Notes:
DAILY SCRUM AT 9:30AM - IF YOU'RE LATE, PAY A DOLLAR!

Team members should talk with each other

This seems like such a minor point but trust me, it's not always obvious. Observe where your team members' gaze during the meeting. If their eyes are on you, that means the conversation is directed at you. You want team members to talk with each other, not to you! Ask questions like, "Why don't you tell him what you just said?" or "Did everyone else hear that?" and move your gaze onto everyone else so that the team member brings everyone else into the conversation. Or, during a lively debate about a feature, simply state, "Keep going, I'll be right back" and step out of the room for five or ten minutes while the team figures it out. Again, your responsibility is to build a productive team. Observe and learn to recognize if team members are using you as a communications crutch during meetings; if this is the case, remove the crutch. They may hobble around at first, but soon they'll find their feet.

Don't over-facilitate

I was once invited to observe a number of ScrumMasters during various meetings at a company with the purpose of giving them candid feedback about their facilitation styles, among other things. I arrived a bit early to one meeting to help the ScrumMaster set up. The ScrumMaster arrived a few minutes before the meeting with 20 flip chart pages, two whiteboards, 10 packets of markers, and a case of sticky notes. She was running around trying to put everything out so I jumped in and helped her so that the meeting would start on time. It seemed like she went a bit overboard on the supplies, but it's better to have too much than not enough, I thought. Well, once the team members and product owner started talking in part I of planning, I noticed that the ScrumMaster was writing literally everything on sticky notes. She had about six different colors in front of her and was trying to categorize what people were saying and put that onto the corresponding sticky note color. Within about ten minutes she had about 45 sticky notes in front of her, of all different colors, and her handwriting was so rushed that she couldn't read any of them. During the first break she was trying to place these sticky notes across the 20 flip charts that she had stuck to the walls. It was one big pile of confusing sticky paper of all types, colors, and sizes. I felt badly for her because she had obviously prepared for the meeting, but overdid it during the meeting, which ended up confusing people and delaying the agenda. During that first break, I helped her collapse some of the categories and advised her to hand out sticky notes to team members so that *they* could capture what was important for them. This helped the meeting get back on track and streamlined the conversation between the team members.

Just enough facilitation is great. Over-facilitation is dreadful.

Sample sprint planning checklist

Following is a sample sprint planning checklist that you may use as a starting point for your meetings. It's exhaustive so that no stone is left unturned, but please tailor to your own needs and keep the lean meeting mind-set. Do just enough to meet the goals of the meeting.

Part I: The WHAT and the WHY (time-boxed to four hours for a 30-day sprint, reduce for shorter sprints)	
ScrumMaster	Opens the meeting.
Product Owner	Presents the product vision and highest priority product backlog items to the team. Sometimes a theme, or overarching goal, will have been established as a result of release planning. If this exists, it is good practice to review this with the team as the selected sprint functionality should support this goal.

Part I: The WHAT and the WHY (time-boxed to four hours for a 30-day sprint, reduce for shorter sprints)

Team	Ensures understanding of the product backlog items by asking clarifying questions in order to identify acceptance criteria. Team members may make suggestions to the product owner based on what they learn about the requirements.
All	Review the Definition of Done to ensure that the entire team understands the quality level that is expected.
Team	Gauges about the right amount of product backlog items on which to conduct detailed task planning during Part II of sprint planning. This can be based on empirically derived velocity.
Team	States the sprint goal. This may have already been defined during release planning; if not, go ahead and define a goal for your sprint based on the selected product backlog (for example, the sprint goal: we will work on the Customer Profile functionality to expand it to include thresholds and other preferences).
Break	

Part II: The HOW and HOW MUCH (time-boxed to four hours for a 30-day sprint, reduce for shorter sprints)

ScrumMaster	Facilitates a quick review of team members' availability. Ask the question, "How much time, out of the next three weeks, do you have available to devote to this sprint?" Make a total team hourly capacity visible to the team members. Task totals for the sprint should not exceed this team total.
Team	Engages in dialogue in order to understand and collaboratively create a design approach to implement the desired functionality in the sprint. All team members participate, not just developers.
Team	Discusses the steps (tasks) necessary to complete the functionality as per the Definition of Done.
Team	Ensures that the total hours for your tasks do not exceed your hourly capacity. Identifies expert and anyone tasks in order to see bottlenecks. Devises a plan for dealing with bottlenecks.
ScrumMaster	Reminds the team of its Definition of Done and asks them to ensure that tasks are in place to ensure completion.
ScrumMaster	Reminds the team that it needs to set aside time for sprint pre-planning meetings, code reviews, sprint review preparation, other tax tasks, and so on.
ScrumMaster	Gets the product owner's involvement if necessary to clarify questions or provide additional guidance.
ScrumMaster	Clears out the parking lot, action items, risks, and decisions flip charts (real or virtual).
ScrumMaster	Asks the team if they can make a commitment to the sprint plan. Facilitates the team to resolve any issues or concerns that may surface.

Commit!

In the sprint planning meeting, I'll ask the team to stop planning once about 80 percent of their team capacity has been reached. After the team understands the work, the details of the work, who's doing what, the risks, and all concerns are voiced, the team should commit to the sprint. I like my teams to actually say the commitment out loud, to each other.

> *Goals aren't truly real until you tell someone else about them. Until then, they're just ideas, just day dreams.*
>
> *— Chris Carmichael, Bicycling Magazine, Jan/Feb 2007*

If you notice that any team members are struggling with committing to the sprint, catch it and discuss it right there on the spot. Perhaps one person feels that she is overcommitted to the sprint, or another person still isn't quite clear about all the acceptance criteria. Whatever it is, get it out on the table so that the team may have a frank discussion and make any trade-offs necessary so that they all have confidence in the plan.

Review the committed stories and make that commitment visible. It's like the weekly goal weight in Weight Watchers. Now there's something to strive for and the urgency is there!

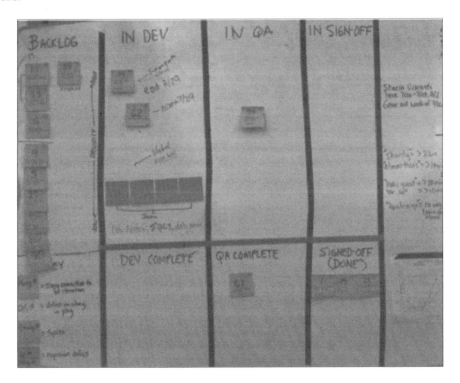

You should also consider asking two additional questions: Does everyone know what he or she is working on right after this meeting? Does anyone need anything in order to get started? This will get the team in the mind-set of work as well as unearth any initial impediments.

Improving sprint planning

You should always look for ways (and suggestions from the team) to make meetings shorter and more efficient. Retrospectives (*Chapter 5, The End? Improving Product and Process One Bite at a Time*) provide an excellent forum for adapting sprint planning as well as anything else that may need improvement. Some ScrumMasters even run a quick retrospective in the sprint planning meeting itself to capture ideas for improvement while they are fresh in everyone's minds! I was hired as a coach at one client to work with a number of teams, one in particular that completed sprint planning in 15 minutes; management thought they were slacking because they planned so quickly! After spending a couple of sprints with them I determined that their planning was sufficient. They completed what they committed to and the product owner was happy with the work. What more can you ask for? As I used to say growing up in Texas, "Don't fix it if it ain't broke!".

Over time, find ways to make your meetings leaner, faster, and more interesting. Prepare for the meeting as well as you can so that the team can just come in and get down to the business of planning.

Summary

You must first understand the reasons behind planning in order to run effective planning sessions. There are meeting mechanics that you as ScrumMaster should follow—game rules of sorts provided by the legacy Scrum literature—and yet even more importantly, you should strive to create and sustain a certain spirit in your meetings. Planning meeting are not crystal balls into which you or the team can look into and predict the future of a project; rather they are the reserved space and time in which a team envisions the possibilities, gets excited about the outcomes, and establishes urgency by acknowledging that only so much can be done in one small time box. Sprint plans are the result of detailed discussions between team members as they figure out how they'll deliver quality results by the end of the sprint. In *Chapter 4, Sprint! Visible, Collaborative, and Meaningful Work*, we will explore how a good plan supports a team as they work together during their sprint, and how plans change to reflect reality, as all good plans should.

Recommended reading

- Xavier Quesada Allue's Visual Management Blog available at
  `http://www.xqa.com.ar/visualmanagement/author/xavier/`

- Cohn, M., *Agile Estimating and Planning* (2006), Pearson

- Demarco, Tom, *Slack: Getting Past Burnout, Busywork and the Myth of Total Efficiency* (2001), Broadway Books

4
Sprint! Visible, Collaborative, and Meaningful Work

I once trained a large company that has an office near Nice, France. On a nice sunny day, in between training courses, I decided to take my rental Peugeot into the mountains over to the Cote d'Azur. While I was driving, I noticed this old medieval city across the canyon and I immediately thought, "I must go there!". So I navigated my way to Tourrettes-sur-Loup via a Hertz Neverlost GPS that spoke French (and because I don't parlez vous Français, I couldn't change the settings to English!). Nevertheless, I finally arrived at the medieval city, and walking along the old, crooked, narrow streets, I fell in love—feeling like I had stepped back in time. I found it interesting that for such a beautiful, quaint, quiet, and peaceful place full of artists, it had quite a turbulent history. The city, strongly fortified by plunging cliffs and stone buildings nested high atop a hill, provided a stellar vantage point highly desirable to various factions of people throughout history; the Romans inhabited Tourrettes-sur-Loup in 262 BC and faced onslaughts and occupancy from Huns, Francs, Lombards, and Italians throughout the centuries. I never would have known this as I sauntered down streets of cobblestone, floating through the buttery wafts of fluffy croissants.

The role of the ScrumMaster is much like the protective cliffs of Tourrettes-sur-Loup: surround and protect the team so that they may reach their goals. Think of the stone cliffs and walls of our medieval city as analogous to the boundaries of a sprint—finite, fixed, rigid, and unbreakable. Within those city walls are a number of things that happen—people work, talk to each other, collaborate, trade, have conflict—all while trying to achieve common goals. The same is true for our Scrum teams. So while the ScrumMaster protects the team from outside interference, he/she must also enable the team members to do their best work. Taking the analogy a bit further, while the inhabitants of a medieval village are trying to stay alive, the Scrum team in a sprint is trying to finish functionality. When a team doesn't finish functionality by the end of the sprint, product visibility is missing. Without visibility, inspection and adaptation cannot happen; thus, the product cannot evolve in a timely fashion. In these modern times of rapidly changing markets, lack of visibility can spell death for a product.

The situations that arise simply from running a sprint will amaze you—organizational culture mismatches, conflicts of individuals due to differing personalities, fear of empowerment, and different learning styles, just to name a few. This chapter will explore what happens within the village walls, or sprint. We'll look at how the work of the sprint happens, how meetings and artifacts come into play, how team members (villagers) interact, and how a protected sprint and team can influence the rest of the organization.

How the Scrum team should work

In *The New New Product Development Game*, Takeuchi and Nonaka described teams as autonomous, focused groups of people, who, when given goals that caused built-in instability had to self-organize around a new directive. In these cases, the manager did not do their jobs for them but rather stayed out of the way and provided everything the teams needed in order to be successful. This wasn't just a hypothetical model; rather, their article was a set of case studies about companies that were actually creating new products this way.

Jeff Sutherland describes the Scrum team as dedicated, cross-functional, self-organizing with a very high degree of autonomy and accountability. Sutherland's description of a Scrum team is similar to the generic definition of any team: a group of people with a complementary skillset and a common purpose. What makes Scrum teams different, then? There are three factors: Scrum team members are empowered to manage themselves, they are dedicated to one project, and they stay on the same team sprint after the sprint, from the beginning to the end of the project. These differences are serious game changers for organizations that use more traditional resource management techniques. If your team does not exhibit those three characteristics, then it is not a Scrum team.

People who are empowered, focused, and engaged have been proven time and time again to be more productive and collaborative. Every time I say this in any class—whether it's for a team or executives—heads nod, eyes light up, and people agree. They can recount projects in which they and their team members were given free reign to do their jobs, and they smile while talking about it. "That was the best team I was ever a part of. Sigh." Yet, everyone goes back to work and back to the way things were always done. Back to the grind, back to working on multiple things at once (or so we think), and back to the exhausting commitments made on our behalf. They cower under the organizational pressures. Don't they remember that Scrum was created to stop this kind of work? That ScrumMasters are chartered to change this sad way of working? All it takes is a small team, whose members work together and make their work visible during a sprint

Working in a sprint

Right after sprint planning, team members begin to work on the tasks they identified in the planning meeting. Usually, programmers begin to write code and unit tests. Testers begin to write test cases. Ideally, they're writing both on the same set of assumptions based on the conversation with the product owner, some parts of which are captured in the acceptance criteria of the story (see *Chapter 7, Scrum Values Expose Fear, Dysfunction, and Waste*). Keep in mind, however, that sprints were designed with a different way of working in mind. In the original Scrum literature, Ken refers to team members as development team members, regardless of what's on their business cards. In other words, everyone is supposed to jump in, no matter what their expertise, and work hard to fulfill the goals of the sprint committed in sprint planning. That means developers could pick up testing tasks, testers could write user documentation or perhaps make a schema change, if that's the way the team chooses to work. Now, in most cases, team members can't learn every skill to the expertise level needed in order to do an expert job at it, but they can learn some. And the new knowledge, skillsets, and so on picked up by individuals over time ends up helping the whole team move faster in the long run. Additionally, teams should be empowered to do whatever is necessary to achieve their goals, yet it's unfortunate that too many teams think of empowerment as a gift that someone must give them, rather than simply a way of being. Learning other skills and taking collective ownership requires real effort. I've overheard comments from team members like, "Working in a sprint is hard. It's difficult and it seems counterintuitive. It means I have to think differently about my job." Exactly!

Sprints shouldn't be just Sprints

I have to admit that I take issue with the word "sprint". When I hear this word, my mind's eye immediately pictures a runner, red in the face, completely out of breath, shaky legs exhausted from pushing his/her body to the point of passing out, sweat flying around everywhere. That is *not* how we want our Scrum teams to experience a sprint. But we see it all the time. Why?

Team members can find themselves in the position of our poor runner for a number of reasons. Sometimes, management thinks that teams should automatically be more productive just because they're doing Scrum. Coupled with a team that cannot say "no" or "that's enough work, and no more," this mind - set will lead to a quick burnout. Other times, teams are just new at the game and need a sprint or two to figure out the new game rules.

You've heard this before: sprints should be run at a marathon pace. Seriously. Teams must conserve energy because when one sprint ends, another begins right away. This means that everything—from meetings, to product backlog preparation, coffee breaks and lunch, to fixing defects and refactoring—should be considered when planning and carrying out the work of a sprint. Hands-on-keyboard time is important, and so is hands-free time. Just because developers aren't coding doesn't mean that work isn't happening. In fact, recent studies show that when our brains get a rest, the quality of work improves. Therefore, when teams plan sprints, they should consider planning for an amount of work that is achievable by working a reasonable workday. Planning for a reasonable workday, as we discussed in *Chapter 3, Sprint Planning – Fine-tune the Sprint Commitment*, allows the team members to work at a sustainable pace, which means that their brains get some rest, which means that they will come to work energized and ready to do their best work every day.

Beware of the old mind-set creeping into the new paradigm

Most new teams initially think about a sprint as a mini-waterfall—after all, that's the paradigm under which they're accustomed to working. However, most teams come to realize that working this way results in defects that must be carried over to the next sprint because the team doesn't have time to fix them in this sprint. In most cases, the resulting pain pressures the team to seek different ways of working since they're not able to actually bring stories to a potentially shippable state within a sprint utilizing the old mind-set.

Symptoms will present themselves as team questions such as, "When should a code freeze happen in a sprint?" or, "When should we hand off to testing?" or a task named "Prepare build for QA" (two days before the end of the sprint). A team that approaches a sprint with the old mind-set ends up carving that sprint into segments. Developers code in their own local branches, only checking in and integrating to the main code branch on the code freeze date. Quality assurance team members then run manual acceptance tests on the integrated build (done only once in a sprint toward the end), sending bug reports back to developers. Developers then run at break-neck speed at the end of the sprint trying to fix the defects before the sprint review. Everybody barely squeaks across the finish line, showing up to the sprint review red-faced and out of breath and sometimes still with hands on the keyboard. This is never a good sign! It's like back when you were in grade school and the teacher started collecting the quizzes and you kept writing right up until the very moment that he/she stood next to you, hand outstretched, toe impatiently tapping. By that time, the quality of your answers probably declined from the pressure and stress. Imagine the quality of code in similar circumstances!

Once a team said to me, "We code all the stories, commit and integrate for a QA build two days before the sprint's end". I asked them how they'd have time to fix all the defects with less than two days to do so. They smugly said, "Well, we'll just add the defects to the product backlog and work on them in the next sprint". Notice how the answer aligned with the way they had always done things, just on a smaller scale called a sprint. I asked them if it was possible to engage testing earlier in the sprint. In other words, could the tester start testing sooner in the sprint, piece meal rather than all at once. The developers looked at me and said, "…sure, we could actually probably do that, but that means we'll have to talk and synchronize more than we usually do". Over time, the developers on this team stopped seeing themselves as merely developers, but as software *craftsmen* who build quality into everything they do. The developers worked with the testers on the team to write test cases first so that everyone would understand the requirements fully before coding began. One could observe developers pair programming from time to time, as well as developer-tester pairs working closely together to ensure that stories were built right the first time. Over time, the testers began to understand more about the architecture, and one tester who had always dabbled in Java was able to pick up some of the easier coding tasks. Slowly but surely, as the team members began to trust each other and learned together, the team became cross-functional and self-managing. Individual roles and responsibilities became blurry; rather, the team members began to think of themselves as team members with responsibility to the customer. As a ScrumMaster, you must be on the lookout for the old mind-set and challenge the team to break through it. Many teams find answers by adopting Extreme Programming practices.

As you can see in the following diagram, a new Scrum team will likely adopt pattern B, which is a fractal representation in each sprint of the larger waterfall. While the customer sees something much sooner in pattern B versus pattern A, "value delivery" is arguable since the resulting code is defective (bugs carry over to next sprint):

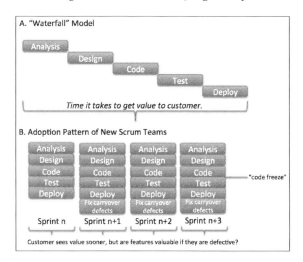

Pattern C is better, as it puts testing ahead of development, and in smaller batches. Teams who stick with Scrum for a length of time realize that this is a much better way to work, evolving into Extreme Programming practices either organically or deliberately. As you can see in pattern C, the customer gets the value when the code for a story passes all of its tests within the sprint boundaries. Also, notice that in pattern C, I've reflected the sprint boundaries as dotted lines because they're merely formalities at this point; features could be released during the sprint since the team has built features of high quality:

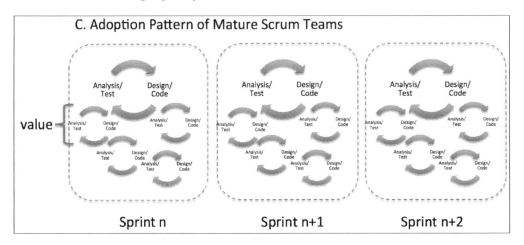

Further evolution (the following pattern D) occurs when teams end up dropping sprint time boxes altogether, simply maintaining a steady delivery of high value/ high quality features in perpetuity:

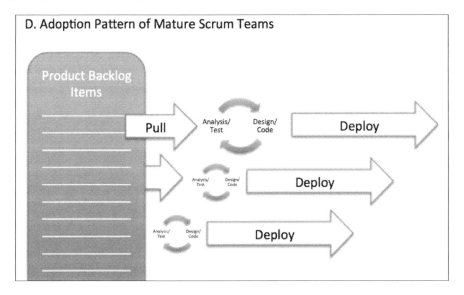

In this pull-based model, the team works on the most important feature, finishes it, and pushes it to production before pulling the next item from the product backlog. This continuous flow is characteristic of Kanban, a set of lean practices that focus on value-driven delivery, just-in-time planning, and whole team concepts.

Throughout these four models you can see that teams follow an evolutionary pattern: first they break down a large release cycle into smaller cycles called sprints; this is the first big jump from waterfall to an iterative model. Then, some teams evolve to reduce cycle time even more by finishing a handful of high priority stories first before working on the next priority within the sprint boundaries. Finally, they reduce their cycle time even further by finding ways to increase their ability to build quality in and release as soon as the functionality is ready. This is the Scrum to Kanban jump; some teams find a middle ground and call it Scrumban. Of course, not every team is able to release features as soon as they're ready. Teams in this situation will deploy to a pre-production or staging environment as they go, as a corral or holding pen for their features as they await the release green light.

Estimating work

In *Chapter 3, Sprint Planning – Fine-tune the Sprint Commitment*, we discussed the traditional Scrum method of breaking PBIs into four to sixteen-hour tasks for the sprint. The reason behind this is that if a work task is small, the team member working on it will have something new to report every day, or at worst, every other day. This visibility into daily status allows for an entire team, then, to jump in and help each other when they can. If you visualize the Scrummage formation in rugby, you can see the similarities, except our Scrum team is huddled around product backlog items, not rugby footballs. Small estimates combined with a daily scrum meeting help the team move the sprint's PBIs together to completion.

When Scrum teams first start out, they focus on planning sprint tasks with lots of detail in order to ensure that they haven't overcommitted, as well as to generate their sprint burndown chart (*Chapter 6*). Due to the repetitive, sometimes boring nature of planning sprint after sprint after sprint, or perhaps to efficiencies gained by establishing velocities, game rules and such, teams that have been together longer tend to spend less time in planning. Some teams organically figure out that estimates impose a fake constraint; in fact, sometimes tasks are completed in much less time when they *aren't* estimated. Parkinson's Law, also referred to as Student Syndrome (Goldratt, Eliyahu M. *Critical Chain*, North River Press), states that, "Work expands so as to fill the time available for its completion". Think back to your university days in which your professor gave you a month to write a paper. Upon assignment, there was not that much urgency. You were probably thinking, "Oh, I have a month. I'll take a look at it at the end of the week. No rush." During that first week, you were distracted with other assignments, campus parties, parent's weekend, and football games. Next thing you know, two week passed in an eye's blink! So you finally sat down and looked at the assignment. The urgency to actually finish this paper didn't hit you, though, until two to three days before its due date. Panic set in the night before. Guess who drank buckets of coffee while frantically writing until the wee hours of the morning that the paper was due? Yes, you! You experienced Student Syndrome first hand. If your professor told you that there was no due date, to turn it in as soon as you could because there are 12 more assignments for the semester, then you probably would have started working on it right away. You were able to actually complete the paper—start to finish—in an elapsed time of only four or five days; the professor's imposed deadline of 30 days actually created a delay in delivery!

As it turns out, many Scrum teams that have been together awhile evolve into the continuous flow practices of Kanban. Instead of focusing on work increments of 4 – 16 hours, Kanban teams focus on the unit of value—the user story—and track the work by reflecting the user story's status. Teams like the Kanban framework for many reasons, one being that the team does not conduct planning for the story until it's ready for work; this just-in-time approach alleviates long, drawn-out sprint planning because instead of the entire team planning multiple stories up front, a subset of the team plans a story as soon as they're ready to take on that story. Using a Kanban system doesn't mean that teams must drop Scrum; you'll likely stumble across Scrumban, a Scrum-Kanban hybrid in which teams have combined the best of both worlds by taking the product backlog, release planning, and cadence and review/retrospectives from Scrum, while utilizing the day-to-day visibility and streamlined nature of Kanban.

The following diagram represents a typical software Kanban board. Unlike our sprint planning task board in *Chapter 3*, this Kanban board only shows stories, no tasks. So instead of breaking down and estimating tasks ad nauseam in sprint planning, the team pulls the highest priority items from the Ready for Work column one at a time and moves it through to completion by working closely together in a cross-disciplined fashion. During the sprint, they move committed stories into columns labeled In Development, Ready for QA, In QA, Ready for Acceptance, and so on, to represent the state of the story, and meet in a daily scrum in which they answer the three questions. A team that I worked with recently updated me and said that the Kanban method helped them double their productivity. Such results are quite common.

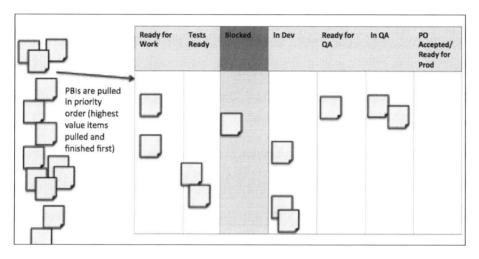

Kanban is a Japanese word that means signboard or graphic. It was created by Taiichi Ohno and applied on Toyota's production lines in the 1950s. Kanban cards signal the need to move materials—or in our case, code—from one step in the process to the next. Kanbans help workers visualize when something is in their queue and ready for their work. Kanban has been applied to software development for at least the past decade and has over the past few years picked up quite a bit of steam. Software Kanbans facilitate a continuous flow of value delivery by requiring teams to work in priority order. Kanbans also help to increase throughput by limiting the amount of work that a team has in progress at once. There are many other characteristics and Kanban game rules; I have included a couple of references at the end of this chapter for your review, and I strongly suggest that you learn more about this way of working to see how your team may benefit.

The misunderstood daily scrum meeting

Just as release plans are revisited throughout a release, sprint plans are revisited and adjusted throughout the sprint during the daily scrum meeting. This meeting, which should be 15 minutes (or less) every day, in the same place, at the same time, is commonly thought of as just a set of three questions that team members answer, going in turn around the circle: what did I do since yesterday's meeting, what will I do by tomorrow's meeting, and what obstacles are in my way?

Daily scrum meetings are meant to be so much more than this. The intent was to help a team synchronize its work tasks so that product backlog items would flow through the sprint as quickly as possible, and to provide visibility into the team's work for anyone who was interested. I'll admit, I've grown tired of these three questions. Maybe it's because I've been doing Scrum for so long, and it's repetitive. Or maybe it's because I've seen too many robotic Scrum team members answering these questions in the groupthink mode, where everybody talks, but nobody really listens. Don't get me wrong, I think that Ken and Jeff created the questions with a good intent. Yet, I've seen too many daily scrums in which the ScrumMaster asks each team member what he or she did, will do, and what prevents moving forward, and each team member answers to the ScrumMaster, which is the problem.

Once again, keep in mind the intended spirit of this meeting. If a team were truly self-managing, then its members would answer these questions to each other, day in and day out, without need for a prompt or reminder like the daily scrum. There probably wouldn't even be a need for a ScrumMaster for a team like this—maybe just a person to whom the team could escalate obstacles for quick resolution. I feel that the daily scrum meeting was a tool created to kick-start team communication for organizations in which this sort of team structure and communication does not naturally occur. Once team members learn to adequately communicate, as well as work together and self-manage, I suppose they could revisit the need for the daily scrum meeting. Most teams I meet, however, never reach this state, and of the teams that do, many prefer keeping the daily scrum because it sets a nice rhythm, it's a habit, and each team member knows exactly where to go to find out what everyone else in the team is up to, and to hold each other accountable. People have told me that the daily scrum puts pressure on them to deliver; each and every day they're renewing their commitment to the team based on what's transpired the day before.

Since I co-train with others, I frequently merge presentations or adapt slide decks based on training retrospectives held with other trainers. The fastest and best way I've found to do this is to meet in a quick planning meeting to talk about who will take various sections of slides over, say, the next two weeks. Once agreed, we divide and conquer. Well, as you can guess, some slides reference others, a change in one could mean a change in other places, the order of slides change, and so on. The other trainer and I could choose to keep working toward our two-week deadline and then come to the end with a bunch of questions and a slide deck that's not done because we failed to integrate early. Or, we could meet at least daily to talk about the progress we've made, the questions that we need answers to in order to move forward, and anything that's blocking us. Daily meetings allow us to synchronize as we go. As a bonus, we also pick up ideas from each other. As a result, we get to the end of the two-week commitment with a much better work product. The daily scrum keeps us honest, makes work visible, surfaces obstacles, and provides a mechanism for team members to synch up on the latest developments in the work toward the goals.

In addition to the daily scrum meeting, which provides a forum for talking about work, sprint task boards and Kanban boards provide visual and tactile expressions of the flow of work. A daily scrum meeting around the task board provides a multidimensional communiqué for all team members: verbal expression via the three questions, visual expression of and reference to a physical task board that is highly visible, and the tactile perspective of moving a task on a sticky note or index card from one status to the next (see *Chapter 6* for more details and examples). Interestingly enough, and I'm not sure that this was intentional by Ken and Jeff. These four components of communication were made famous by Neil Fleming in his **VARK (Visual-Aural-Read/Write-Kinesthetic)** model, which describes people's preferences for taking in information. Daily scrum meetings around a task board hit on all four preferences! There's something for everyone, and if you're multimodal, even better.

In medieval times, the church was the meeting place of the town, located in its center, surrounded with markets of local produce, meats, cheeses, drink, as well as a go-to for medical and spiritual healing. Announcements were made about local goings-on, and church bells rang in the villages to signal when people should work in the fields or come in for the day. Daily scrum meetings are similar. There is a regular meeting place, decided upon by the team (but usually not in a church!), and the team also decides when the meeting is held every day. The ScrumMaster is, in the beginning, like the church bells, keeping the cadence for the sprint and setting the rhythm of work. The team members are the messengers of their own work; with each team member voicing his or her progress and obstacles, the other team members can listen for opportunities to help as well as potentially resolve issues. This in and out, back and forth, work and inspection of work, is a pattern of behavior in Scrum teams. Scheduled times, rituals, and exchanges of information were integral to the life of the village, just like it is integral to the success of a Scrum team.

Three questions

Team members answer three questions in the daily scrum meeting: What have I done since yesterday's meeting? What will I do by tomorrow's meeting? What blocks me from completing my work?

What did I do since yesterday's meeting?

By answering this question, all team members let each other know what they did prior to today's daily meeting. While it is informational in nature, more importantly it's an alert so that action can take place. Let's say that Bob mentions that yesterday he checked in code for the user login story. Let's explore the conversation in a run-of-the-mill Scrum team and again in a proactive, above-average Scrum team.

Run-of-the-mill scenario: Bob tells the ScrumMaster that he checked in code for the user login story. The ScrumMaster says, "Great, Bob—did you update the sprint backlog? Are you stuck on anything? What will you start on today?" Bob answers, and then it's Jose's turn, then Ramesh, and so on. Not bad, but it could be better.

Now, let's look at the same scenario but in a proactive, more mature Scrum team:
Bob (to the other team members): "Hey guys, I checked in the code for the user login story. All unit tests and integration tests passed. I learned from the customer that the user gets three tries and if his/her username or password is entered incorrectly, their account should be temporarily suspended. I don't think that was in our original set of acceptance criteria, but it wasn't a big deal for me to do. I had some slack."
Jose says, "Oh, I need to write some additional functional acceptance tests to cover the three-tries scenario. Thanks for letting me know, Bob. I'll pick that up today. Yesterday I verified that all known defects against the user profile story have been fixed. We can call that story Done as long as Kumar (product owner) accepts it. ScrumMaster, could you make sure that Kumar takes a look at the profile story in the sandbox environment and gives it his OK? I haven't been able to reach him."

Do you see the difference? I see the first scenario all the time; I'd say it's the way nine out of ten teams run their daily scrum meetings. The first scenario is like a bunch of villagers waiting on someone to tell them how to survive, whereas the second scenario is a collaborative dialogue about what's been done, what's been discovered, and a proactive engagement from each team member about what needs to be done next. The second scenario represents a village that is not waiting on a leader; it is taking the responsibility upon itself to communicate about what to do next. The second scenario represents shared leadership and self-organization. I found the preceding picture to represent the spirit and the sort of language one would hear when observing an energetic Scrum team's daily scrum meeting.

The first question (what did I do since yesterday's meeting), if approached proactively, might answer the second question (what will I do by tomorrow's meeting?) and sometimes the third (what blocks me?) for free. Sometimes, what a person did yesterday doesn't affect anyone else, so they talk about that, then they jump to what they'll take on tomorrow; perhaps that opens up a dialogue like the one between Bob and Jose. Maybe not. That's the level of detail that we cannot predict. That's why the daily meeting is there – for team members to synchronize so that they learn from each other and figure out and vary their approaches to problems that present themselves in the sprint.

What will I do by tomorrow's meeting?

Team members gain an understanding of what's coming in the next 24 hours when they each answer this question. Hearing this information allows team members to think, "How might I be impacted by what my fellow team members are working on?" Again, the point is not to report out to the ScrumMaster, but for team members to proactively identify and possibly address impacts or conflicts together.

What blocks me from being able to do my work?

When a team member runs into an issue that prevents him or her from completing a work task, the risk is that the feature may not be complete by the end of the sprint. As we discussed earlier, that's like the death of the village, except in this case, it's the possible death of the team's ability to inspect and adapt its progress toward the sprint goals. The team needs to know anything and everything that might impede a person's ability to make forward progress during the sprint, and the ScrumMaster takes on these impediments if the team members cannot solve them. I've seen just about every obstacle one could imagine: VPN tokens quit working, sustaining issues pulled team members from the Scrum team to "firefight", someone's home computer crashed and they live too far from the office to come in every day, someone's dog ate the product requirements document (good dog!), someone broke the build, someone isn't playing nice with others. Yes, some impediments do involve people, and that may be brought to your attention in a one-on-one, or you may directly observe this "unspoken impediment" during the planning or daily scrum meetings.

An impediment is anything—a person, a chunk of code, a failing test, a busted VPN token, an interpersonal conflict—blocking a person or a team from completing work in a productive, efficient manner. The ScrumMaster must vigilantly remove obstacles from the team members' paths so that they may deliver on their goals.

Impediments come in all forms, shapes, and sizes. Let's say that one of the team members attended an Agile testing conference and learned how acceptance test-driven development can improve the rate of story acceptance, but none of the team members know how to do it. They'd really like to learn more about it as they've heard it can help them improve quality. The ScrumMaster would recognize this as an impediment—not that it prevents today's work from happening, but rather that if the team learned how to do ATDD, they'd be able to do tomorrow's work a bit more effectively. The ScrumMaster decides to discuss the value of ATDD with the product owner prior to the planning meeting so that the team is able to spend a little time in the next sprint to explore various test-driven frameworks to figure out what may work for them. The ScrumMaster also jots down a note to see about asking an Extreme Programming coach to come in during the following sprint. By doing so, the ScrumMaster is tackling an impediment stemming from lack of knowledge or understanding. The ScrumMaster in this example is doing a good job of empowering the team by listening to and acting upon the expressed needs. Through this, the team realizes that the ScrumMaster truly is trying to help, which opens the door for similar conversations in the future.

Sometimes obstacles aren't explicit, but rather observed. For example, when facilitating sprint planning, the ScrumMaster observes that one boisterous "Type A" team member keeps shutting down another quieter team member during team conversations. The ScrumMaster makes a mental note to make more eye contact and express active listening cues (like head nodding) to encourage the quiet person to say what he/she is thinking. A ScrumMaster realizes that anything that gets in the way of collaboration is an obstacle. In this case, the obstacle is missing information—the words *not* coming out of the quiet team member's mouth—and that single missing piece of information could be just what the team needs in order to move ahead. An obstacle like this may be corrected on the spot, or the ScrumMaster might have a one-on-one conversation after the meeting.

Do we have to meet every day?

I frequently hear complaints from team members that they just don't see the value of meeting in the daily scrum meeting every day, and so they all get together and lobby to attend only once or twice per week. I've found that most of the time, the root cause of this problem is that the teams really aren't teams; instead, they're a collection of individuals working on their own independent tasks, and often they are on more than one team. So you see, the *spirit* of the meeting isn't there because the team members' loyalty does not lie solely with that team. There is no value in the daily standup for them. They aren't interested in what anyone else is doing, they're only doing their part, they have many other things to do, there's not a lot of time, and the daily standup feels like a boring status meeting run by the ScrumMaster. I don't blame them for checking out!

So how do you get a team to get value out of the daily standup? Remind them that they are a team. Remind them of their goals and hold them accountable until they begin to hold each other accountable. Support them by working hard to remove impediments; let them know that you hear their voices. Remind them of the product vision and the goals for the sprint. And if your team members are on more than one team, you certainly have a bigger obstacle to fight. Tackle this one first!

Keep an impediment backlog of issues that come up in the daily standup meeting and retrospectives, as well as obstacles that you may illicit from one-on-one meetings, your own observations, or from interacting with the team and other stakeholders. You should maintain this backlog just like any other backlog—the most pressing issues go at the top. We'll go into much more detail about impediment backlogs in *Chapter 6, The Criticality of Real-time Information.*

Who's allowed to attend the daily scrum?

You may have stumbled across Ken Schwaber's quip about pigs and chickens; the former having skin in the game (the team) and the latter just laying eggs and waddling off (stakeholders). Keep in mind that the spirit of the daily scrum is to promote visibility of work; that means *anyone* should be able to stop in and listen if interested in the team's work. The pigs/chicken story is a reminder that only the team may talk during this meeting; otherwise, it might be difficult keeping the meeting to only 15 minutes.

I urge you to open this meeting to outsiders until they give you good reason to disinvite them. I have used this meeting to build trust in situations when others in the company didn't think the team was working hard. I have seen CEOs attend this meeting because they were interested in hearing about issues. The trouble arises when the people who aren't committed—the chickens—start clucking, I mean talking; they certainly have ideas about the product and it may be important to capture those ideas, but the daily scrum meeting is not the place or the time.

> I used to keep a rubber chicken, the kind you get from a magic shop, on the table in the team's war room. When a chicken would start talking, I would hand the rubber chicken to that person—everyone would giggle, and the offending human chicken would zip it. It was a light-hearted way of reminding everyone who indeed had full rights to this meeting, and who didn't.

And no, I don't ask my team members to stand during the daily scrum. This rule came about several years ago by someone who noticed that people get really antsy when they have to stand around for longer than 10 – 15 minutes. Thus, in order to keep meetings short and sweet, the daily "stand-up" meeting was born. I personally don't run into problems with time in my meetings, so I don't use this rule. But if it helps you and your team, by all means stand up!

Look ahead at the next sprint's product backlog items

I cannot stress enough the need for the team to look ahead at the candidate product backlog items for the upcoming sprint during *this* sprint. This step is vital to ensure that the product backlog items are ready for work; that is, they are small, independently valuable pieces of work with estimates and an idea for how they'll be accepted when they're done. You'll hear this idea referred to as a "Product Backlog Refinement" or "Product Backlog Grooming" or "Story Review" meeting. There is no official name for this discussion; the most important thing to remember is that you need to make it happen! I simply ask my teams to reserve a couple of hours every sprint to look ahead at the product backlog items for the next sprint; I personally like to call this the "Next Sprint Prep" meeting. In the following diagram, you can see that this look-ahead is only done for the very next sprint and does not go out any further into the future than that.

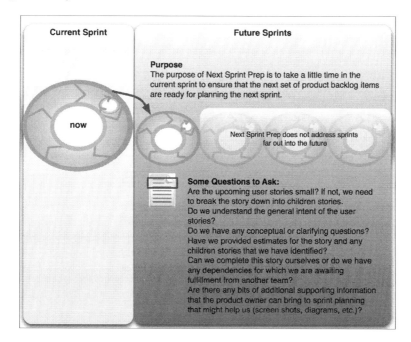

It takes a village – communicating during the sprint

Let's go back to our village metaphor. Let's say that we decide to open up a new Scrum village in the south of France — we'll call it Cap d'Scrum. The city walls already exist, as well as a few homes, a pub, and a blacksmith shop. We invite a few dozen people to live there, give them some seeds, a donkey or two, three or four cows and some chickens, and tell them that this is their new home. What do you think would happen? Would they just sit around? Would they wait to elect a leader in order to be told what to do? Probably not. They'd start exploring, figuring out what resources they have at their disposal, talking about what they need to do next (plant seeds, milk cows, maybe even start building a fence for the cows and donkeys). Someone would volunteer to plant the seeds because maybe they had a little bit of experience doing that before; maybe someone else is good with animals, so they take on the tasks of milking, and one guy doesn't know much about building a fence but he's willing to try. Everyone jumps in. And they're all accountable to one another for survival — each has to ensure that he is doing his task for the greater good of the village. People learn new things and develop new skills, build a church, a dry goods store, a cobbler shop, and a Starbucks with Wi-Fi. And then someone figures out a way to tax everyone and now we have a new government.

We should think of our Scrum teams the same way (minus the taxes!). Let's put them in the village (inside the fixed dates of the sprint), give them a couple of donkeys (in this case, product backlog items), and let them go. They will figure it out. There are a few ideas at play here: emergent leadership, trust, and trial and error. It is up to the ScrumMaster to cultivate and allow each of these things to happen.

The challenge is that villagers have different personality styles. Our carpenter might be very meticulous, organized, a perfectionist, and a bit on the introverted side as he communes with hammers, nails, and wooden boards all day long. And our cobbler might be very outgoing, creative, and jovial. The cobbler has to go to the carpenter for shoe lasts and is taken aback by the smithy's terse communication style. The cobbler wants to explore different ways of creating the shoe forms, discuss and consider different kinds of feet, different types of wood to use, and so on. The carpenter is trying to figure out how one size will fit all so that he can be done with the cobbler and go back to fence-building. This creates tension. The cobbler thinks that the carpenter is grumpy, close-minded, and abrasive, while the carpenter thinks the cobbler can't make up his mind and has too many ideas to be useful. Maybe they end up not able to work together at all. Their personality styles cause conflict — what Bruce Tuckman referred to as "storming" in his stages of group development. When we ask team members to work together, the best case scenario is that they are a collaborative bunch, rolling up their sleeves, and energized about their work.

The reality is that it takes a huge amount of effort, in most cases, to create this reality, simply due to the complexities of intrapersonal communication and personality styles. This is the complexity that Dr. Stacey describes in his latest works, referenced in *Chapter 1, Scrum – A Brief Review of the Basics (and a Few Interesting Tidbits)*.

Individual influences to the work of the sprint

It is important for ScrumMasters to understand personality and learning frameworks so that he/she may more readily recognize what's really going on when a team's members move from the "Forming" stage into the "Storming" stage. One such framework is called the **Five Factor Model (FFM)**; basically, five dimensions that describe the human personality (refer to `http://en.wikipedia.org/wiki/Big_Five_personality_traits for more information`). These certainly come into play when a team's members get to know each other.

Factor 1 – Openness

How open-minded and curious are the people on your team? Do some want to explore different ways of designing or coding a feature, while others have already made up their minds about how to proceed? For the latter, are they set in their approach, not wanting to listen to the ideas of others? One example that readily comes to mind is the architect and the developer. The architect wants to figure it out all up front, think about it incessantly, create the perfect solution that will scale, extend, and so forth. The developer just wants to get started. He/she knows that technology and requirements will evolve, so why not let the architecture evolve along with it? Getting these two to see each others' points of view can be a big exercise in patience and will try your facilitation and persuasion skills, for sure. In a case like this, I'll invoke Occam's razor and ask the architect and the developer if they can agree to move ahead with the simplest theory, try it out, and analyze what happens; maybe create a research or spike story to work on. Encouraging an experimental mind-set can sometimes help people get through this seeming impasse.

Some team members are not curious simply because they are accustomed to having a manager create and hand out their tasks to them; they are not responsible for the solution, the manager is. So they close off their curiosity; they're reserved and focus on consistent delivery, not innovation. Trial and error is seen as a waste of time. Now comes a new ScrumMaster who believes that the team should think for themselves and devise their own solutions. This can be very frightening for the team's members who feel put upon and as if the ScrumMaster is a threat. A ScrumMaster in this situation must proceed slowly, ensuring that the team feels ready to take on new challenges and not overwhelming them by putting too much on them too quickly. If I have a team in this mind-set, I'll partner with a manager or tech lead who can simultaneously help them and challenge them to take risks in the planning meeting. Sometimes hearing that it's OK from a manager creates the safety for a team to try.

Factor 2 – Conscientiousness

Would you call yourself a planner? Always prepared for the next meeting, the next day, the next week? If so, you have a high level of conscientiousness. Being able to plan for a release or a sprint makes you feel comfortable because a plan is in place and you can now make steps toward that plan. Scrum team members with a higher conscientiousness like planning for sprints and they *prepare themselves* for these meetings by reviewing product backlogs, thinking through acceptance criteria, and envisioning solutions before the meeting even starts. It's one thing to plan, and an entirely different (yet related) thing to prepare. Everyone on the team should prepare to interact with the team by reviewing important product information, using their imagination or creativity to solve problems, and by coming to meetings with a sense of openness and gratitude for fellow team members. Diligent preparation makes for productive planning sessions.

I work with an advertising agency that has a big creative group and an equally large development group. Creative people and developers work together on cross-functional teams. I see the conscientiousness and open-mindedness factors at play all the time at this agency. The creative person wants to explore many different ideas, mock up look and feel, branding, images, colors, and the like. They're not always very organized about the way they go about the development process, often pooh-poohing the notion of planning and deadlines. One artist I met said to me, "You just can't plan or put a deadline on creativity". To some extent, she has a point, that yes, a person could keep creating and there might never be a perfect solution. But think about actors in a theater.

Tickets to the opening night are sold months in advance; the curtain opens and the show happens, regardless. Actors rehearse and apply what they learned through rehearsal so that by opening night they're ready *enough*. The actors continue to adapt with each subsequent ensemble, or production (Devin, Lee *Artful Making*). So if the team—creative and development team members alike—do their best to prepare, do their homework, think through problems together, then they are apt to find solutions even in the face of deadlines. Preparation is the openness to what's possible; planning is the act of figuring out what's possible. Team members need both levels of conscientiousness, but they don't always come that way.

The customer needs a product. And the developer just wants to get started, yet is held back by the creative person who feels that the perfect design should first be in place. This causes immense tension. Balancing the need for creative thought but also making forward progress for the customer can feel like a tightrope 20 stories high for a ScrumMaster. Both needs are correct. Help the team understand their different problem-solving approaches, and use these differences to their advantage, not disadvantage. I've seen teams overcome this in a number of ways. The creative person pairs with the developer to create the initial wireframes; the developer begins implementing wireframes without all the production assets in place, using placeholder images until assets are available; the team adopts an open mind toward receiving change requests from the customer after he/she sees it in the sprint review, buffering the plan to accommodate this unknown.

Factor 3 – Extroversion, are you an innie or an outie?

Extroverts are obvious. They're outspoken and energetic in social situations. They seem to get a high from these interactions, never tiring of engagement with others. Introverts are quite the opposite—they are quiet in social scenarios, stick to themselves, and usually don't like to draw attention to themselves. Imagine now a sprint retrospective where each person on the team is to contribute ideas for team improvement. This will be right up an extrovert's alley. He/she will have an idea for everything. In fact, they won't shut up. The introvert, however, is perfectly content with letting the extrovert talk for everyone and can't wait for it to be over so he/she can get back to work. How do you balance this as a ScrumMaster without shutting down the extrovert and embarrassing the introvert? Facilitation skills can really come in handy. If you notice that you have one or two "quiet ones", change your approach: the next question that you ask, request a response from everyone. Go around the room round-robin style. Make sure that everyone speaks up. Another technique is to break out clusters of team members to work in small groups. For example, during a retrospective I'll ask the team to divide into clusters of 2 – 3 people to have smaller-scale discussions about what worked and what didn't.

Sometimes an introvert can more easily find his/her voice when they only have to talk with one or two others, versus a whole team of nine. As a first step, simply identifying which category your team members fall into can help you explain some of the behavior and think about how to address it. Giving everyone an equal chance and using positive facial expressions and other non-verbal cues can also help those who are quiet to open up.

Factor 4 – Agreeableness

This factor doesn't rate how much you go along with everyone else. Rather, it looks at the degree to which you are compassionate and cooperative rather than suspicious and antagonistic. It's important that team members cooperate, work together, and care for each other. It's perfectly fine for someone to have an opposing viewpoint; in fact, it helps the team think more robustly about solutions. However, it is important that this opposing viewpoint's source is truly a result of robust thinking, and not sourced from fear. Trust is one of the facets of agreeableness and not surprisingly, it is the single-most important requirement for a performing team.

Factor 5 – Neuroticism

Neuroticism is a person's tendency to express negative emotions such as anger and anxiety. Ordinary situations seem threatening and daunting, causing the neurotic person much anxiety. Some people, on the other hand, are happy-go-lucky, relaxed in the face of daunting situations. Neuroticism is a psychological dysfunction, and many people have this trait. So the answer isn't "do away with it" — you can't. Rather, it's how to leverage that trait for the good of the team. I can recount a team discussion once with a neurotic tester who ran around exclaiming that the QA sky was falling every day. The sky never fell. But it gave everyone else on the team a new perspective for risks and for keeping an eye on quality, as annoying as it could certainly be sometimes!

It's important for you to understand your team members and equally important to understand your own personality traits. After all, you are a team member too. You can take the big five personality test at http://www.outofservice.com/bigfive/. And, good news, a person *can actually* evolve his or her personality with self-awareness, diligence, and periodic introspection (sort of like an interpersonal retrospective!).

What's 'Norm'al for one team is not for another

Teams that move into a Norming phase establish game rules for behavior. They feel mutually accountable for the goals of the sprint because they have set the goals themselves. Game rules help the team keep its focus; norms are rules that the team follows and emerge from the team's history and experiences. You can imagine that a team's members are much more committed to the norms they've set for themselves rather than rules set for them by managers or others. It is imperative that a ScrumMaster is secure enough to create an environment in which team norms may emerge. And it's important to know that one team's norms will be very different than that of another's. One team I worked with had a rule that if a developer chose to pair with another developer on a user story, then the code did not have to go through a code review; the team found over time that pairing resulted in much better code quality as a result, allowing a formal code review bypass. I've personally found that having a team understand and define Done can provide a great way to devise the first team norm; having a frank, open talk about how a sprint's feature quality can unearth perceptions and opinions about quality, team roles and responsibilities, and accountability. Most importantly, the team makes a decision about Done with the product owner based upon what it feels is acceptable and achievable.

In the following graph, I've layered team characteristics and leadership styles onto Bruce Tuckman's model (forming-storming-norming-performing). As you can see, when a team's members don't share the same vision and do not have a high level of trust, the team is in a state of forming. The team members really don't know each other very well; they don't understand how their personalities interlace. As a team's members become more comfortable with one another and form trusting relationships, you'll see them argue, or "storm". This is a very good sign, actually, as difficult as it can be to facilitate. Arguing is a signal for the ScrumMaster to invoke a hands-on style; the ScrumMaster should, at every chance, facilitate the team members to create game rules for themselves. Once a team begins to create rules for itself, everyone has a clear picture of how to act and knows what's required of them. Life gets easier. When this happens, the ScrumMaster can turn his/her attention to larger system (or organizational) issues:

As team members move toward a high trust level, share a common purpose, and self-direct, the ScrumMaster has more time for the role of change leader:

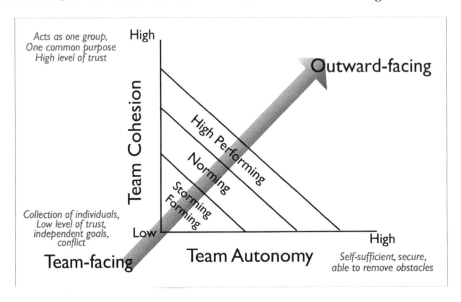

A corporate culture and its impact on teamwork

Think about your corporate culture: does it support collaboration and creativity, or is it focused on creating internal competition and/or obsessed with controlling everything. Collaborative workplaces are "open" and "sharing" and place high value on teamwork, participation, and consensus. Creative cultures encourage risk-taking and experimentation and initiative and freedom of the individual. In a control corporate culture, rules and processes govern behavior and management wants security and predictability. Competing organizations emphasize winning and competitive action (Bruce M. Tharp, http://www.haworth.com/en-us/knowledge/workplace-library/Documents/Four-Organizational-Culture-%20Types_6.pdf).

Think about your company's mind-set and the way that Scrum will fit—will it be like putting a square peg in a round hole? Your company's culture will have a direct impact on your team members and the way they work together, especially at first. A culture of collaboration and creativity will likely embrace Scrum and its values, whereas a culture of competition and control will create many obstacles for you to remove. Here are some points to begin thinking about, and we will explore this in more detail in *Chapter 7, Scrum Values Expose Fear, Dysfunction, and Waste.*

Team assumptions about management

In a pre-Agile assessment I conducted for some retail application teams, a few team members responded that they felt there was quite a bit of management "secretism". Turns out that this stemmed from the micromanagement of people—managers were assigning them to secret projects because the managers were afraid to make all work in progress visible. How did this impact the work of the sprint? Team members did not make their tasks visible. There were missing JIRA tickets; daily scrum updates were vague. Team members didn't truly synchronize, nor were they too concerned with what the other guy was doing because everyone just needed to get back to work! Understanding your team members' assessment of management could lead to important insights into the work patterns you've observed.

Corporate mind-set opposes the Agile manifesto

Will your organization frown upon a sustainable pace of team members? In other words, will management be OK with no more overtime? Will they readily accept the fact that plans will be buffered, and those buffers will be visible? This can make or break your Agile attempts. I've seen so many "Agile" or "Scrum" implementations that are just a façade; that is, teams do the practices, but none of the values are embraced. In this situation, team members loathe Scrum. Be ready to walk the talk when it comes to how many hours team members put in during the sprint.

Fear of empowerment

I've seen many new Agile teams push back hard on the ideas of self-management and empowerment. Team members in this situation feel comfortable being told what to do; they fear taking accountability for delivering a quality product. This fear is usually due to observing, or being the focus of, a negative reaction. A team member may be afraid to take ownership because if it fails, he/she feels that they might lose their job, or not get that raise, or possibly be yelled at by the product owner. You need to get down to the root cause of any fear on your team that may be holding them back from being productive, accountable team members. And do your best to eradicate the reasons for the fear. I recently spoke with struggling team members who expressed fear that because the client cut funding for an adjacent team, they worried about that happening to them too. This had never come out before and was key in helping team members build empowerment.

Employees feel like headcount

If this is the case, you might observe that your team members are "checked out", or alienated. If employees do not feel valued, they will not step up to the plate. You'll see Groupthink symptoms during the sprint; people will be concerned with only their tasks. In a company that pits one department against another (the competitive culture), you might see infighting and finger-pointing between a developer and a tester on the team, for example.

Scrum—or any Agile framework—was designed so that people could work in a collaborative and creative open space. There is a big separation that a ScrumMaster needs to be mindful of (and perhaps to remind others of): what happens inside the village, between the team members, is up to the team. Marketing, sales projections, contracts, services, and so on, are business-critical activities that should not force a team into subpar behaviors. Don't compromise! The ScrumMaster should communicate this to others in the organization and to help the team members find their best working their best working styles and patterns.

I created the following flow diagram after spending time over the years with many unhappy teams. There is a direct relationship between low morale, production issues, and bad engineering practices. Lack of process, or the wrong process, contributes to micromanagement, which drives low morale and a low-quality system. You have a great opportunity to affect change—start with the team in the sprint. Help them learn how to collaborate, self-manage, and help them make their work visible. As a result, they'll find new meaning and a sense of purpose in their work lives. Happy workers create high-quality products that customers love!

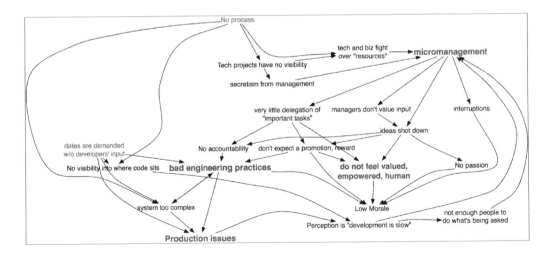

Summary

The ScrumMaster's responsibility is to do anything necessary to help the team find success. This means removing obstacles and protecting the team from outside interruptions. However, other obstacles present themselves while a team is working — surfacing as personality, cultural, or values conflicts or mismatches. "Sticking to your guns" — that is, upholding your responsibilities as a ScrumMaster — provides an opportunity for both your team and the surrounding organization to change. If you relent on your responsibilities, it's likely that the team and the organization will remain in status quo.

Recommended reading

- Adkins, Lyssa. *Coaching Agile Teams: A Companion for ScrumMasters, Agile Coaches, and Project Managers in Transition* (2010), Addison-Wesley

- Kanban, general at `http://en.wikipedia.org/wiki/Kanban`

- Scrum-ban write-up available at `http://leansoftwareengineering.com/ksse/scrum-ban/`

- Ladas, Corey. *Essays on Kanban Systems for Lean Software Development* (2009), Modus Cooperandi Press

- *Scrum and XP from the trenches, Henrik Kniberg's free whitepaper* available at `http://wwwis.win.tue.nl/2R690/doc/ScrumAndXpFromTheTrenchesonline07-31.pdf`

- Bruce Tuckman's model available at `http://www.sandy-campbell.com/sc/KTC_Module_2_files/KTC%20Module%202%20%E2%80%93%20Tuckman%201965.pd`

5

The End? Improving Product and Process One Bite at a Time

The End.

Those two words signify finality, completion, and by their terseness, create an abrupt stop. Every child's storybook ends with these two words; and when we said them aloud with our parents at bedtime—The End—we knew it was time to turn the lights out and go to sleep.

A sprint starts with a sprint planning meeting and ends with the sprint review and retrospective. These meetings are the "bookends" of the sprint time box. At first glance, it appears that the goal is for a Scrum team to get to the end of each sprint having completed "potentially shippable product increment" or "features that work", after which they hold a sprint retrospective to discuss process improvements. This is certainly part of the goal.

The other, and probably more important, purpose of these meetings is to temporarily pause development so that the team and project stakeholders may figure out how to better proceed in the next sprint. Unlike the end of our children's bedtime story, we don't just turn out the lights and go to sleep; rather, we stop to figure out how to make tomorrow better. Teams *pause development* during the review and retrospective so that they may figure out the improvements they need to make to both the product and the process. This inspection allows them to start the following sprint from a place of enhanced learning and knowledge about what to build, and how to build it from both a technology and process perspective. It's no wonder, then, that most teams take three to four sprints to jell, find their mojo, and hit their stride.

The sprint review is not merely a demo of functionality; rather, it is time set aside so that the team may discuss important discoveries made during the sprint, as well as show the resulting product increment to stakeholders. Retrospectives should not be mere touchy-feely whining sessions; the team should use this time to figure out how to improve its delivery process.

A team should not think of Scrum as something to transition to; instead, a team should look at Scrum as something to transition *through*. The end of every sprint provides an opportunity for a team to reflect on the events of the previous sprint to discover processes, technology, actions, and/or behaviors that need to change and come up with decisions and actions that will carry those improvements forward. The sprint review and retrospectives hold great potential for team members to apply what they learned in order to improve the product and process for next time. Sometimes teams realize that they want to bring in an Extreme Programming practice or two, or perhaps they might like to experiment with Kanban. The important thing to remember is that Scrum exposes the weaknesses and tells a team exactly what they need to fix in order to be successful. It is up to you to facilitate a team to become the best it can be, especially by focusing on these two "end" meetings.

Ken Schwaber says it best: "Scrum is like inviting your mother-in-law to come live with you. You know, the mother-in-law who always thought her son or daughter could have married someone better than you. You're inviting your mother-in-law to come live with you specifically for the purpose of pointing out your weaknesses and flaws so that you can understand how to improve." I can't think of a better analogy! Have you felt like work became more difficult after implementing Scrum? If you are nodding your head right now, you're not alone—many teams and managers have said that development, or work in general, seems more challenging after implementing Scrum. Retrospectives reveal issues and roadblocks to effective, efficient development, but the irony is that those roadblocks were *always* there; by implementing a sprint, which is essentially a lean cycle, in which the team focuses on creating working features, Scrum squeezes what may have previously been a 9 – 18 month cycle time down to only one month, or less. A ton of stuff can get in the way when a team delivers features this fast. Just like your mother-in-law might tell you that you should take out the garbage more often, organize the office, lose some weight, trim your roses, and so on, Scrum will let you know exactly what needs to be fixed—from mind-set, to quality focus, to whole team support, to modern tools that support Agile development. Anything that gets in the way is an opportunity for improvement. Let's look at these two meetings and learn how they help us to start a new sprint with a new beginning.

Sprint review – inspecting and adapting the product

They were anxiously awaiting the start of the 10:00 a.m. meeting. All crammed into the testing lab; five to nine people at each workstation, 12 teams in all. They had worked hard all sprint, 30 days of figuring out how a third-party application would integrate with theirs, the ins and outs of differing roles and permissions models, two sets of business rules from two different systems that didn't always jibe. They were excited, nervous, and a bit fearful about unveiling their findings to the rest of the company. It was their third sprint review and they were getting closer to a marketable release. It was time to show the world what they had done.

The clock struck 10, and with a room full of support and services staff, managers from sales and training departments, executives, and even a few customers, the ScrumMasters sprang into action. They introduced the purpose of the sprint review, quickly gave a rundown of the features each team would demo, team velocities, and a summary of obstacles the teams encountered during the sprint. After this introduction, the group of 30 or so external stakeholders was divided into 10 groups of three or so, and the horn blew. Small groups of stakeholders visited each team's workstation, experienced the features hands-on, discussed ideas, and gave feedback. Every 15 minutes, the horn sounded and the stakeholders migrated to the next team's demo. Every person at the meeting, whether a stakeholder or team member, had a clipboard to write ideas, feedback, discussion points, and possible issues, while ScrumMasters took notes as they listened to discussions. Once all the stakeholders had viewed each team's functionality, everyone took a pizza break and reconvened some time later to discuss feedback about the product en masse. This science-fair-style sprint review was the most exciting meeting I have ever attended; even if your sprint reviews are for a single team and a single product owner, you still want to create similar outcomes.

- The teams were thrilled to show off their work, and more importantly, they really wanted to know what others thought about it. And this is the exact mind-set that you want to cultivate in your team: a desire to know what others think about the emerging product. This is quite different than the waterfall mind-set of, "Don't show the customer anything as they might change their mind!"

- Executives were so excited to actually see a market-worthy product emerging; seeing it early gave them all sorts of new ideas for features and enhancements. Iterative, incremental delivery provides opportunities for others to insert their ideas. Of course, it's very important to have a product owner who can balance all the excitement and new ideas!

- The visiting customers found it intriguing that they were invited to give their ideas as well; they had never been treated so specially by a vendor before and were appreciative of the chance to weigh in. I strongly suggest inviting actual customers, and/or end users, to the sprint review; they will appreciate the chance to give feedback. This gesture also creates customer loyalty and builds team excitement because team members get to talk to real live people using their product!

- Likewise, managers and staff from support, services, and training were also very excited because they had important information from the field about how certain features needed to work. They were able to see the product well ahead of its scheduled release, which made them very happy. When you set up your team's sprint meetings, talk with other department representatives to see if they may benefit from seeing features in the sprint review.

Let's go back to our science fair sprint review. After the feedback session, one ScrumMaster showed a combined release burndown chart for all the teams (this was not a simple chart to create at the time as Agile project management tools did not yet exist!). As a result of seeing the features and the release burndown, stakeholders were able to layer on their best ideas for shaping the product and collectively, in real time, understood the status of the project. They also learned in the meeting that if they wanted the product owner to add their ideas to the product backlog, then items of equal estimate would need to drop below the release cut line. This concept was surprisingly acceptable to everyone. The meeting was collaborative in nature, not a one-way street in which a project manager read a status report.

You may recall from training that sprint reviews should be informal, and they shouldn't involve fancy slides or other dog-and-pony shows. A sprint review is like pulling out the magnifying glass: remove it from your pocket, look into it to see what you need to see, learn, and make decisions based on what you've seen. And the "you" can be anyone: you, the product owner, a stakeholder, a team member. The sprint review is a learning opportunity.

Product owner acceptance

While the team certainly seeks feedback from the product owner and other business stakeholders and users, it is ultimately the product owner's responsibility to accept the work of the team. This prevents chaos and confusion. The product owner acts as the filter for a myriad of requests that come into the product backlog and sorts those requests and ideas based upon his/her knowledge of the market, user needs, and so on. By owning prioritization, the product owner thus owns the success of the product—he/she acts as gatekeeper for features going to market and owns the decisions about the right feature set for the delivery timeframe. Therefore, the product owner must have "ownership" during the sprint, and in the sprint review, to say if the resulting functionality is appropriate or not.

Scrum requires a dedicated product owner for many reasons:

- The team needs to understand the product vision—the big picture or problem to solve—so that they know what it is that they're ultimately trying to do. The product vision guides a team's decisions, from release planning to sprint planning down to daily discussions.

- Even though teams do their very best to plan a sprint, they will have questions or need clarification during the sprint itself; therefore, team members need a business expert, the product owner, who can quickly answer questions about user or business needs as they're working in a sprint.

- The product owner provides consistency; that is, the same person helping the team understand the requirements is also checking the implementation to ensure that the needs are met. Product owner acceptance of the potentially shippable product increment is an important part of the sprint review discussion. In this way, the product owner is the ultimate decision maker who ensures that the results of each sprint support the product vision.

From time to time I consult in the Washington DC area. It's fraught with frustration for me as I usually hear from teams that they don't know who their product owner is! In fact, one team said that it had to answer to 13 Senators, of which none wanted to take ownership of the product because if something went wrong, they didn't want the responsibility to fall on their shoulders or to be perceived as supporting a program that was outside party boundaries. Their team floundered because every time they would implement one Senator's wishes, another wouldn't like it and would change it. And so on! Multiple owners caused extreme chaos for the team members; one of the challenges for their ScrumMaster was to work with the Senators and their assistants to create a single backlog that they could somewhat agree upon in order to shield the team from this morale-busting environment. The ScrumMaster was also very keen on buffering for uncertainty and change during release planning meetings.

Prior to the sprint review

While technically signifying the closure of a sprint, the sprint review more importantly provides the team with an opportunity to hear how the product will (or won't) meet the users' needs. This is a big event and it should be exciting! This is the time when the team shows the product increment--one of only three Scrum artifacts--so that it may be inspected and changed if necessary. Again, visibility is the heart of an empirical process.

There are some simple things you can do to make this meeting successful:

- Prior to the meeting, talk with the product owner; identify and invite anyone who may have an interest in the outcome of the project. Send these invitations out right away.

- Close out stories that have been accepted during the sprint, by updating the tool or the task board; calculate velocity if you are able to (see *Chapter 6, The Criticality of Real-time Information*, for more about velocity).

- A few days before the sprint review, get the team and product owner together to look at the next set of product backlog items. In addition to other benefits as discussed in *Chapter 4, Sprint! Visible, Collaborative, and Meaningful Work*, this makes the sprint review more efficient; as feedback and new ideas are discovered during the meeting, a well-prepared product backlog is much easier to re-prioritize and move things around.

- A day or two before sprint review, perhaps in a short extension to the daily scrum, discuss who will demo what. I'm a firm believer that the team members should demo the features; after all, they built them! Better yet, ask the team how they can set up the demo so that the product owner and other stakeholders may get a hands-on during the meeting. Do a run-through of technology the day before; ensure that the projection equipment works, that the conference room is (truly) reserved; that the telephone or conference call system is good to go, that sample data is ready, and so on.

- Finally, prepare or remind your product owner about his/her responsibilities in this meeting. Listen for and capture feedback for new product backlog items, have "hands on the demo", answer questions from stakeholders regarding vision, roadmap, or release inputs or impacts.

As you're preparing for and visualizing this meeting, don't forget to create an agenda for the meeting attendees and possibly a script for yourself. Items that may appear on your sprint review script and/or agenda should be as follows:

- Features/stories to be demoed

- The Definition of Done (was it met?)

- Number of unit and functional tests written and automated; passed/failed

- Number and severity of defects discovered/fixed in sprint

- Number and severity of defects placed in product backlog

- Velocity review; how many points were targeted for the sprint? How many were finished?

- Release burndown chart

- What obstacles were encountered during the sprint? What issues or risks are still present? What has been escalated?

- What else do you want to say about the team, the sprint, and the product?

- Any aha moments?

I have included the following sprint review checklist to help you identify anything that may be missing from your agenda. Again, craft an agenda that keeps **LEAN** meetings in mind: Limit the agenda to its purpose; **E**ngage everyone; be an **A**gile facilitator; and prepare to help others **N**egotiate:

Who	Item
ScrumMaster	Short introduction by ScrumMaster welcoming all attendees, reviewing purpose, agenda, and time boxes for the meeting. Reiterate the use of parking lot and action items.
ScrumMaster	Recap the Definition of Done. Give a short introduction of the user stories that the team will show and won't show during the meeting. If velocity is known, provide that information to meeting attendees. Take notes while product discussions ensue between stakeholders, product owner, and team members.
Team	Provide a demo of the functionality completed during the sprint.
PO	Get hands-on if possible; try out the functionality. Have discussions with the team and other attendees as needed regarding new ideas to add to the product backlog.
PO	Accept the stories. If a story is unacceptable, please give a reason to the team ("story does not meet Definition of Done", or "there are obvious defects with the feature", and so on). Velocity points are given based on stories that are finished—so it's important that finished (or Done) has been defined!
ScrumMaster	If the team is working toward a long-term release plan, present a release burndown chart showing the amount of work remaining as a result of the accepted work of this sprint.

During the sprint review

The sprint review should be a *meaningful dialog* between the product owner and team members about the existing product and its capabilities, how well it serves the user or market needs, and what new ideas have emerged as a result of seeing the features. Dialog infers two-way communication. The review should not be reduced to merely a team presenting to an audience. It might start out that way but then discussions should quickly follow.

Set the context

As ScrumMaster, your responsibility is to ensure that the meeting is conducted in a logical format, that the product owner sees what he/she needs to, and that other stakeholders are aware of what's being demoed (and just as importantly, what's not). Setting the context and expectations of sprint review attendees is critical for a smooth meeting.

Give a visual

Visuals, whether diagrams, mockups, and so on, can help the team and stakeholders understand how this sprint's stories fit within the big picture, especially in the early stages of the project. I personally like to create a simple visual to walk through what will and won't be shown during the meeting. In the following diagram, I've attempted to give you an idea of how a visual can facilitate this understanding in your meetings. Prior to the team showing any functionality, I would show this screen cap via projection and put a big sticky note on it that summarizes what hasn't been done yet:

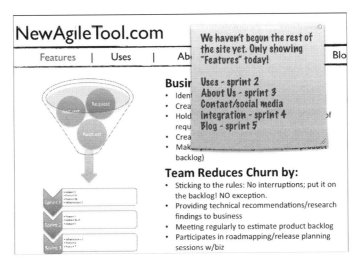

Another really cool way I've found to do this is to create a **Prezi** (www.prezi.com) to show the project at a high level and then zoom or drill down to only the stories that will be shown at this sprint's review. That is a very effective way to underscore the limited nature of the meeting, and also helps all attendees gain an appreciation for the overall scope of the project at a very high level. The following screenshot is a Prezi that I threw together that would help the review attendees understand the site map. I color-coded the Home page to visually indicate that page as the focus for our meeting. I can embed a link to the Home page from this summary view so that the team can click and demo the home page, all from this visual dashboard. Try it!

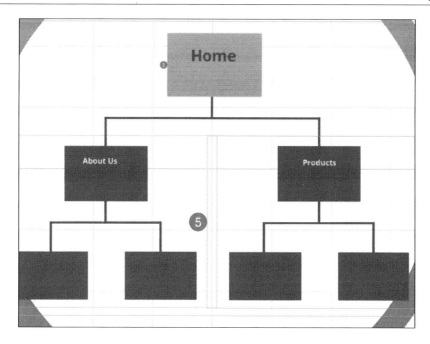

Keep your stories straight

It's also very easy to set the context for a sprint review by creating a quick list of the committed sprint stories. During the "demo" portion, you can read from the list and say, "Bob will now walk us through the login story." Bob does so. You can then ask, "Product owner, do you accept this login story? Are there any changes that you'd like to put in the product backlog?" If the product owner accepts the story, put a check mark next to it and then go to the next one in a similar fashion. If the product owner does not accept the story, the story gets an X, with follow-up discussions about why it was not accepted. Ideally, the team is working from a physical task board—you could just walk up to the board and write a check mark or X next to each item (better yet, have a team member do this!):

Rank	Story	Accepted?
1	Login	✔
2	User Preferences	✔
3	Landing Page widget	✔
4	Secure log off / cache clean up	✘
5	SMS Notifications	✔

In the preceding snapshot, you can see that the team did not complete story 4 for some reason. If this were to happen to your team, you would first discuss during the review why the team didn't finish the story. Keep it at a summary level (no problem-solving!). The root cause is usually that one of the acceptance criteria was missed, the Definition of Done was not met, or the team ran into an obstacle. For example, during the sprint review, the team mentioned that they had three outstanding defects of showstopper proportions for story 4; as a result, neither the team nor the product owner could consider the story as done. If the team does not bring this up during the retrospective, then please mention it. The team must first talk about what they can do to ensure story completion for next time, as well as why the number five priority was completed ahead of number four.

Keep everyone focused

I've seen all too many meetings in which a stakeholder gets sidetracked about a feature that's not yet implemented. If someone gets distracted about functionality that's not in place yet, you might say to him, "The feature that you keep asking about has not been developed yet. It is in our list and is currently priority #47. It should be available for your comments in sprint 19. Please talk to the product owner if you need to discuss priority or implementation details ahead of time. Let's move on." You must be assertive; remember that in doing so, you are creating an energetic meeting environment that people *want* to be a part of.

I worked with a ScrumMaster at a small startup who mentioned that he was scared to invite the CEO to the sprint review because the CEO might change his mind. As much as I tried to persuade him to think of this as an opportunity to educate the CEO, he "didn't want scope creep" and would rather get "spec sign-off" than invite the CEO! I tried to reassure him that if the CEO were to add something to the backlog, then something else must drop. Easier said than done: the ScrumMaster knew from many times in the past that the CEO wanted everything in the original scope PLUS everything that he discovered along the way. Not only was this a challenge for the ScrumMaster in figuring out whom to include in the sprint review, but this also exposed two bigger issues: the mind-set of the CEO and the team's inability to say, "No".

Does a Scrum team demo incomplete work?

This question comes up quite a bit, especially by new teams. It really depends on your situation. I have a general rule that teams should not demo anything that is not done; however, I will make an exception with new teams since they're learning the ropes. Let's say that my team didn't finish three out of five stories and their sprint progress report looked like this:

Rank	Story	Accepted?	Notes
1	Login	✔	
2	User Preferences	✔	
3	Landing Page widget	✘	3 outstanding defects
4	Secure log off / cache clean up	✘	Test cases not written
5	SMS Notifications	✘	No test cases, no doc

You can see that I added a Notes column to show specifically what wasn't done for each story. I would have had to prepare this prior to the meeting by talking with the team members and comparing completed work to the Definition of Done. Any outstanding work would show up on this progress report so that I could give a quick summary in the sprint review. It clearly illustrates the progress of the sprint by focusing on working functionality, not percent complete.

See the whole

In addition to helping stakeholders see how far along the product has come in this sprint, it is also a good idea for the ScrumMaster to help them envision the overall status of the release (if the team has been asked to create and follow a release plan). At a minimum, I like to show the team's velocity chart, with estimated and actual velocities for each sprint like the following one:

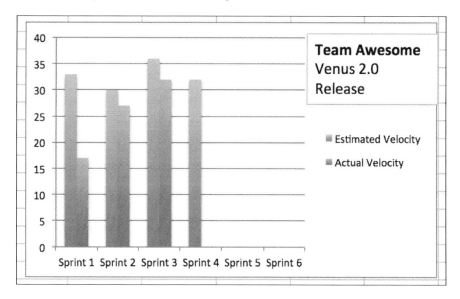

And the following is a release burndown that shows the amount of remaining work (see more about release burndowns in *Chapter 6, The Criticality of Real-time Information*):

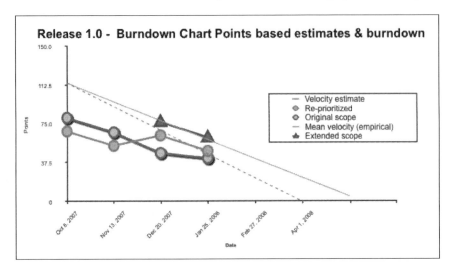

It can also be interesting for stakeholders to see other information about the sprint. While certainly not required, I find it helpful sometimes to paint a picture of where a sprint's investment actually went. For example, in the following graph, you can see that in the latest sprint (4), the team took on more spike/research work than in previous sprints. I might explain in the sprint review that the stakeholders will see a little less functionality than in previous sprints because the team did some research to figure out how to leverage Facebook's API. The team would also make the results of their research known, just like they would demo the results of implementing stories. Remember, a Scrum team makes everything visible during a sprint review!

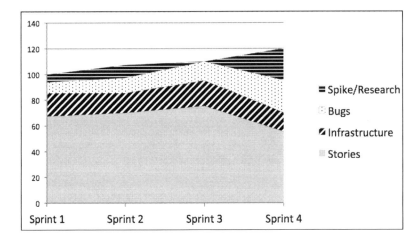

Possible outcomes of a sprint review

By now you understand that the features shown in sprint reviews create a starting point for conversation. The functionality shown in sprint reviews—especially the early sprint reviews—is likely to not be correct; in fact, perfect delivery of a sprint is not really the goal. I can imagine that statement might surprise you, but the sprint review, while it feels like "the end" of the sprint, is actually the beginning of new ideas, thoughts, and interesting considerations for the product. That is why it is imperative that the ScrumMaster works with the product owner to ensure that the right people are in attendance.

There are several possible actions as a result of the discussions in a sprint review. First, the product owner can simply accept the work of the team. The stories delivered meet the Definition of Done and pass the functional acceptance criteria; the product owner says they're accepted and the team gets the points for the work. Conversely, any stories not started or still in progress are moved back to the product backlog, points are not given, and the product owner considers the unfinished work in addition to and in light of the stories already marked for the next sprint.

The product backlog is expected to change as a result of the sprint review. Sometimes, the product owner has an **IKIWISI** moment (**I know it when I see it**). That is, having reviewed the features in the sprint review, the product owner now has a better understanding of what he/she wants (or doesn't want). The product backlog is then refined to reflect this deeper understanding of needs:

- The product owner may remove or add stories as well as change the priority of stories based on what was discussed in the sprint review or based upon new information from other stakeholders or customers.

- If the team's velocity was higher than expected, the burndown will be steeper, resulting in an earlier-than-planned release; or the product owner could decide to fill up the original release deadline with more functionality.

- Conversely, if the team is not burning down enough functionality, the product owner may need to consider extending the release date, dropping features or stories, or perhaps looking at funding another team to work on the same product backlog.

- If the team doesn't finish everything in the sprint, the product owner has the right to discontinue work on any in-progress stories. That is, stories shouldn't automatically move to the next sprint; the product owner must approve to push them forward.
- The product owner could say, "That's enough, ship it!" This is why maintaining a high-quality level is so important! If the team has a bunch of clean-up work to do in order to ship it, then they're not very agile, are they?

In addition to making these decisions, product owners need to communicate the impact of these decisions to other stakeholders. Most product owners have steering committee or core team meetings to update other organizational and customer stakeholders about these decisions. For example, marketing professionals need to know if the product owner and team extended the release date, as this will impact their marketing campaigns. Another example is a client engagement manager who is responsible for transitioning a client to the new platform; he/she will need to know what to communicate to the client and when.

Don't surprise the product owner

Ideally, product owners are on call during a sprint to review stories as the team completes them. The sprint review is a safety net: in case the product owner was not available during the sprint he/she may give feedback during the review. I advise my teams to never surprise the product owner; in other words, they should not make assumptions about functionality. If there is even a question or doubt, call the product owner, walk over to his/her desk, or get his/her attention in the daily scrum.

Sprint reviews for continuous flow frameworks

In *Chapter 4, Sprint! Visible, Collaborative, and Meaningful Work*, we briefly discussed teams that evolve into Kanban practices. In the case that your team is using or thinking about using these practices, the sprint review may be handled a couple of different ways:

- The team can hold a mini-review with the product owner as soon as a story is ready. This means that a product owner may have several little review discussions per week as team members complete stories. The purpose is to catch any changes or new ideas before the team pushes the story to production. I've observed some teams give a heads-up in the daily scrum, hearing comments such as, "Hey guys, I'm going to finish up Stock Alerts by noon and I'm meeting with Kumar at 1 p.m.; anyone else have something to show him?" This style is definitely a bit more ad hoc, but teams do get into rhythms and make game rules so that it's manageable. This is probably the most agile a team can get—well, you could always take it a step further and get the customer in the room with the team every day! You know, XP style!

- The team could still hold sprint reviews every two weeks, for example, in which they would show every story that was finished in that two-week period. Stories would have been integrated and built to a preproduction or sandbox environment and pushed to production as soon as the product owner accepts them during or right after the sprint review. The danger here is that something from two weeks ago might need rework versus the first option in which a team would catch it right away.

There is no right or wrong answer if doing Kanban or a Scrum/Kanban hybrid. The point of it all is to get product owner or customer input and validate that through a review of functionality as soon as possible.

Sprint review – a time for collaboration and trust

A discussion about the product's features can open the door for new ideas. Someone from Sales might have a comment about a user story shown in the review based on previous talks with a client who would like to sign a contract, but is stalling because he/she needs a particular set of functionality. Or perhaps the support staff currently must provide a manual workaround to customers for particular types of data entry and they bring this information forward in the sprint review. This enlightens the product owner, who can now create a new product backlog item to automate support's response. Team members and stakeholders should view the sprint review (and really, Scrum in general) as an opportunity to shape the product, and, as in the following diagram, the product owner listens to these valuable contributions to understand if they may be important or impactful enough to be prioritized in the product backlog. The sprint review is a living example of the Agile Manifesto's "Responding to change over following a plan" as well as "Customer collaboration over contract negotiation".

In Scrum, we invite feedback and yes, sometimes, often, that produces change requests. ScrumMasters must encourage others to embrace the new ideas that emerge early and often during this pause in development called a sprint review. The resulting discussions, transparency, and mutual understanding builds trust between business people and the delivery team through time.

Sprint retrospective – inspecting and adapting processes and teamwork

Many people don't realize that the sprint retrospective was not a part of Scrum originally. It was not a part of Ken's first book but was included as a part of his second as a bona fide step in the framework reportedly based on influences in 2001 by Norm Kerth, Diana Larsen, and Esther Derby.

The retrospective is the time and place dedicated to process improvement; in other words, it is a focused space for the team to think about how the last sprint went, what worked well, what needs improvement, and collectively what they will do to change it for the next sprint. A team discusses anything that may be relevant, whether it's a technical impediment that challenged the team, such as CI, test automation, and so on; organizational impediments; a misbehaving ScrumMaster; behavioral and social challenges; and issues preventing collaborative teamwork. The retrospective is not a time for inspecting people and finger pointing, but rather a time for improving process and building a team, which sometimes means having frank discussions about team conflict.

And for heaven's sake, just because the Scrum literature says that the meeting is time-boxed to three hours does not mean you have to take three hours in this meeting! The time box means don't go over three hours; if your team can get in and out within 30 minutes and feels like a good discussion has been had and improvements have been identified and assigned, then get in and get out! No need to waste time!

SCRUM is not an acronym for Serious Crud Required by Upper Management

I once facilitated a group retrospective for three Scrum teams working from one product backlog. There were about 25 people in the room who had completed three sprints. I began running through my retrospective script. Nothing seemed to have gone well; nobody said anything positive as much as I probed, questioned, and asked several times in several different ways. Onto the next question: "What could be improved for next time?" I started to see the group come alive. After a couple of ideas were exchanged, one guy said very loudly and bluntly, "I feel this is just a way for management to try to get more out of us." In a large room now silenced, this one guy's voice seemed to echo. I asked, "Would you mind sharing more about that with the group?" Boy was he pleased to. He began to talk about how their little company was bought by a larger company five years ago. He (and others chimed in at this point) felt that the acquiring company never cared about them. He said that the new managers were never interested in him or his work; they just cared about the bottom line. In fact, several of his coworkers had been laid off three weeks before this retrospective. So he felt that Scrum was just management's way of trying to get more with less.

I looked around the room and a couple of people had started crying. They were very upset about this! They had been very proud of their work up until the acquisition and never felt appreciated afterward. So they decided, once management said to do Scrum, to check out. They really didn't care about things like the Definition of Done, sprint deadlines, testing, or their work in general anymore. They never saw a customer. They never heard from their product owners (who were doctors and nurses). They were sad and demoralized. And they took it out on me as the "consultant who's going to fix them", fixing me instead. I was stunned. I didn't know what to say, exactly. I felt as though I was being thrust into the role of a psychologist and I do not have a degree in psychology. I tiptoed around... don't even remember what I said exactly... but learned that several of the mainframe guys had been employed for 20 years and were just waiting to retire. They didn't care about radical change or improving work processes; they just wanted to do their work and go home. Overwhelmed, I managed to somehow convince the teams that there could be some other benefits to working this way—autonomy over tasks, teamwork, no more multitasking. They agreed to give it a good try but still felt like SCRUM was an acronym for Serious Crud Required by Upper Management. As of today those teams are still sprinting, though their managers have managed to create what I call "managed Scrum", which is nothing like real Scrum. Managed Scrum is basically the Scrum framework, but where managers control everything; they standardize meeting templates, Definition of Done templates, they break down all the tasks for the teams, team members report to them in the daily stand-up meeting, managers assign people to teams and then rip apart teams and form new teams based on a Taylor-istic mind-set about expert-to-task resourcing. Teams don't self-organize; there's no autonomy. It's probably the worst form of hybrid Scrum I've ever encountered. The people on these teams were very unhappy as a result of managed Scrum. It's sad. It's not what they expected.

Ikujiro Nonaka, in *The Knowledge Creating Company*, tells us that, "The employees' sense of identity (must align) with the enterprise and its mission." Clearly the team members at this company did not share the mission or identity with its acquiring company, and that mismatch in mind-set and values was discovered through the Sprint retrospective. All other issues were mere symptoms of this larger diagnosis. But, it didn't matter anyway since managed Scrum was implemented. The managers didn't really care about letting the teams control their own destiny, becoming truly self-organizing.

I've included this story because I think it represents the extreme of what a retrospective can unearth. It's crazy how the sprint health can often be a reflection of the emotional health of the team members. Sometimes, no matter how well you prepare, the retrospective can surprise you. Leverage each retrospective as an opportunity to try new techniques; becoming a better facilitator will enable you to handle these curve balls with grace and leadership, and build a better team in the process.

Unearthing information for improvement

Most retrospectives don't play out like that one. You won't typically find yourself suddenly thinking that you need a Ph.D. in Psychology. They're usually very straightforward. Following are a few steps that will help the team have meaningful discussions and get good retrospective results. Esther Derby, who wrote *Agile Retrospectives*, recommends five retrospective steps (`http://scrumpedia.com/ concepts/sprint_retrospective`).

Set the safety

The first rule of a retrospective is that only the team members and anyone whom the team members invite may attend. Oleg, a VP of Development I once helped implement Scrum, decided to plop down in a seat during the team's retrospective meeting. He was excited because he heard that this is a meeting in which great things will happen. Before the meeting started, I asked Oleg if anyone on the team invited him. He said, "No, but the team will say anything in front of me! We have so much trust!" I wasn't convinced, and try as I might, I was unable to pry him from his chair. The retrospective started. What do you know—everything that the team members talked about was positive, happy—everything was perfect. Oleg left about halfway through the meeting, excited that everything was going so well. As soon as he left the meeting, the team members collectively sighed relief and then said, "Ok, now let's talk about what really happened!" They were not at all comfortable airing their dirty laundry in front of Oleg; they didn't feel safe. If you have trouble keeping managers out of the retrospective, you may need to engage an ally—ideally, someone at a level higher—who can help you coach the managers and clear the room at the appropriate times.

Back in 2003 when I first started doing Scrum, it was generally agreed that the product owner shouldn't attend the retrospective; however, that opinion has now changed (for the better, I believe). I've seen the perception of the product owner change from adversary to an ally. Truly, he/she is the customer or customer's representative and has the biggest stake in the project's outcome; therefore, yes, the product owner should be in this meeting. *The product owner is part of the team.*

From time to time, you may need to set the safety within a team. For example, you might notice that one team member routinely picks on another. You might ask a question during the meeting like, "You guys all agreed that respect was one of our core team values; how can we stick to this value today?" and see if the team self-corrects. Perhaps the situation requires a one-on-one conversation with the aggressive team member. Maybe you need to eventually escalate this to the person's manager. If you are unsure or hesitant about conflict resolution, check with your corporate training department to see if any classes are coming up. This is a popular corporate course and there are many online seminars as well. Facilitating conflict resolution takes practice and courage! With patience and hard work, your retrospectives will turn into team-building exercises!

Recall sprint events

What happened during the sprint? Having team members think through the sprint the start to finish will give them some insight into what worked well and what didn't (the next two questions). Try to keep the team from making judgments at this point; just the facts, ma'am. Sometimes it helps to put a timeline or calendar on the wall to help the team remember what happened. You can also have team members get up and write on the timeline, or for shy teams, write on sticky notes and you can post them on the wall. This gets the information out there in a visual and tactile manner; again, many different modes for learning.

Ask – What worked well for us? What didn't work so well for us?

Once the team has warmed up and has thoughtfully considered the sprint, you will now have the team write events on stickies and place those stickies into one of two columns: what worked well, and what did not. Please ask this question and refrain from telling the team what you thought worked and didn't work well. This is imperative! If the team is to own its actions and ultimately be responsible for itself, then it must identify areas of improvement on its own. The following figure presents the five steps of a well-run retrospective:

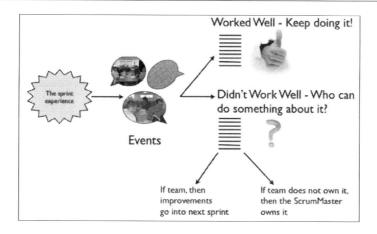

Who owns the improvement?

In other words, who can fix the issue? Is it something that the team can resolve, such as "more unit testing"? Or is it something that the ScrumMaster needs to take for the team such as, "Stop Bob from being pulled into other projects?" Deciding who owns the improvement does the following two things:

- Helps team members realize that they *can* decide for themselves what they would like to do to improve the situation for the next sprint

- Ensures that the ScrumMaster is taking responsibility for removing impediments in a visible, public way

Any items that the team members cannot resolve for themselves go into the ScrumMaster's impediment backlog for action. Focusing on ownership of the problem is a real way to build team empowerment in the sprint retrospective. After some time, a team should be able to resolve most of its issues, handing off the most severe ones to the ScrumMaster. If an impediment cannot be resolved after some time, it might be a constraint--a fact of life that the team will have to deal with and work around.

Impediment Backlog

Resolved?		Sprint	Impediment
yes	✔	1	Daily scrum meeting stretched to 30 minutes. Gotta keep this to 15!
yes	✔	1	We did not have small stories coming into Sprint Planning; will work ahead with PO to decompose stories; pull in Bobby and Ramesh to this discussion
no		2	Team needed an architect to mentor and we didn't have anyone available; sprint 4 will cover new technology; will line someone up now
no		2	Team needs a test automation tool
no		3	Team wants to explore continuous integration; will investigate some common agile tools
no		4	Sprint Backlog was not updated consistently by team members. Will keep an eye out for this in next sprint.

Prioritize and assign action items

Evolution doesn't happen overnight and neither do improvements for a Scrum team. That is why it is imperative that the team members prioritize the actions that they would like to take to improve life for the next sprint. Bite-size pieces, if you will. Action items should have owners and due dates, which may simply be "by end of sprint 7". The following table shows some common problems and one team's solutions (your team's solutions may differ):

Problems	Solutions
Definition of Done isn't clear; we thought we finished all of our sprint work but didn't get points for three stories in sprint review	Define done and enforce it; answer "how do we know when a story is finished?" (ScrumMaster will put it on the team wall after meeting today). Check in every day or so to remind each other of the Definition of Done.
We plan for engineering work and builds but not testing and bug-fixing time	Deploy to the development branch daily so that testing can happen early and continuously.
	Notify team of check-ins so that everyone on the team knows what's ready for testing (our tool can be configured for notifications; in the meantime, Katie (a Scrum team member) will update the team twice per day when new code has been merged. Bob (another Scrum team member) will configure the tool to send automatic notifications by next Friday.
We run out of time in the sprint because we have to fix production issues	Plan 60 percent of the Scrum capacity for new work, 40 percent for production support. Commit to less (whole team can do this starting with tomorrow's sprint planning meeting).

Make REAL action items

I like teams to express action items in terms of REAL. REAL action items are first, **realistic**. They are achievable, earthly endeavors. Real in this context means down-to-earth tasks that a team can achieve. No pie in the sky. A team can **estimate** how much time it will take to finish the action item. Will it be done by the end of the next sprint, or will it take six months? For example, setting up, configuring, and training everyone on Jenkins for continuous integration might be a longer-term action item, while keeping the daily scrum meeting to 15 minutes is instantaneous. A person or team can actually do REAL action items; the team can **assign** a member to shepherd its completion. Finally, we can **learn** from REAL action items and share that learning with the rest of the team.

Any time humans reflect upon an experience, they recall information that is sometimes unpleasant or uncomfortable. Discomfort can spawn change; that is, a person, or a team, can decide to remove the negative reinforcer of, say, an unhappy customer, or a broken build, or too many defects. REAL action items help the team visualize the steps to resolve the unpleasant situation. You must take the team all the way through to action items; don't just stop at recalling the events. Nothing is likely to happen as a result.

I've included the following sprint retrospective checklist for your use:

Who	Item
ScrumMaster	Short introduction by ScrumMaster welcoming all attendees, reviewing purpose, agenda, and time boxes for the meeting. Reiterate the use of Parking Lot and Action Items log.
ScrumMaster	Start with the prime directive: "Regardless of what we discover, we understand and truly believe that everyone did the best job they could, given what they knew at the time, their skills and abilities, the resources available, and the situation at hand." (Norm Kerth, `Retrospectives.com`).
Team	Discuss the events that occurred during the sprint.
Team	Divide these events into positive events (helped us succeed) and negative events (wish to improve).
Team	For the "wish to improve" list, select two or three items for improvement. Make a REAL goal—**R**ealistic, **E**stimated, **A**ctionable, and **L**earn (see following). The ScrumMaster takes on any obstacles the team does not feel it can remove or affect (adding them to his/her Impediment Backlog).
ScrumMaster	Review the actions that have resulted from the meeting; all action items should have owners. Close the meeting by emptying the Parking Lot.

Some different retrospective techniques

Many ScrumMasters use the plusses (what works well/keep doing) and minuses (what needs to change/stop doing) model for retrospective (see the diagram at the end of the *Why should we care about reviews and retrospectives?* section for an example of plusses and minuses), which works well, but it can be too simple sometimes, and too repetitive. The ScrumMaster runs the risk of creating a stale environment when he/she uses that technique over and over again and doesn't experiment with anything else.

+ (do more, keep doing, we like it)	- (stop doing, change, it's not working)
Tasking work in sprint planning	Need more discussion during design sessions
Release and roadmap helpful	User stories were too big for sprint
Daily scrum led to important discoveries	Need to think about who's demoing what
Everyone contributed	

Here are four ideas for extending the retrospective; perhaps something here could work with your team's personality (or serve to bring out your team's personality):

Change the scenery

Have coffee. Seriously. Go to the coffee shop with your team, order up a tall latte (with skim milk), and talk about the sprint. Take a little notepad with you, discuss what the team would like to do about the issue, and see if anyone can step up to the plate. Sure, you don't have the luxury of a whiteboard at Starbucks, but you have the benefit of caffeine, free Wi-Fi, and pound cake. The point is that sometimes changing the scenery can get people thinking differently about their circumstances. Plus, it's not a bad way to do a little team-building.

If you're close by a park, step out with the team for an hour. Call the meeting "Ice cream in the Park + Retrospective". Sometimes feeling like a little kid opens up the creative mind. Get giddy, get ice cream, have some fun in the name of serious work.

Visualize the future

Ask the team to draw a picture of the characteristics their successful team will exhibit in the future. Ask if a couple of team members would be interested in showing their drawings. Ask others if they agree with the ideas in the drawings, and if so, what will it take for the team to get to that future state?

Here's an idea for getting your team to think about what's possible. Set up the retrospective and ask your team members to bring their laptops (this will immediately pique interest because normally laptops in meetings are a no-no). In the retrospective, explain that you would like the team to write an article for Wired Magazine that describes a super cool, highly collaborative and creative team—them! Have the team members get creative about the scenario and the article tone. Then have them answer the following questions:

- Which day-to-day actions do you feel made our team a smashing success? What difficulties did you encounter? How did you overcome them? (These do not necessarily have to be real events; the team can make up examples.)

- What differences do you see between this perfect world scenario and how you operate in real life today?

- What ideas for improvement would you like to try in the next sprint?

- What game rules could we create to guide us in the future?

- What could the ScrumMaster do to help the team get closer to being written about in *Wired Magazine*?

This exercise touches on many dimensions. The basic retrospective questions are hidden in the first and second questions. Action items are covered in the third and fourth questions. The last question addresses ownership. The entire exercise provides a creative outlet in which the team can visualize what it could possibly attain. Sometimes a mental picture of the end state can inspire the team.

Team cave art

Primitive storytelling was done verbally through narratives, music, rock art, and/or dancing. Have each team member pick a medium through which to present his or her ideas. You'd be really surprised to see what people come up with! Lee Devin and I used to hold a one-day workshop about extending ideas from theatre to development teams for better collaboration. At the end of the day, after several warm-up and creative exercises, we asked the team members to use what they learned about improvisation and rehearsal to solve their biggest (real) team impediments. Thinking this way allowed team members to identify and explore solutions they had never before considered.

Retrospective yoga/meditation

Once a team asked if they could do 10 minutes of yoga prior to the retrospective. I believe in the spirit of trying my boundaries as a facilitator. Well, I was more than happy to oblige, and participate! This little joke ended up turning into several teams meeting on a daily basis (for months!) for 11 a.m. yoga (read a great blog post by Dan Oestreich about Touchy-Feely at http://www.unfoldingleadership.com/blog/?p=472). Actually, I've had several teams approach me about doing yoga, meditation, or a walk around the block as a warm-up to retrospective.

Okay, let's face it. While retrospectives are serious work, some developers may check out when you start asking them to draw their experiences on a rock or sing a ballad. I heard this once: "This is a warm and fuzzy meeting, and I don't do warm and fuzzy." You must set the tone in the meeting that this is real work. I always open with the fact that this is about process and making our work lives better, that team members create their own realities, and what is discussed in the retrospective is confidential yet we expect that high-priority actions will be implemented. If I feel that warm and fuzzy isn't going to fly with my team, I'll quickly turn it technical by asking instead, "What issues or challenges did you run into when developing your feature to the Definition of Done?" Ah, this unearths all sorts of gems. I highly recommend adapting your style and techniques to that of your team, yet don't be afraid to try something different now and then. Keep in mind, however, that if you push your team members too far out of their comfort zones, you run the risk of shutting them down. Either way, so what if you fail? You just opened the door for others to, also. After you blush from embarrassment, do a silly walk, and press on.

Why should we care about reviews and retrospectives?

The review and retrospectives are the backbone for organizational evolution.

> *To create new knowledge means quite literally to recreate the company and everyone in it in a nonstop process of personal and organizational self-renewal.*
>
> — *Nonaka, Ikujiro, The Knowledge Creating Company*

Just like the snake sheds its skin every so often to reveal shiny new scales, an individual, a team, and an organization must shed its old culture skin by creating new knowledge and sharing stories about the new way of doing things. One excellent place to start is in the retrospective. And during those times of reflection, a team can dig up challenges as heavy as boulders.

An example of this presented itself to me a short time ago with a client. We were in the very first sprint review. The team was very proud of itself, as it should have been—they achieved a lot in their sprint. However, I noticed that they were scurrying right up until the very last minute before the meeting started; I observed developers literally running around from cube to cube right before the meeting. While demoing one of the features, it crashed. Red-faced, the backend developer said, "Well, it worked right before the meeting." And I'm thinking to myself, "Yeah, it worked with duct tape and bandages." The team got through the rest of the demo and then it was time to talk velocity. I asked the product owner if the features were acceptable to him. He said yes, but not the one that crashed. I reminded the team that the crashing feature was worth eight points, and since they committed to 32 but didn't get eight, the actual velocity then was 24. This made the team unhappy. They tried to blame everything—that someone else broke the build, that the environment wasn't set up properly, and so on, eventually saying that the issue was brought forth in a module of code that they didn't originally write, so they shouldn't be responsible for it. The feature worked before the meeting and they felt they should get credit for it. I sat there, pensively. I then asked, "Well, who would be responsible for fixing that bug before deployment?" They said, "Well, we would be because the original team that wrote that code is no longer here." Then I asked, "If you are responsible for fixing it anyway, how does that relieve you of the responsibility in this sprint?" To this they just answered, "Well, we'll just fix it at the end. We want the points." This discussion revealed an issue that I see quite a bit: teams that are preoccupied with winning points instead of completing high-quality features, and end up gaming the system in order to get more points. They're missing the *point*, obviously, so as the coach I had to remind them of why teams estimate in points in the first place, what a point represents, what *done* really means, and why they should care. I have to admit that this wasn't popular with the team at first; they weren't happy about it. But I think that over the next couple of sprints they got it, especially when they were hit with production issues in old code in the middle of peak retail season, defects that could have been caught with performance test cases and a good Definition of Done.

The beauty of the retrospective is that the team takes charge of its solutions. In the following diagram, you can see the traditional versus Agile ways of problem solving. The traditional approach is owned and executed by management; whereas the Agile team has ownership and responsibility to solve its own problems. A person gains knowledge, experience, and insights into challenges through his/her work each and every day, and often has ideas for improving his/her environment. Traditional managers, however, manage their workers toward a predefined set of expectations and outcomes (Taylor's scientific management). In a situation like this, a worker may never escalate learning because the manager may reprimand or otherwise negatively impact the worker. Therefore, new insights and learning often stay with the individual when working in the traditional model. Agile team members also individually gain knowledge, experiences, and insights while working in sprints, yet they are empowered as a team to solve their own problems and to escalate the ones that they cannot solve. When team members are engaged to solve problems together, the knowledge that each person acquires during the sprint is shared among everyone on the team. The team, rather than just one person or a person's manager, shares their perspectives and collaboratively solves the issues. This often leads to greater outcomes.

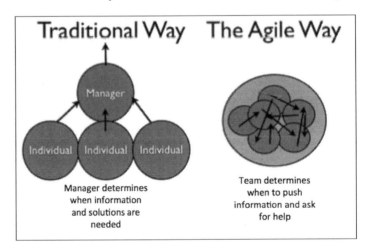

Summary

Retrospectives provide teams with the ability to solve their own problems and escalate any issue that they cannot solve for themselves. Reviews and retrospectives offer visibility into product and process so that both can be adapted, giving the organization the ability to improve by listening to knowledge workers, rather than managing, measuring, and punishing them for challenging the status quo. Scrum sprints allow for the most important work to happen in short cycle times; anything that jeopardizes completion of the product increment must be dealt with immediately. Scrum often leads to innovation by the issues it exposes, but only if the ScrumMaster and/or team can engage in focused, relevant discussions of the challenges. If issues are surfaced but no action items result, the process will surely stagnate. As you accept the role of the ScrumMaster, please be sure that you're ready for your Scrum mother-in-law to live with you!

In *Chapter 6, The Criticality of Real-time Information*, we will discuss ways that you can help the product owner and Scrum team broadcast information at the right level, to the right audience, at the right time.

Recommended reading

- Visit www.businessballs.com for all sorts of workshop exercise ideas. I love this site!

- Derby, Esther and Larsen, Diana, *Agile Retrospectives (2006)*, Pragmatic Bookshelf

- Kerth, Norm *Project Retrospectives (2001)*, Dorset House.

- Nonaka, Ikujiro and Takeuchi, Hirotaka, *The Knowledge Creating Company: How Japanese Companies Create the Dynamics of Innovation (1995)*, Oxford University Press

- Visit www.prezi.com for a simple but effective way to create a visual dashboard for sprint reviews. You'll be hooked!

6

The Criticality of Real-time Information

I lived in the NYC metro area for years, and I get particularly grouchy and disgruntled when my travels require that I take a train *from* Penn Station. Several train lines depart from Penn Station — New Jersey Transit, Long Island Railroad, Amtrak — to name a few. NJ Transit and Amtrak trains share a central schedule, a big board, about the size of five ping pong tables put together end to end, with letters and numbers that click-click-click like the shuffling of a card deck as it shows basic information about the incoming/outbound trains, departure times, and track numbers. While a good way to distribute basic information, the issue is that the tracks are updated within mere minutes of departure time, which means that large crowds stand underneath and around the suspended dashboard, nervously awaiting track information. Click-click-CLICK! The track number appears! Five hundred people clog one skinny escalator as they attempt the descent to their track; other passengers run around the waiting hall searching for staircases or other escalators, often bumping into each other. It can be quite dangerous! I've always hated this last-minute reporting; it causes lots of tension and stress.

If I were King of Penn Station, I would place mini-schedules in every coffee stand, retail shop, restaurant, and hallway so that passengers could dine, shop, and stroll while being able to view information about their train from practically anywhere within the station. This new system would allow passengers to queue when they wished, unlike the old system that forces them into nervously watch a clicking board with hundreds of other anxious passengers. This solution might also boost commerce as people could spend more time shopping and eating instead of waiting under a big sign.

You see, real-time information can help our rail travelers make important decisions about how to spend their time at the train station, sparing them inconvenience and aggravation. Similarly, the burndowns, backlogs, and other real-time information provided by Scrum teams enable product owners and stakeholders to make good decisions and spend their time appropriately.

Without inspection, adaptation cannot occur; that is, evolution in product and process can only occur when results are made visible. *Chapter 5, The End? Improving Product and Process One Bite at a Time*, focused on reviews and retrospectives—the *end* meetings that actually create a new beginning. But Scrum provides us with some very good basic techniques to promote the broadcast of real-time information throughout a Scrum project, so that the appropriate levels of decisions can be made.

In the Agile world, the word "control" has a negative connotation. It is typically used in the phrase "command and control" to depict old-style management techniques. However, think of control more of like a shared state between the ScrumMaster, team, and product owner; this state is reached by visibility, influence, and teamwork and not by micromanagement by a manager. I think it's perfectly fine to have "control" in a project if the right people are controlling the right things. In this chapter we will discuss how various stakeholders can achieve this shared state of control by utilizing real-time information. As a ScrumMaster, you will learn how to make your team's information available at the right time to the right people so that they may make the best possible decisions. Visibility also builds trust between business and technical people, which is a great thing to have in situations—like product development—that require collaboration to achieve the greatest outcomes.

Yesterday's news is old news

Humans want the latest information. We want to hear news as it happens, not days later. It's interesting that as high-tech and special as we think we are, cool real-time apps and gadgets have been around way longer than we think. In fact, it was all the way back in 1881 that the Theatrophone was invented in France so that people could listen to live opera, theater, and news over the telephone lines. In 1884, King Luis of Portugal couldn't attend opera in person, so he used Theatrophone to dial in! You know, this sounds eerily similar to our modern WebEx or GoToMeeting applications!

Today, we can subscribe, trackback, post, ping, poke, and utilize any number of ways to stay in touch and to have news data fed to us. Take social media; we follow our favorite "Tweeps" to hear what they have to say as they say it and we see what our friends are cooking, who they like, and what they're doing today by reading our Facebook news feeds. In fact, we usually read the top of the feed for the most recent updates, losing interest in older, outdated, possibly irrelevant updates. Old news is simply not interesting or valuable; maybe only when we need to research something, or for entertainment value as we look at those old high school photos and yearbook letters from our high school friends. Most major newspapers have taken double-digit hits in subscriptions and sales over the past decade as we increasingly choose to read their news via electronic means. We want information, and we want it now! Yesterday's news is old news!

Much as the general population wants to hear the latest news and information about, well, anything, so do our project stakeholders. Scrum provides this visibility in simplistic ways; so simple, in fact, that some people try to overcomplicate it. ScrumMasters rely first on broadcasting and then on reporting if necessary.

Getting the message

Communication is simply the relay of information between two or more people. With all of our technological advances, we can communicate just about anywhere, with anybody. Communication *with intent* is making sure that the message that was intended is indeed the message that was heard. For example, if I show your three-year-old a pie chart describing investment capital expenditures for fiscal year 2011, is that really communication? No! Even though your little tike might be impressed with the pretty colors, he/she probably doesn't get the message!

In our projects we have many different stakeholders with different needs for information and communication frequency. From executives, to managers, to vendors, and team members—good communication helps people see the big picture, and how the steps they are making every day get them closer to the goal. What happens if communication is not done well? Many studies show that most projects fail due to breakdowns of communication, yet what's interesting is that even in these projects deemed as "failures" I'm sure there were plenty of Gantt charts and status reports and the like. So in these projects deemed as failures due to lack of communication, there actually happened to be a whole heck of a lot of communication. So what gives here? If, like our three-year-old, people aren't *getting it*, then the format, the timing, or the audience is wrong. The challenge in any project is to ensure that the communication vehicle is appropriate for the audience.

In his *Agile Software Development* book, Alistair Cockburn explains that two people, face to face at a whiteboard, is the richest and most effective way to communicate. The least effective, least interactive is communication by paper. Think about project communications the same way. Whenever possible, teams should update stakeholders in a face-to-face manner. Also, they should regularly, if not continuously, broadcast important information about their work. Finally, a ScrumMaster may need to make a team's progress visible via a report as needs arise, but this would be the last resort and probably not as effective as the other means. In this chapter, we will explore the following categories of communication:

- **Face-to-face**: Daily scrums provide day-to-day insight into what the team is doing during its sprint. The team runs it via face-to-face communication (or via conference call if they are distributed) and opens the door to others who may be interested to observe or listen. As you learned in *Chapter 5, The End? Improving Product and Process One Bite at a Time*, the team shows stakeholders the product increment in the sprint review so that feedback may be given in real time. The ScrumMasters's job is to help the team get the right people in the room so that they may gain visibility and have important conversations.

- **Broadcasts**: Scrum provides simple broadcasting tools such as burndown charts as periodic updates for project stakeholders. The frequency of broadcasts depends upon the needs of the stakeholders and the project's horizon (daily, weekly, monthly, quarterly). The ScrumMaster ensures that information is broadcasted in appropriate manners, at appropriate levels, at appropriate times.

- **Reports**: These are for people who aren't there. Reports simply won't be as effective as broadcasts, but there will certainly be a place and time for reports in your projects.

Traditional status reports depict perceived information about work or task status, while working software—Agile's status report—is about real, tangible features. The Scrum process is like a microscope; it allows stakeholders to view the project ecosystem at different levels so that they may make timely and good decisions. ScrumMasters must get the right people to look through that microscope. Scrum helps us set expectations around value delivery and broadcast information relevant to those expectations:

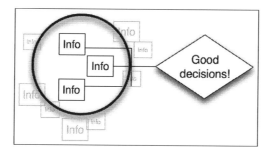

Through the Scrum microscope

Communication should be timely, streamlined, reflect reality, and include the appropriate decision makers. The level of information should be appropriate to the audience.

Just like any microscope, our Scrum microscope has a set of objective lenses; the view of a project is very different depending on the strength of the lens chosen. When we want to see a general shape of something, we'll use the 1x or 2x strength. This might be appropriate for, say, a product vision statement or product roadmap. When we want to see every last detail, we'll use the 64x. The daily communication of the team is like the 32x or 64x lens—all the detailed work tasks, team member interactions, code and tests being written and executed, discussions, and dependencies between team members. We don't need 64x, though, for reporting to executives. They may want to see information at the 2x or 4x level. As a ScrumMaster, you must understand that providing visibility and information is one thing, but providing visibility and information at the right level to the right audience is quite another. Good communication in a project is much, much more than just updating a sprint burndown chart. You must play the role of the biology lab instructor, helping your students understand which lens to use, what they will see, and what to make of it.

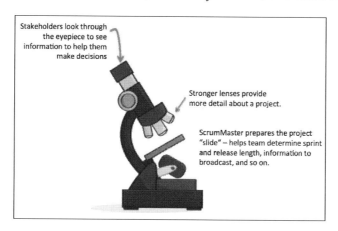

The following figure shows the various communication points—or times to bring out the microscope—for a project with both sprints and releases. Notice that communications in a Scrum follow a pattern, or rhythm. For example, during the sprint, one big daily conversation (called a daily scrum) is held so that team members may inform each other as to what's happened, what will happen, and issues that may be hindering progress, as well as to provide visibility to other stakeholders.

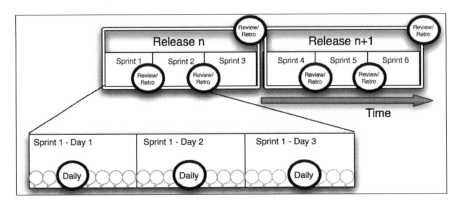

Sprint reviews and retrospectives magnify relevant summary information about a sprint—progress toward story completion and process adaptations. Release reviews and retrospectives magnify information pertinent to the release level—stories and value delivery, time and cost.

1x magnification – product vision/initiatives

Level 1x magnification is the big picture view. If you were to look through the Scrum microscope with the 1x lens, you'd see broad shapes and outlines, product visions, programs, projects, ideas, and initiatives. Most ScrumMasters or teams have nothing to do with this level of planning or visibility.

A CEO might want to know, for example, the status of the laptop project. All he/she needs to hear is, "…it's on time for September in order to meet the holiday demand." And he/she is on their way. The CEO doesn't need to know that Bob on Scrum team 3 had a dentist's appointment and will be out for an afternoon, possibly causing Sally's task to be delayed. I know this is an extreme example, but it reminds me of status meetings long ago in my waterfall days when the Gantt chart of activities was presented to executives. Talk about getting lost in a project plan in a meeting that would drag on forever!

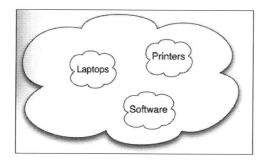

Even though they may have nothing to do with creating it, Scrum team members should be able to peer through the 1x lens so that they understand the reason why work has commenced, the big problem or business case that they're trying to solve. It amazes me to observe so many teams that don't get the big picture. This limits good decision making; teams with blinders on can't quite see where they're going and often don't make the right decisions. It's those little day-to-day decisions that lead up to the big solutions, so if the end state is unknown or questionable then the tasks to get there will be unknown or questionable as well. It's imperative that everyone "starts with the end in mind" as Stephen Covey once said. If your team is not sure of the vision statement, have your product owner stop by the team room and discuss it with a team and then write it on a big flip; if you have a distributed team, post the vision statement on the home page of the team's project wiki after a quick conference call. Make it front and center!

2x magnification – the product roadmap

Peering through the 2x lens, we see a bit more detail underneath each initiative. For example, we zoom in a little on the laptop project and see a roadmap that spans four quarters, with high-level themes for each quarter:

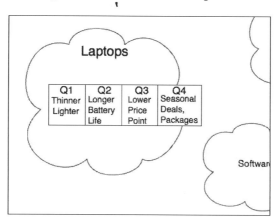

Again, ScrumMasters and teams are probably not as involved with this level of magnification as they are with, say, release planning (4x), but they should be aware of any available roadmaps and make sure that product managers consider technical input when crafting them. For example, it would be wise to engage an architect or another technical team member during a roadmapping session in order to gauge the feasibility of features. If the product manager for our new laptop wanted a screen that's paper thin, the architect may know what, if any, technologies exist to support that request. Or he/she may feel that the idea is feasible but has a hunch that the cost would be high and might call for a different battery configuration. Another example is that perhaps the product manager wants to win new market segments with a new set of features. The architect, or a technical team representative, may understand that this requires new hardware that is very expensive; upon hearing this, the product owner decides to shelve the request. The early technical input and high-level cost information can help a product owner decide early if a feature set is worth the investment. You should ensure that your product owner is sharing roadmaps, if they exist, with the team on a recurring basis. Again, this is necessary information that supports the product's vision, and team members can make better decisions with this knowledge.

It's equally important that product managers and executives understand the reality of development, that is, how teams progress toward the goals of the roadmap and release plan. The ScrumMaster is a critical link between stakeholders who need to understand a team's ability, or velocity, for strategic planning purposes.

What if you don't have access to this level of information? Believe it or not, I've met teams who don't know who their product owner is. So the first step is to identify your product owner, and he/she may be up the food chain; perhaps he/she is a director or even a VP of product management! Approach this person to request a half-hour of his/her time to set the vision stage for the team—a project kickoff (or reset). If the product owner is not available, seek out an assistant or other proxy who is available. Most good product managers have a product vision statement and a roadmap (regardless of if they're "agile"), so ask that your product manager share these assets with the team. If he/she says that they've written it down so why don't you just have the team go read the document, remind him/her that this is probably not the best way to communicate such important information. Most product managers are more than happy to oblige.

4x magnification – the release plan

Looking at the project through the 4x lens shows more details. As you zoom in, you can't see everything on the project slide, so the release plan detail for the first quarter comes into view. Many stakeholders like to look through the 4x lens; everyone seems to be interested in the team's progress toward the release plan. The 4x lens can help everyone understand if the team is on track and moving according to plan, as well as what changed in the plan. Keep in mind that the 4x view will change through time as the product owner thinks of new features, the team increases its velocity, and so on. Just like living micro-organisms under a real slide, the view through our Scrum microscope isn't static, and more things seem to wiggle around as the magnification increases:

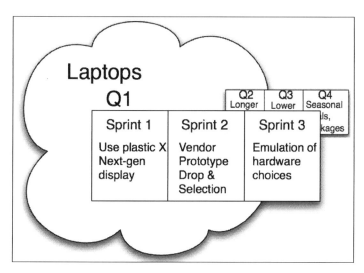

In *Chapter 2, Release Planning – Tuning Product Development*, we discussed how to engage the team in release planning in order to discover the subset of the product backlog—the release backlog. Let's consider now how to best communicate information about the 4x lens view—the release plan—to various project stakeholders.

Release the burndown baseline

This is simply a view of how many units of work are planned to remain at the end of each sprint over the span of a release. This is the outcome of the product owner meeting with the team to estimate product backlog items and project the release date and targeted functionality. In this case, the team estimated their release backlog items in points, which represent a relative size of one story to the next. This team planned for about 130 points of work for the entire release and forecasted completing an average of almost 20 points per sprint. The release burndown baseline shows how much work is *anticipated* to remain at the end of each sprint. As the team makes progress, they can overlay reality.

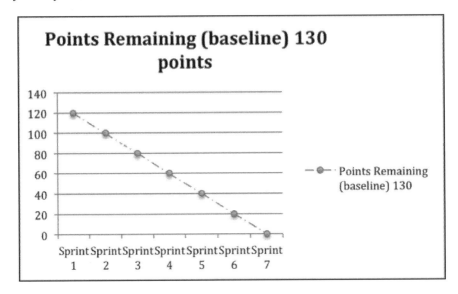

It is very important that the release burndown baseline is communicated as just that, a baseline of a forecast.

Baseline with updates

At the end of every sprint, you should invite stakeholders to peer through the 4x lens to see how the team is doing compared to the plan. You have many possibilities in which to help them see this information: face to face, broadcast, or report. You may decide to utilize one or all three methods, depending upon the needs of the project's stakeholders: communicate the release plan face to face during the sprint review, post the updated release burndown to the wiki, and send a summary e-mail to executives. The following release burndown chart shows the team's original baseline and actual burndown. Even though the team thought, in release planning, that they'd have about 80 units remaining after Sprint 3, they in fact had around 90 units of work remaining. I've circled the variance in the amount of work forecasted in the original baseline, and the amount of work that remains to be done (solid line) as of the end of Sprint 3. The third dashed line is a projection of how many sprints the team will need to finish all the remaining work. As you can see, the projection is now 10 sprints. This is very important information for stakeholders; for example, the product owner has early visibility that some features may not make it, or that he/she should consider extending the release date. Also, stakeholders from marketing and sales may need to realign their external messaging to customers.

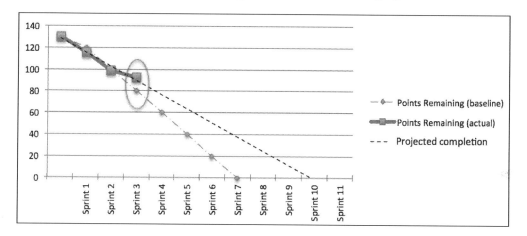

It's very easy to put an Excel spreadsheet together to get these views. Following you'll see the release backlog behind the baseline and release burndown charts. You can see that the team's estimates and actuals were spot on for Sprints 1 and 2, but that they did not complete features F.2, H, I, and J by the end of Sprint 3. A team's release burndown only takes into account work actually done (based upon the Definition of Done and the product owner's acceptance of the product increment!):

Release v1.0 Plan					
Rank	Item	Story Estimate	Velocity (0 if not done)	Remaining per baseline	Remaining per actuals
1	Feature A	1	1		
2	Feature B	2	2		
3	Feature C.1	1	1		
4	Feature C.2	3	3		
	Sprint Totals	**10**	10	120	120
5	Feature C.3	5	5		
6	Feature C.4	3	3		
7	Feature C.5	8	8		
8	Feature D	1	1		
9	Feature G	3	2		
	Sprint Totals	**20**	20	100	100
10	Feature E	3	3		
11	Feature F.1	5	5		
12	Feature F.2	1	0		
13	Feature H	2	0		
14	Feature I	3	0		
15	Feature J	3	0		
	Sprint Totals	**17**	8	83	92

The preceding spreadsheet also shows sprint cut lines within the release, or where each sprint's goal ends. Cut lines move up and down as the team establishes a velocity, the product owner adds new items to the product backlog or changes priorities, and so on.

Team velocity chart

A Scrum team is supposed to end each sprint with a number of stories or features that are done. Users stories are usually estimated in a coarse way; many teams use points (but it is perfectly fine to use man-months or any other system you might want to use, as long as it's kept high-level and not confused with actual time).

As I mentioned in *Chapter 5*, the velocity chart basically shows how many units of work a team completed in a sprint. Over a number of sprints, velocity should begin to stabilize and becomes useful for forecasting future releases and sprints. Teams may also want to show committed and actual velocities per sprint, in order to show better planning and attainment of goals over time. Keep in mind that before a team runs a sprint, velocity is either a *planned* velocity or an *estimated* velocity; once the sprint is over, the team has an *actual* velocity (or simply, velocity).

It is important to remember that confidence and certainty will grow over time the longer a team is together as they learn more about the technology and requirements and by working with each other. It can take three to four sprints for a team to jell in its dynamics and stabilize its velocity. As ScrumMaster, you make velocity visible by turning the 4x lens on the Scrum microscope. This is important information for most, if not all, business stakeholders.

A Gantt chart in an Agile project

Yes, it is perfectly acceptable to depict scheduled features via a Gantt chart view as in the following figure. I've had to provide this view in several situations in which executives weren't quite accustomed to or comfortable with the burndown concept. They were very familiar with a Gantt view, so I decided why not use it! As you can see in the following figure, a Gantt view is simply a different way of viewing the release plan over time. Please do not jump to the conclusion that teams are entering actuals into a timesheet as per the traditional way; rather, the ScrumMaster just enters a few milestone activities to represent features/stories, and level-of-effort activities to represent sprints. The team is responsible for tracking its tasks at the sprint level, which occurs independently of this view. This Gantt chart view is easy to create and maintain.

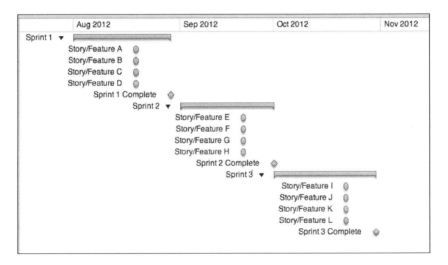

I've provided you with some simple ways to depict release status. Please use them and then devise your own; you can get very creative with these views. Remember, first choose face-to-face communication of this information by presenting it during sprint reviews, then broadcast it by putting it out on a wiki or project dashboard. Create a report, if you must, for other stakeholders.

8x magnification – the product backlog

Clicking the 8x lens into place, you now see a deeper level of information: the entire product backlog. As I mentioned in *Chapter 2*, since the product backlog is the link between long-term and short-term planning, used by numerous stakeholders, it must be in a language that everyone can understand. Otherwise, you have the Tower of Babel effect, where business-speak and tech-speak co-exist but without shared understanding. The user story format prevents or remedies this situation. Stories greatly facilitate communication between the business and development, and help product owners negotiate depth of feature delivery. While large requirements docs are muddy, difficult to wade through, and bog us down, user stories are light and easy to organize in a product backlog, and require us to expand upon them only when necessary at the last responsible moment (16x magnification). Stories also help product owners think like users and that allows for the better prioritization of users needs. Finally, stories facilitate vertical slice development (that is, creating features that work cross-component).

What does your user want?

I'm not going to rewrite the user story book here (you absolutely must read Mike Cohn's *User Stories Applied*) but I do want to discuss the communication benefits of a well-structured story. User stories follow the format: As a [user] I want to [do something] so that [I get value/benefit]:

rank 2	size 8
User Story	
As a <u>seller</u> I want <u>an option for buyers to buy my products now</u> so that <u>I don't have to wait on an auction.</u>	

User stories identify three main parts: the actor, the action, and the benefit. Traditionally written on a 3x5 index card, they hit on all three learning modals: visual, auditory, and tactile/kinesthetic. A story is never perfectly written; rather, it is a placeholder for several future conversations that have an increasing level of detail.

Stories are relatively easy for business stakeholders to write because they tend to talk about users all the time anyway. Stories, while not intuitive at first for developers, are an easily learnable format and help development team members visualize a real live human and what he/she needs to do or would like to do in the system. This visual is very important as all team members can put themselves into the shoes of users. User stories provide a great reporting mechanism; in other words, the product owner and business will understand, "we've implemented the login story" instead of "we've implemented a backend SQL query to return an error on incorrect login credentials."

The product owner lives in 8x magnification. It is also very important that he/she invites other business stakeholders to peer through the eyepiece to see the product backlog as well. You should help your product owner if you realize that this isn't happening.

16x magnification – the sprint

Turning the lens to 16x, you dive into a bit more detail, going from stories in a prioritized product backlog to stories contained within a sprint along with their tasks, hourly estimates, and status, as we discussed in *Chapter 4, Sprint! Visible, Collaborative, and Meaningful Work.*

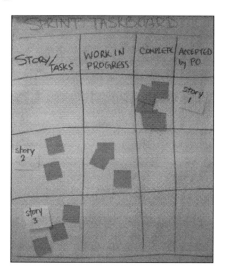

User stories in sprint planning

User stories facilitate sprint planning because they keep our conversations limited and they ensure full understanding of what's needed by the user. One way we can ensure understanding is through conditions of satisfaction, commonly referred to as acceptance criteria.

Acceptance criteria

The product owner and team agree to the acceptance criteria in sprint planning; they spell out the expected behavior of the story. I like to have my teams complete the sentence, "We know this story is done when the user can do [this, that, and the other]." In the acceptance criteria for our "sell it now" story, the product owner has explicitly stated the selections the user must make in order for the item to be saved as a sale versus an auction. Separate stories exist for View Item, then Purchase Item, and Get Notifications for items. Acceptance criteria help the team understand a user story's boundaries:

rank 2 size 8	**Test that:**
User Story As a <u>seller</u> I want <u>an option for buyers to buy my products now</u> so that <u>I don't have to wait on an auction.</u>	a. Seller can select "buy it now" or "auction" via radio button on item description page b. Seller can set a minimum price (this is a required field) c. Seller can choose to include shipping in the cost of the product or require that the buyer pay shipping (also a required selection on item description page)

If there were no acceptance criteria for our "sell it now" story, for example, one person on the team might assume that it is just the seller functionality, another team member may assume that it encompasses both seller and buyer functionalities, and yet another team member may assume that it includes sell, buy, and search filters. You can see that without acceptance criteria, a story's description is incomplete and ambiguous and can lead to many issues in a sprint such as low story completion or late code commits (and eventually, an unhappy product owner!). Acceptance criteria may also include guidance for validation, error handling, hardware needs, performance, and so on. If the team has a question in sprint planning about a requirement of a user story, the product owner answers it then and there and either writes it as acceptance criteria or creates another story to do in a future sprint. Acceptance criteria help the team see where one story ends and another begins.

When the entire team understands the acceptance criteria, this knowledge can greatly reduce, or eliminate altogether, questions at the end of the sprint such as, "Did we really agree to do that?" The acceptance criteria provide a handshake between the product owner and the development team that they have outlined, to the best of their abilities, the way the features should work upon implementation. Acceptance criteria provide a good starting point for writing functional acceptance tests.

Definition of Done

Whereas the acceptance criteria spell out the functional or behavioral expectations, the Definition of Done is the *quality* goal for any story that is committed in a sprint. A common Definition of Done is, "Stories have been coded, unit tested, integrated into a build in x environment, all regression tests automated and show as passing, performance thresholds exceeded." The team and product owner determine the Definition of Done through an open dialog about what's technically possible by the sprint's end. Once the Definition of Done is determined and agreed upon, it is put on the physical or electronic team wall so that the team doesn't forget.

With clear acceptance criteria and a good Definition of Done, team members clearly know when they're done with a user story. And for sprints, our 16x magnification, delivering user value is the most important objective of a Scrum team. User stories facilitate that.

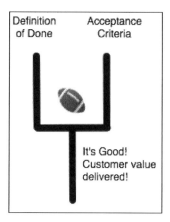

Sprint goals

A team should be able to summarize its committed stories in a sprint goal. This is important to 1) ensure that everyone on the team knows what it's supposed to do at a high level, and 2) provide good summary-level information so that others outside the team can understand—without having to go into excruciating, often non-interesting detail—the overarching goal of a sprint. Goals might be enable users to pay and talk about us via social media or move our first terabyte of data. ScrumMasters often communicate sprint goals to others in the organization. This is like inviting them to the microscope at the beginning of each sprint to look through the 16x lens.

Sprint reviews

As we discussed in *Chapter 5, The End? Improving Product and Process One Bite at a Time*, the sprint review is the time for the team, customer, and stakeholders to *zoom in* on what's been done thus far in the product. It's the best form of status. Period.

Remember that the information discussed in sprint reviews can also include other information that is helpful for decision makers. This information was discussed in 4x magnification as release plan updates to the baseline. However, a ScrumMaster may decide to include information about various impediments, unmet dependencies, or other such information in a sprint review if it is timely and appropriate for the attending stakeholders.

32x magnification – tasks, daily scrums, and other information

This is the most detailed view of the work, and it's owned by the team and mostly referenced by the team. We covered this view in great detail in *Chapter 3, Sprint Planning – Fine-tune the Sprint Commitment*

Daily broadcasts

Scrum has built-in daily broadcasts. Daily scrums and sprint backlogs provide the basics, but there are many permutations of how these basics are implemented. Teams end up customizing their daily scrum, sprint backlogs, and other formats.

Daily scrums

We took a deep dive into the details for this meeting in *Chapter 3*. But it is important enough to mention again that in addition to a synchronization meeting for the team to course correct to meet its sprint goals, this meeting also doubles as a daily magnifying glass so that others can see how the team are doing. Anyone is invited to stop by. But only the team members talk. Any questions or issues should be taken up with the ScrumMaster after the meeting.

I've observed and have used different questions in this meeting to drive different results or behaviors. A couple of examples are as follows:

- On whom will your work have an impact?

  Having team members answer this question can get them thinking proactively about alerting others on their team when their task may impact another's.

- What did you learn that others on your team might benefit from knowing?

  This is a great lens through which team members may view the daily scrum—the sharing of new knowledge for the greater good of the team.

Sprint backlogs

Tasks are the work steps necessary to complete a user story. A user story is a container for work tasks. The team's progress, or the project's progress, can be communicated based on the number of stories done and not done. The day-to-day self-management of the team is done at the 32x level, with acceptance criteria and the Definition of Done as goal posts for each story.

The team's collective set of tasks forms the sprint backlog. This is basically the team's to-do list. They own it and manage it. That means they can remove tasks, add tasks, split tasks, add increasing estimates to tasks—any action that portrays the remaining to-do's in the most realistic light possible—without having to ask for permission to do so. The sprint burndown chart is automatically generated if using a tool, and manually generated pretty easily on a wall chart usually by the ScrumMaster. The sum of the individuals' updates gives a feel for how the team is doing as a whole, every day of the sprint.

In my early Scrum days, I was especially frightened by the idea of a team updating their own tasks. This was because as a project manager, one of my main responsibilities was to schedule the project. Every task in the project plan had dependencies, estimates, and so on, and a change in one task could impact the critical path, then the end date, then the executive dashboard, which meant the executives would breathe down my neck for an explanation of schedule changes. Therefore, I wouldn't allow anyone access to my project plan in order to avoid such a disaster. When I became a ScrumMaster, I had to mentally separate the different levels and needs for planning. I realized that I could still have a project plan, if I needed it (this later morphed into a release plan), and the team could manage the day-to-day tasks with their own tools and techniques.

In the following sprint backlog, you can see the items from the product backlog (Automated Download, Check Free ACH) along with their tasks indented beneath them. You may also notice that each task has a team member assigned, a status column, and estimates in the columns to the right. Day 1, or sprint planning, was October 23. Team members update each column with a new assessment of the amount of task hours that remain on each and every day of the sprint. Ideally, the amount of task hours decreases every day during a sprint, "burning down" to zero remaining on the final day of the sprint.

Project: Financial Tracking System Sprint 1 Backlog	Responsible	Status	23-Oct 1 266	24-Oct 2 250	25-Oct 3 232
Automated Download		In progress			
Coding	Tom	In progress	0.5	0	12
Code Review	Edna	Not started	1	1	1
Unit Testing	Tom	Completed	0.5	0	0
Prepare System & Acceptance Test	Tom	Completed	0.5	0	0
Change Controls for Migration to Prod	Bill	Completed	0.5	0	0
System Testing	Marcie	Not started	3	3	3
Acceptance Testing	Elli	Not started	3	3	3
Acceptance Testing	Patti	Not started	3	3	3
Acceptance Testing	Mark	In progress	3	10	2
(Remember to include Nicole from Support)	Marcie	Completed	0	0	0
Project Space	Tom	In progress	6	4	3
Audit Review	Robin	Not started	0.5	0.5	0.5
BOS Update	Marcie	Not started	1	1	1
(Remember to notify Samantha for update)	Marcie	In progress	0	0	0
Check Free ACH		In progress			
Coding	Edna	In progress	3	5	3
Code Review	Tom	Not started	1	1	1
Unit Testing	Edna	Not started	4	4	4
Change Controls for Migration to Prod	Bill	Not started	0.5	0.5	0.5
System Testing	Marcie	In progress	3	1	3
Acceptance Testing	Marcie	In progress	3	4	3

Sprint burndown chart

The sprint burndown chart is generated from the sprint backlog and is simply a plot of the number of hours remaining over the days of the sprint. This view, while mostly used by the team to assess its sprint progress (and make course corrections if needed), is also appropriate for anyone outside the team who's interested to see how the team is doing. In the following burndown chart you'll notice the jagged line, which represents the day-to-day remaining hours. You'll notice that the burndown is not linear. The *perfect* line that you see in the Sprint 1 Burndown is a guideline; that is, if everyone burned down linearly every day, the result would be zero on Day 13. It's just a visual guide. You can see that our team's first sprint isn't going so well. If we were to draw a trend line, the team would need an additional three or four days to finish the work. Since sprint time boxes aren't flexible, the team and product owner have an early indication from this burndown that a story or two must be dropped from the sprint and put back into the product backlog.

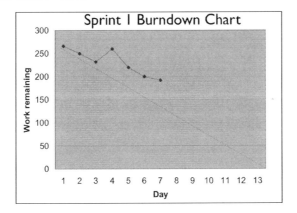

Some teams create a hand-drawn burndown chart to put on the wall next to the physical taskboard, eschewing Excel or any other tools altogether. Instead of hours, they'll simply count the number of tasks remaining every day. It helps when each task is eight hours or less in order to normalize. This works great for teams as it is simple and very effective.

The visual information in the sprint burndown chart is not a tell-all but can provide some important clues as to what's happening. The team can use these early indicators to spur a conversation—in real time—to course correct during a sprint. Look at the following burndown chart; that team won't finish anytime soon! In this case, you would get the product owner and the team together to see if some lower-priority stories could be cut, or perhaps discuss terminating the sprint altogether (see *Chapter 7, Scrum Values Expose Fear, Dysfunction, and Waste*).

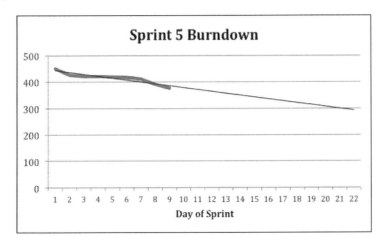

In the following Sprint 6 burndown chart, you'll notice the opposite scenario. The team was trending to finish on Day 10 of a 24-day sprint (yes, early!). At that point, the product owner and team met in a quick mini-planning meeting to identify stories that they could pull into the sprint in order to fill up the space; you will notice the upward tick of hours remaining around Day 10 based on the tasks and hours the team entered after discussing the new stories with the product owner:

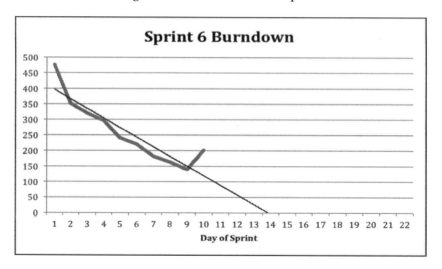

In Sprint 7, the support team escalated some severe production issues to the Scrum team; the task hours for these interruptions plus the original scope is represented by the line with triangles in the burndown. You can see that the team had buffered for potential interruptions—the burndown of the tasks from sprint planning (bold line) is trending to finish by day 18 of a 29-day sprint; the trend line for the production fixes plus the original sprint commitment (line with triangles) shows completion by the end of the sprint. The team is looking good for Sprint 7!

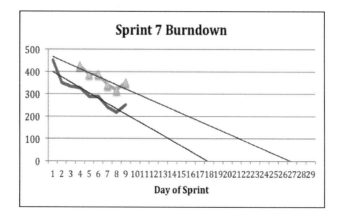

The scenario represented by Sprint 7 is not ideal; Scrum was created with the goal of controlling chaos by eliminating interruptions. However, some teams have no choice: they must support earlier versions of a product while also implementing features for a new version. In the case where interruptions cannot be corralled to a different team (or a subset of team members), the team must buffer for the "known unknowns" to the best of their ability in sprint planning. In other words, it doesn't make sense for them to allocate 100 percent of their six-hour day to new features when they know that they will be interrupted with production issues. That would be wasteful planning. Rather, they may decide to plan tasks only for 70 percent of their available six hours per day, reserving roughly two hours a day for interruptions. The ScrumMaster would take on an impediment to help the team reduce the number of production issues in the long run. The ScrumMaster might also consider showing a graph in the sprint review that shows the amount of time or points going toward new features versus production issues.

What burns down can also burn up

Some teams like to burn up the number of points earned for stories as they're completed in a sprint. This model is widely used, especially among teams using Kanban or a hybrid. The burn up chart simply shows the cumulative number of points earned over the days of the sprint:

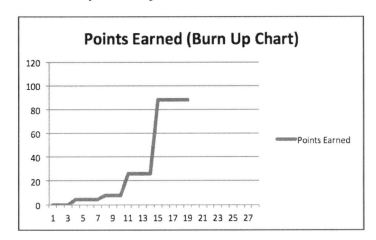

Don't forget to broadcast the need for the product owner and team to prepare the product backlog for the next sprint (see *Chapter 4, Sprint! Visible, Collaborative, and Meaningful Work*, for "Next Sprint Prep" information in the *Look ahead at the next sprint's product backlog items* section). This is like jumping from 32x back up to 8x magnification in order to prepare the next set of stories for the upcoming sprint. Many teams forget to switch out their lenses. Don't let it happen to yours!

64x magnification – read all about it, in the team room!

The team room is the team's hub, its domicile, its commons area, and its cave (Alistair Cockburn). The team owns the setup and organization of their space, establishing game rules for communication to ensure that they are getting through their sprints as effectively as they can, as individuals contributing to a team's success.

I'm a big believer that collocation works really well for teams. I've seen it in action numerous times. However, not every team—or their managers, for that matter—will be thrilled about the idea initially. One team I worked with recently realized that there might be some benefit to collocation but they wanted to try it out first on a temporary basis. So they convinced a couple of their colleagues to trade cubes so that the entire team would be at most two cubes away. They say that if they like that, then they'll get facilities to rework the cube structures into something more enveloping and permanent for the team. As ScrumMaster, I did not force collocation on the team. Rather, I dropped a hint that this might be a good way to work, and the team figured they could at least try it in some form, and move forward if they liked it and if it worked for them. That was their decision, not mine. I just supported it however I could, and I'm anxious to learn the results of their experiment.

People who sit close by each other tend to overhear each other's conversations; some conversations are relevant to work, others are just noise. Team members should have the ability to set ground rules for themselves about when it's okay to be approached and when it's not, for both team members and those outside the team. Some teams do this by updating instant messenger with a status or otherwise denoting open time. One team I met put a crime scene tape around its office area border to signal to external stakeholders that it was not OK to approach them.

Simple conversations become broadcasts in a team room. I've seen it in action many times: two developers will start talking about a problem, and you'll see others on the team slowly migrate over and start chiming in about their perspective or solution. Next thing you know, the entire team is now in the center of the team area discussing the issue and collaborating toward a solution. Then they each go back to their workstations, and it's quiet for awhile. Next issue comes up, some talking, more join in the conversation, and so on. It's this pulling apart and merging back together of people and conversations that is a natural rhythm of communication in development, in our daily scrums, and throughout the project. Just like you'd see a lot of wiggling about on a slide under a 64x lens, so you will in the team room.

Monitor this!

I've seen a few team rooms/areas outfitted with TV monitors that broadcast critical information for the team (and observers!). One example of this was a production support team that could view the number of calls (with severity and escalation) in the support center's queue. Another example was a company that had monitors showing a measurement of the number of conversions per minute. If conversions increased, they released the right features. If conversions decreased, they might roll back the feature that they feel caused the drop-off. Talk about real-time measurement of business value! Another team had monitors that showed pass/fail status of their integration and regression tests with green and red indicators, along with bar charts for how many defects were found versus fixed. This allowed them to quickly discern when things were getting out of control.

Scrum microscope summary

The following summarizes, in detail, all the magnifications that we have seen so far:

Lens strength	What do you see?	What should you broadcast?	Who's primarily responsible for this level?	Who's the traditional audience?
1x	Project vision statements, project names and descriptions, big ideas, initiatives	Broadcast these ideas to the team, especially product vision statements.	Product owner, product manager, CEO	Business stakeholders, but encourage a team audience.
2x	Product roadmaps, market analysis, user personas	Broadcast this information to the teams working on the initiative; also, broadcast team sprint reviews and velocity to the product owner and other stakeholders as requested.	Product owner	Business stakeholders, but encourage a team audience. Become the link between long-term and short-term planning (or assist your product owner in doing so).

Lens strength	What do you see?	What should you broadcast?	Who's primarily responsible for this level?	Who's the traditional audience?
4x	Release plan	Get the team and product owner together to plan face to face. Broadcast baselines, updated burndown charts and cut lines in sprint reviews, and by posting on project wiki (or similar). Broadcast any obstacles that get in the way.	Product owner, ScrumMaster, team	Project manager or product manager. Scrum changes this by advocating team participation. Help the product owner prepare burndowns
8x	Product backlog	Ensure that the product backlog is visible and that the product owner maintains and ranks it for the team. Encourage team participation in story writing, estimation, and defining acceptance criteria before or in sprint planning. Broadcast any obstacles that get in the way.	Product owner with help from the ScrumMaster, if needed	Product owner, leads, or managers. Scrum changes the rules in that the product owner works directly with the team to flesh out product backlog items.
16x	The Sprint	Broadcast meeting times and places, sprint goals and commitments, Definition of Done. Broadcast any obstacles that get in the way.	ScrumMaster and Team	Project manager or line manager. Scrum changes the rules – the team makes and owns its commitment and goals and defines Done with the product owner.

Lens strength	What do you see?	What should you broadcast?	Who's primarily responsible for this level?	Who's the traditional audience?
32x	Day-to-day work	Daily scrum time, obstacles that need to be escalated, sprint burndowns, backlogs, velocity, interruptions, and Definition of Done (as a start). Broadcast any obstacles that get in the way.	Team	Project manager or line manager. Scrum changes the rules—the team makes and owns its tasks, updating those tasks, and task assignments. Encourage stakeholder observation in the daily scrum.
64x	Team room	Nothing, unless asked by the team. Sometimes posting game rules in the team's room will keep them mindful of their working agreements.	Team	Project manager or line manager. Scrum changes the rules—the team is empowered to own its space and do whatever is necessary to complete the work. Encourage face time with business stakeholders. Thwart obstacles and interruptions.

When physical taskboards and conversations aren't enough

Let's face it, not everybody in the company will walk by the team area, study the physical taskboard, ask questions, and so on. For many, this pie-in-the-sky Agile just won't exist (or won't immediately exist). Perhaps the project is just too large to scale up these face-to-face conversations and bug-in-a-jar visibility? How does a ScrumMaster help the souls who won't leave their desks, or who cannot be there in person?

Invite stakeholders to sprint reviews

As mentioned in *Chapter 4*, sprint reviews are wonderful opportunities for stakeholders to learn what the team have implemented, as well as to give their feedback. Work with the product owner to figure out which stakeholders should be invited, and send the invitations early so that folks can get this important meeting on their calendars.

In lieu of (or in addition to!) sprint review attendance, perhaps it's possible to set up a sandbox environment so that stakeholders can at least preview the functionality as early as possible. I've done this quite a few times for Support and Training departments and it was a wonderful way for them to get up to speed on new features, and update their support and training documentation iteratively and incrementally. We really don't want stakeholders to have any excuse for not seeing early and frequent builds of functionality. One simple fix: post a link to the demo sandbox front and center on the project's wiki home page, or send that and a sprint review invitation by e-mail blast to the entire project team's distribution list.

Create and distribute reports

Some stakeholders won't stop by dailies, attend reviews, or otherwise play in the sandbox. How do we engage those people? Reports!

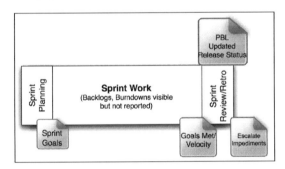

In situations of large projects or distributed teams, lack of good reporting can lead to an inability to act, respond, or adapt. While face-to-face communication is nice, Scrum teams and ScrumMasters in large programs need vehicles through which they may scale communication. All the backlogs, charts, and views that I've shown you thus far may be easily turned into reports. See www.HelloScrum.com for more templates.

Waste and obstacle removal

In addition to broadcasts and reports to the right audience at the right time, obstacles need visibility so that they may be resolved as soon as possible. If a team cannot resolve its own issue or obstacle, then the team escalates it to the ScrumMaster. The ScrumMaster in turn attempts to remove the obstacle; when he/she cannot, the issue is escalated to the "Waste and Obstacle Removal" Scrum team. What is a Waste and Obstacle Removal Scrum team? Well, you know all the managers (like me in the beginning!) running around asking, "Now what do I do since my teams manage themselves?" Well, this is where they go to work. And I'm sorry that the acronym is WORST—that was not intentional , but I bet you'll remember it!.

The Waste and Obstacle Removal team is responsible for improving the effectiveness of the software development process by removing impediments from Scrum teams. This is a group of volunteers and they don't manage a Scrum transition (worst mix of words ever!) but rather facilitate issue resolution so that teams may work effectively and productively. That means that the WORST needs to know what's plaguing teams. Setting up an "obstacle broadcast" board—especially in the situation of multiple and distributed teams—is a highly effective way of doing this. ScrumMasters (and team members!) can also meet on a recurring basis to look for patterns of issues and recommend solutions.

I have contributed to a few such teams. At one company, we called our team the ELMO team; that is, Engineering Leadership Office (we put the M in because we happened to like the Sesame Street character). Another team of a client called themselves the Firefighters. I've also heard many organizations refer to this team as the ATT team, or Agile Transition Team.

Whatever the team is called, its purpose is critical: pave the way for Scrum development teams to be as effective as possible. This team organizes itself as an actual Scrum team, runs sprints, and makes its product backlog and velocity visible to development teams. The teams themselves should be the product owners of the management Scrum team's product backlog and attend sprint reviews.

Look at the following management team's backlog. You can see the clear mission described as "always being 30 days away from potentially shippable." For this development group with a decades-old legacy client-server product, 30 days was as close to potentially shippable as they could get. This was also in 2003, a time in which Agile tools for integration and version control weren't as readily available as they are today.

Anyway, the "stories" in this process improvement backlog are comprised of two things: escalations from ScrumMasters and observations/action items regarding process improvement, quality, visibility (reports/metrics), and learning. There is nothing in here about commanding, controlling, running a schedule, and so on. This process improvement backlog represents the nature of what a management team should do in an Agile setting: support the teams, and let the teams self-manage. This is in many cases a huge change of mind for management teams, yet you can see the immense value in the kinds of tasks that the management Scrum team addresses! Remember as you're talking with managers in your organization: managers form a team to support the Scrum teams:

Management Scrum Team Product Backlog
Mission: Always be 30 days away from shippable!

Rank	Item	Status	Estimate	Sprint start	Sprint Finish	Owned by
1	Ensure Scrum Process is happening	in progress	40	1		Bob
2	Teach teams about design driven testing	done	8	2	3	Bill
3	Improve engineering practices (refactoring, code standards, reviews, etc.)	done	13	2	4	Ibrahim
4	Create a release plan for 4.0	done	5	2	2	Jennifer
5	Work with product owners on ROI/feasibility/architecture for next release	in progress	8	3		Matt
6	Define management reports	done	8	3	4	Stacia
7	Establish productivity metrics, trends and history	done	5	1	4	Stacia
8	champion long-term integrity of the product	in progress	40	1		Joel (PO)
9	Better defect management process	done	5	3	3	Bill

What does a ScrumMaster have to do with the WORST? Well, a ScrumMaster is the go-to person for a team member or team when they encounter an obstacle. In many cases the ScrumMaster can handle the issue himself/herself; however, when he/she cannot, a clear escalation path is necessary. That's where WORST comes in. I feel a pun coming on: "WORST" case, issues are escalated here!

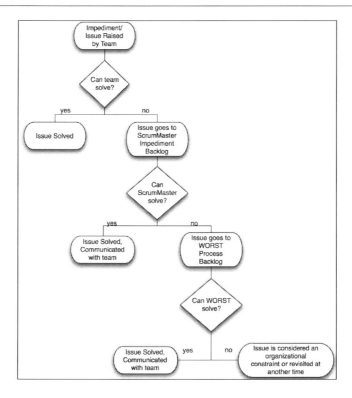

In the preceding flowchart you can see that even though we may consider an immovable issue as an organizational constraint, this item should remain in the WORST backlog for review from time to time; that way, as the organization changes its culture, mind-set, practices, and so on, this issue can be opened again to see if there is room for change.

Following are the types of issues that a ScrumMaster might have in his/her impediment backlog:

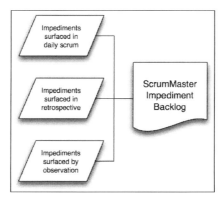

The task of the ScrumMaster is to discern the difference between what appears to be an obstacle versus what really is an obstacle. For example, team members I worked with once said, "We don't feel the need or see the value in meeting in a daily scrum meeting." Well, instead of saying, "OK, little team, run off then and try meeting twice per week and see how it goes", instead, I tried a root cause analysis, asking five Why's until the team revealed the true issue. The discussion went a little something like this:

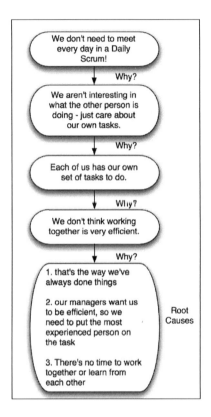

From this five Why's exercise, I had a clear direction. First, I needed to work on the mind-set of the team by providing examples and case studies of teams that used Extreme Programming practices. Secondly, I needed to talk with the team members' managers to figure out what they were communicating in the name of efficiency. Finally, I knew that in the next sprint planning I would suggest that the team buffer its sprint plan to save time for learning from each other. I knew, although management might need some convincing, that co-learning creates much stronger teams in the long run, even though it might feel like a short-term inefficiency.

Another team I was a ScrumMaster for said in retrospective that they felt that they wanted to share more knowledge with each other because when this one particular guy was out of the office, the team just couldn't proceed. This information turned into several action items for me:

- Emphasize knowledge sharing—allow the team to explore mechanisms for knowledge transfer either by pairing or by holding team training (each person takes a turn at teaching the team something)

- Schedule at least one brown bag session per sprint per month, ideally more often

- Post topics on wiki so that the rest of team can sign up if interested

- Encourage team members to share their experiences (that is, what the problem was and how you solved it)

- Support pairing on development and testing tasks

Pairing took some management convincing and a "let's try it approach". Bottom line: ScrumMasters must work with managers to pave the way for improvement and change, and make all impediments visible, from 1x to 64x, so that they may be resolved.

 An excerpt from my 2003 journal: July 24—"during planning, need to relay to the team that I'll be on vacation the week of 8/25. Can they survive with a guest ScrumMaster during that week? Would they prefer a new SM altogether? Am I hence voted off the island? J".

Summary

The Scrum meetings and artifacts help the team broadcast real-time information so that timely decisions can be made. The ScrumMaster must help teams maintain crystal-clear visibility and often help them create a communications plan. Most ScrumMasters take on these administrative tasks to shield the team from that burden. ScrumMasters should use face-to-face, broadcasting, and reporting methods—or all three—as appropriate for the situation. Use reports as a backup in case certain stakeholders cannot make it to the appropriate meetings.

Scrum helps teams and project stakeholders deal with reality by focusing on the quick resolution of obstacles facing teams. ScrumMasters must set up an obstacle broadcast and work closely with managers to quickly surface and help resolve anything preventing forward progress.

Scrum helps us see the truth: good, bad, or ugly. Sometimes the truth isn't what people want to hear. However, with an understanding of reality, an organization can make higher-quality decisions based on reality rather than hopes, dreams, or wishes. In the next chapter, we will focus on how a courageous ScrumMaster can help build an Agile culture.

7

Scrum Values Expose Fear, Dysfunction, and Waste

By reciting the Hippocratic Oath, physicians all over the world swear to ethically and honestly practice medicine. The original version of the Oath, penned in the late fifth century B.C., has changed drastically throughout the centuries—various groups of physicians at various points in history didn't like, for example, that the original version swore to *Greek* gods, while others were concerned that the Oath didn't subscribe to certain political views. Therefore, they changed the Oath to reflect their beliefs. Today, in fact, some newly minted physicians refuse to take the Oath at all (even though most medical schools offer some form of it at graduation ceremonies, if not for purely ceremonial or traditional reasons). You see, the Hippocratic Oath was a way of trying to instill values, ethics, and professional integrity in those practicing medicine, but the problem with it is that not all humans share the same values or political and religious views, and those views change with the times. As a result, it has been impossible throughout the centuries to settle on an all-encompassing Hippocratic Oath; people have diluted it over hundreds of years.

The same thing has happened with Agile! Although Agile practices were certainly around long before 2001, Agile was formally created by the authors of the Agile Manifesto in 2001 (`www.agilemanifesto.org`). Like the Hippocratic Oath, it is a set of values and principles, and frankly, people have been trying to water it down ever since it was written because the values contained therein didn't perfectly fit within their organizations. As a result, teams have ended up running planning meetings, sprint reviews, and story pointing exercises purely for ceremonial purposes, losing or forgetting the original intent. People in these pseudo-Agile companies changed the rules because the values were too difficult for them to uphold. I hear it all the time: "We do something like Scrum. We call it (insert one: fragile, waterscrum, scrummerfall, scrumbut, frankenscrum, pseudo-scrum)."

I'd estimate that half the people I meet think that if they implement Scrum "correctly", all will be better. Scrum is simple, too simple, in fact. How many times I have wished that there were a Scrum book that would tell everyone exactly how to do things! But it's not a methodology; Ken and Jeff have purposely kept the process light all these years. It is a framework meant to expose dysfunction and waste for the purpose of a driving change—and one company's dysfunction and required changes will be very different from another's.

Did you realize that as ScrumMaster, you're the person in charge of driving change? Being a change agent is no easy task! You must make sure that you want to do it and that you can embrace what this role throws at you. You will run into obstacles—some tangible and some you'll have to sniff out. Change agents are not always popular and greeted with enthusiasm and support! As a ScrumMaster, should you choose to accept this mission, you will begin a life-long process of learning to influence, guide, and teach. This chapter will help you identify resistance, waste, and dysfunctions as you apply Scrum practices and values. Remember, to be Agile is to embrace both values and practices; without values, practices are meaningless. And without rituals, or traditions, it's difficult to reinforce values. Can you support both? Can you deal with the culture confusion that Scrum naturally creates? The first step is to recognize that people struggle when confronted with change.

Prepare for change aches and pains

Virginia Satir was a psychologist and therapist who created the Change Process Model that describes how people accept and adapt to change. The following diagram, adapted directly from her model, shows what happens when people are asked to move to Agile ways of working. Over to the left, the existing (or late) status quo is the waterfall way of thinking and doing things. When confronted with the foreign element—or "let's do Scrum!"—people resist and attempt to revert to form, or to what's comfortable. When the pressure remains on to change, chaos and depression can and often follow and performance suffers.

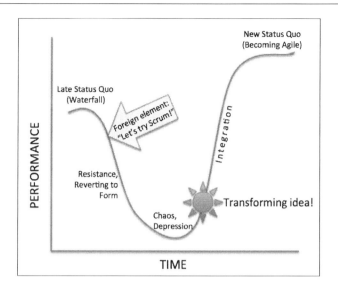

At some point, people will recognize a transforming idea to help them out of the "slough of despond" or "valley of despair". As they integrate the new ideas, they eventually realize a new status quo—in our case, they become Agile. Because a Scrum team focuses on continuous improvement through retrospectives and other means, the team realizes over time that the new status quo is actually a *state of evolution*, represented in the right-hand side of the diagram. With the introduction of Agile practices and values, people, teams, and the greater organization will struggle with early change. People become more comfortable with change if they're in charge of the changes, and if they have a safe environment within which they may try new ideas:

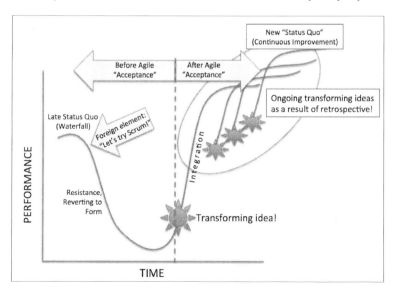

The Transforming idea is when a person or the team says, "OK, let's accept this thing called Agile and give it a try"—we'll call this Agile *Acceptance*. Once that happens, people present numerous transforming ideas through time, each ideally bringing the team to the next level of performance. There is always the real possibility that a new idea for change won't work, and that the team's performance may suffer as a result; it is for this reason that ScrumMasters attempt to create a mind-set of *fail fast*. Ideally, these setbacks should be short-lived as the team reflects and tries new ways to change. The ScrumMaster supports teams by escalating obstacles they encounter as they struggle up the other side of the cliff—hopefully to reach the new status quo!

The ScrumMaster is a change agent, someone courageous enough to apply the Scrum framework along with its values. A good ScrumMaster realizes that the framework without values is weak, and opens the door for managed Scrum, which you don't want. You see, when you exhibit behaviors of a ScrumMaster—the way they were intended to be—you can expect a reaction, and that reaction won't always be easy to deal with. Here you go with getting a team to deliver features every two weeks; in an organization in which people are accustomed to hiding behind project plans, this might freak people out a little! Some people will love it and others will fear it.

The five core values of Scrum

The Scrum values are important because they transform the way teams work and create collaboration opportunities between business stakeholders and teams, ultimately replacing hostility with trust. Any company or team can implement sprints, backlogs, and burndown charts (that's the easy part), but a company or team that embodies and lives the values will excel.

Scrum value	Antithesis
Commitment	A manager committing on behalf of others
Focus	Suboptimization
Openness	Secrecy
Respect	Position, power, and control
Courage	Caution and contracts

Scrum values are interrelated. For example, when a team commits to a sprint, everyone else outside the team should *respect* them to get the work done. The team displays *courage* by *committing* to show their work at the sprint review. As ScrumMaster, you must get your team to live the values by doing the practices; if you have to pick one or two out of the five, start with courage and openness:

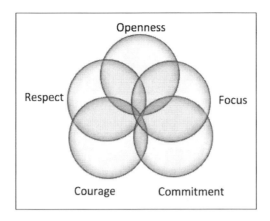

The Scrum values won't match everyone's existing personal values. Value mismatches are a way of life. Values are beliefs or philosophies that are meaningful to a person, and we each hold different beliefs about what's meaningful or important. This is one fundamental reason why Agile methods are so difficult to implement: values differ. But without values, and without at least agreeing on some common ground, we lose our direction. Without values, the organization's compass is broken.

Why have people watered down Agile principles? If an organization's culture is collaborative and creative, for example, Scrum will fit with little to no need to dilute it. In this case, there is no drag. The values will be easy to incorporate into the culture because they closely align with the existing mind-set—the people in the organization feel safe and free to try new things. However, if the prevailing culture type is command and control, Agile runs the risk of dilution, or rejection.

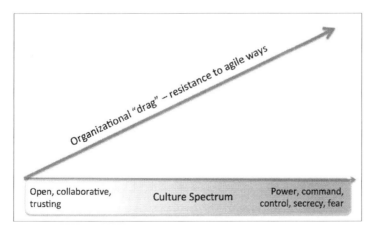

There are many reasons for this. Process people see procedures, org charts, pay and compensation, job descriptions, budgets, and performance appraisals. They do not readily see the political system, cultural norms, unwritten rules, grapevine, relationships, informal leaders and influencers, and informal reinforcement. Both dictate and define an organization's culture. Add fear to the mix — people are afraid to work in a new way, with a new set of values and rituals. So they make excuses that they don't really need to change all that much. And they start loosening the requirements, watering them down, to fit into something that's not so scary or upheaving. It's easier that way. Culture confusion — the result of trying to inject a new way of thinking/being/behaving in an organization — can spell the demise of the new way. It is up to the ScrumMaster to clear the confusion and pave the way for a real change. You can rate your organization in *Chapter 9, Shaping the Agile Organization.*

You know, when I am training for a marathon, I must stick to a very strict mileage and nutrition regimen. Every week or two there is the dreaded long run. This long run is essential to prepare the body and mind for a long period of running. Each time I set out to do my long run, I get myself amped up, repeating, "I will run 15 miles (or whatever the goal is) today." I say this again and again, as a mantra. This becomes super important while I'm at around, say, mile 11, and I'm starting to get tired. The lazy part of me says, "Oh, it's OK! You can quit at mile 13; that's a half-marathon and that's good enough!" But the disciplined part of me says, "…no, you must run 15 miles. When you're in the real race you can't just quit at mile 20 — you have to go the distance — all 26.2 miles!" If I were to start cutting corners during my training program, I wouldn't be able to perform during the actual race. The strict regime allows me to push myself and reflect on where and how to improve. Without this consistency and mind-set, training is for naught, and let me tell you — it's not easy! It is the path of *most* resistance. Likewise, when we water down Scrum, we lose the boundaries that expose the changes that need to be made. We lose our discipline and focus and as a result our efforts become futile. To be Agile is to embrace both values and practices. Without values, practices mean nothing. And without creating new rituals and traditions, it's very difficult to reinforce values.

Scrum value #1 – Courage

John Wayne once said, "Courage is being scared to death… and saddling up anyway." Courage is the ability to confront fear. A bit stronger than risk-taking, which is a calculated undertaking, courage is the decision that you make in order to face something head on, whether or not you know the consequences. Maybe we get fed up one day with the bureaucracy and just march up to our manager and tell him/her like it is. Maybe we say, "To hell with it" and start leaving on time every day. Perhaps our team is growing tired, so we muster up the courage to tell others that we can't sustain this. There, we said it. Now we can sort through the consequences and just move on. Living with the same bad set of circumstances every day is living a lie. Eventually, the lie catches up with you. Clear your conscience, step up, and set yourself free.

 Organizational drag factor #1: FEAR. Only through the decision to be courageous can one conquer fear.

Many people work up courage when the consequences of *not* facing something begin to outweigh the consequences of facing it and getting it over with.

As ScrumMaster, you must be courageous enough to give the message that nobody wants to hear. You must get up every day, look at yourself in the mirror, and say to yourself that you will be courageous. Nothing will ever change if you do not. Courage happens to be contagious, interestingly enough.

> *When a brave man takes a stand, the spines of others are often stiffened.*
>
> — *Billy Graham, American evangelist*

Free the spark

I feel so badly when I see fearful employees. They mill around. They don't speak up; rather, they silently comply. They're defeated. They clock in, type on a keyboard, and clock out. They aren't happy, and one day will realize it and leave. They're like corporate zombies.

Cautious employees want to cover their … hind ends, so to speak. Many invent sign-offs, document reviews, and ultimately contracts because they can point the finger at someone else and avoid reprimand. I hear it in the words people choose: "I'm waiting on the product owner to *sign off* on that story," or, "I threw it over to QA," or, "The customer wants to change the scope *again*!" These words are the language of contracts. Contracts are documents intended to put the risk onto someone else. Just like business contracts, person-to-person contracts are meant to transfer blame, and nothing slows progress more than the blame game.

Organizational drag factor #2: the blame game. Scrum counters this by giving explicit responsibility to only three roles.

Perhaps the biggest managerial challenge facing the 21st-century company will be finding ways to free that spark, resident in employees, from the organization's tidal pull to keep doing the same old things.

—*Walter Kiechel III,* `http://hbr.org/2012/11/`
`the-management-century/ar/7`

One way of freeing such a spark is to squelch fear. Since all the drag factors you will encounter share the common denominator of fear, it is important that you make a conscious decision to go through each day with at least a bucket of courage. is to help a team commit to a sprint, and then commit to remove obstacles for that team, whatever they may be. Start here.

Scrum value #2 – Commitment

Commitment is a promise or a serious pledge made by a person to do something for somebody. A commitment says, "You can count on me." Imagine if people did not make commitments. We would have no presidents because they would quit whenever the road got tough. Teachers might show up to teach our children, or maybe not. Church services would not begin. Commitments are important as they hold groups of people together, help them reach goals, and ultimately succeed.

Scrum teams were designed with commitment in mind—team members plan and work together to deliver the best possible product or product increment. This is what Takeuchi and Nonaka observed in the successful projects and first Scrum teams of the 1980s. This means that teams must commit to finding the courage to say "no" whenever someone asks them to do something in half the time. Imagine if marriages were sealed with someone else saying, "I do" on the bride and groom's behalf? Wedding surrogates, anyone? One of the ScrumMaster's responsibilities is to get the team to take responsibility for their commitments and honor them as serious promises.

There is a television show called *Extreme Makeover: Home Edition* in which construction crews either remodel or build—from scratch—an entire home within seven days! They are driven by a larger purpose of changing the lives of impoverished families, and this commitment and vision drives the daily actions and integration between the various construction crews. The crews seem excited and motivated to work very hard, and are often caught on camera crying or otherwise very emotional when they see the happiness on the faces of the families for whom they've so diligently worked.

In what ways do Scrum team members commit?

- Firstly, a Scrum team commits to work together to achieve a sprint goal; they will do anything within reason in order to meet that goal. Scrum teams undergo a lot of pressure when they take on this sort of commitment; they have to reach a consensus in planning, often without a complete picture; they commit each day in the daily scrum actions for the following day; and they show their work at the sprint review.

- The product owner, in return, commits to providing product vision and clarification of product backlog items; he/she promises to be there to help the team along the way should questions arise. He/she also commits to being in the sprint review and, ideally, looks at completed functionality *during* the sprint, not waiting until the end.

- The ScrumMaster commits to protecting the team and making sure that they have everything they need in order to meet their commitment. The ScrumMaster looks after both the product owners and the technical team members to ensure that they are happy, motivated, and energized about their work.

Even though it might not look like an episode of *Extreme Makeover*, with tears in everyone's eyes at the end of the sprint, the team should feel a sense of pride and accomplishment as their commitments are realized.

During the writing of this book, the Northeastern United States was severely impacted by Hurricane Sandy, which caused over $50 billion in damage. In Lower Manhattan, many basements and sub-basements, some of which house data centers for major corporations, were flooded with up to 30 feet of water. Gas was scarce due to electricity outages all over New York and New Jersey. I received an e-mail update from my website platform provider who had a data center in Lower Manhattan that sustained complete loss of power despite multiple levels of redundant systems. To make it worse, backup fuel and building infrastructure was completely destroyed. However, this company's customers experienced no downtime. How did this happen? Well, the employees of this company banded together and *manually carried fuel up 17 flights of stairs for three days* until an interim fuel supply and pump could be installed. When I received the e-newsletter detailing these valiant efforts, I realized what a great example of commitment these employees displayed. My website platform providers will forever have my loyalty because they were loyal to me.

People are much more committed to work that they themselves commit to versus commitments made on their behalf. There's nothing worse than your manager committing for you and then asking you (nicely, of course) if you can do the task. You know, pull a rabbit out of your hat! And you, the nice development team member that you are, don't want to say "no", so you say, "Sure, I can do that in one week even though I originally said two," and then grumble your way through a week of overtime (without extra pay). Now your manager sees what a hard worker you are and says to other managers and colleagues that, "I know the perfect guy for the job! Bob can do it in half the time and never says no!" Meanwhile, you (Bob) grow more resentful by the day. You'd much prefer that your original estimates were taken to heart, but now you don't want to let your boss down after he's/she's spoken so highly of you. Your boss doesn't realize, however, just how many corners you've cut—that you have written a couple of shaky code modules in the effort to appease your manager and meet his/her unrealistic commitments. Your quality of life suffers. With each new commitment, you walk around with increased feelings of guilt instead of pride in your hard work. You don't know how to stop it.

When people cannot make commitments for themselves, their morale, and possibly their health, suffers.

Commitment exposes fear of dedicated, cross-functional Scrum teams

The traditional style of *allocating resources* is to put the right expert on the right task at the right time. This necessitates that:

- Experts and their skills and talents are known

- Tasks are planned to the most detailed level, ahead of the work

- Tasks must finish on time so that the experts can be scheduled accordingly across multiple initiatives, which means that managers must make sure their people are doing their tasks on time

Each of these preconditions are disqualified, however, by using some basic common sense: a manager may know a person's domain expertise, or what language they code in, and so on, but that manager cannot possibly know a person's expertise in various contexts, different systems, and different circumstances working with different people. Secondly, a manager can do his/her best to plan tasks upfront, but as soon as the project is underway, those tasks, estimates, and finish dates are out of date due simply to the day-to-day complexity and variation of people, technology, and requirements. Finally, tasks never finish on time. They finish early, late, and drag on forever. You don't need much effort to dispel these myths. It boggles the mind to consider the amount of management overhead needed to run a traditional resourcing system like this.

Organizational drag factor #3: the management controls workers' commitments and doesn't want to relinquish control to the workers.

However, the prevailing mind-set in most companies—a carryover from traditional management thinking—is that managers can plan for efficiency when experts are assigned to do the tasks they're best at. Companies with this "total efficiency" mind-set struggle with the dedicated, self-managing, cross-functional team empowered to make their own decisions. Managers with traditional management tendencies end up thwarting good efforts. The trouble with the traditional mind-set is most basic: knowledge work is *not* an assembly line with a known outcome and defined process.

Let's explore *resourcing* in both traditional and Scrum examples and then talk about human resource/traditional management drag factors.

Expert-to-Task or ETT model of human resource allocation

Let's take Bob, an expert Java developer. Bob is so good that all the managers want him on their respective projects. There are four projects underway in parallel at the moment, in various phases of traditional development, and Bob's dance card is full. He is allocated to the following four projects as follows:

- Project A – detailed design phase: Bob is needed for detailed design and proof of concepts, 8 hours per week

- Project B – coding phase: Bob is needed for 14 hours per week

- Project C – coding phase: Bob is needed for 10 hours per week

- Project D – testing phase: Bob is needed to fix bugs, eight hours per week

Bob is allocated 40 hours a week because that's the amount of time that developers are expected to work. Let's say that the company pays Bob an annual salary of $120,000 ($10,000 per month). They pay $2,500 for 40 productive hours per week, or roughly $60 per hour.

There are hidden costs that eat away at Bob's productivity. First of all, he's not really available 40 hours per week for creating value. Bob's resource plan does not include time for context switching. Studies show that Bob loses 30 – 50 percent of his productive time to context switching. Management pays him $2,500 per week for really only about 30 hours of productive work per week. The company loses $625 per week for Bob because of the waste of context switching.

Additionally, Bob spends a lot of time waiting on other people to finish their tasks, send him a document, or answer his e-mail. He must also send code downstream to other developers and fix bugs that have been found by testers. Because of the handoffs, Bob spends a lot of time waiting. Studies show that workers lose 15 – 25 percent of their time waiting for handoffs in traditional processes. Let's be conservative and say that Bob loses four of his work hours per week; that's another $250. Total so far: $875 per week lost.

It gets worse. The QA team interrupt Bob to fix some defects that he caused. Studies show that "inspecting quality in" causes a loss of 15 – 25 percent of productive hours due to rework. Let's be conservative and say that Bob gets interrupted with production defects to the tune of eight hours per week. That's another $500 per week lost to bad quality!

Wasteful Activity	Studies show	# hours / week waste for Bob	$ in waste/week
Multitasking	25-60% waste	10	$625.00
Wait time/handoffs	15-25% waste	4	$250.00
Defects/rework	15-25% waste	8	$500.00
	Totals	22 hours/week waste	$1375.00 out of $2500 salary per week
		1000 hours/2000 hours wasted per year per employee	$60,000 out of $120,000 wasted per year per employee
Does not include management overhead, cost of low morale, relearning, sickness, and other wastes.			

The situation only gets worse. Bob's resource plan does not include time for non-hands-on-keyboard work like meetings, bug scrubs, design sessions, troubleshooting, status reports, documentation, ramping up new hires, and so on. So now Bob is working lots of overtime to keep up with everything (and is probably not getting paid to do so). Even though the appearance is that Bob is working hard and doing a lot, the company is paying for bad estimates in other ways: Bob writes more bugs and his health suffers. Bob's healthcare premiums were just increased because he keeps going to the doctor for a nagging upper respiratory infection. Because he comes to work while ill, he's caused three other people to miss work.

The tasks that Bob's work is dependent upon don't finish on time, which causes Bob to have to go to this manager and that manager to find out what to do next, resulting in wasted time. It also takes two line managers and a project manager to create and run the schedules. And tasks don't finish on time and projects are not predictable, so that costs as well. If we think it through, the REAL costs of scheduling Bob the traditional way are mounting. Using conservative numbers, the company pays Bob $10,000 per month but only gets about 15 hours of truly productive, value-added time per week, losing roughly half of his salary, or $60,000 approximately, to wasteful "resource staffing" models. Multiply THAT across the organization and the amount of wasted dollars is mind-boggling.

Yet, traditional organizations continue to allocate resources this way because they feel that it would be wasteful to put a cross-functional team together whose members must ramp up and learn from each other. The mind-set is a carryover of Frederick Taylor's scientific management principles; that humans are just cogs in the process, that managers know best, and that managers can measure and tweak plans and process to get the most productivity. That works for some types of systems, yet it is not the best way for knowledge work.

This style of resource allocation looks good on paper. It has the look and feel of total efficiency. If executives see that we're using Bob's expertise when and where it's needed, this appears to be the best use of Bob's time. What they don't see is all the hidden costs and the hidden risks of creating silos of people; nobody knows what's going on in Bob's head, nor in any of the other experts' heads. This sort of bottleneck is not only challenging to work around on a daily basis but also represents a huge business risk. If any of these experts were to get hit by a bus, the company would be in big trouble.

Team-to-Backlog or the TTB model of human team allocation

A lean Agile organization seeks to create knowledge. The antiquated ETT allocation model does not seek to create knowledge in others; rather, it seeks to put the right person on the right task at the right time, and manage worker and task until Done. Yes, there is the short-term benefit of efficiency. But it is short-lived and quickly outweighed by the costs of lost time to context switching, management overhead, short-sightedness on the part of the individual knowledge worker, upfront planning costs, defects, and knowledge that stays only in one person's head. The alternative is Team-to-Backlog, or TTB, allocation. That is, dedicated team members—made up of cross-functional skill sets—who work together and stay together indefinitely. The short-term loss of TTB is more than made up for by the long-term gain.

The TTB model provides the right level of abstraction for two very specific and different needs. The local need—the need of the team members—is to manage their day-to-day work tasks in order to meet a common goal. The day-to-day complexity of human interaction, variability in productivity, breakthroughs in knowledge, and so on, is too slippery for a manager to *manage* like in the ETT model. Rather, the team members are the right people to manage this as they are closer to the work and have a better understanding of each other's needs. A level up, managers' needs, simply put, require that they understand progress toward overall business initiatives. The TTB model gives them the ability to know, every day in real time, the progress that a team is making toward product backlog and sprint goals. This information is broadcast via sprint backlogs and burndowns and release backlogs and burndowns. This greatly reduces the amount of management and project management overhead in the ETT model.

Short term, a new cross-functional Scrum team will struggle with roles and responsibilities, but with a ScrumMaster who creates an environment in which it is safe to struggle and experiment, the team will figure out productive and efficient ways to work together. This is what we refer to as emergent process and emergent leadership. After some time, team members learn from one another about various responsibilities so that the entire team can move together in lock step. There is a cost associated with the time required by the team to figure this out. But once they figure it out, and go through the prerequisite storming phase, they move into a high-performing state and their productivity outweighs these short-term costs by leaps and bounds. In fact, Jeff Sutherland says that Scrum teams are, "twice as productive, with a 40 percent defect reduction and radically improve the fit of the product to customer needs" (http://jeffsutherland.com/ PracticalRoadmapGTFS25Nov2009.pdf).

 Organizational drag factor #4: team members are initially afraid of empowerment.

There are many long-term benefits of staffing this way. First, the individual on a team progresses to a mind-set that embraces a continuous state of learning. For knowledge workers, this is huge. In fact, studies show that many knowledge workers value learning new things more than a salary increase. So there is the continuous state of learning plus the morale boost by being free to learn. Secondly, management overhead is greatly reduced. Thirdly, the Scrum team itself says what they can take on and does not allow interruption to or deviation from its goals (unless of course an early sprint termination is requested by the product owner). So the additional costs of insurance and sickliness and all those things that arise from worker stress are now reduced. Healthy, happy workers who trust each other are very productive! This is not new news!

At Pixar, a staff of writers, directors, animators, and technicians move from project to project. As a result, the studio has built a team of moviemakers who know and trust one another in ways unimaginable on most sets. Animation days at the studio all begin the same way: The animators and director gather in a small screening room filled with comfy couches. They eat Cap'n Crunch and drink coffee. Then the team begins analyzing the few seconds of film animated the day before, as they ruthlessly "shred" each frame. Even the most junior staffers are encouraged to join in. The upper echelons also subject themselves to mega doses of healthy criticism. The proof is in the product. The average international gross per Pixar film is more than $550 million, and the cartoons are critical darlings — the studio has collected 24 Academy Awards.

— An excerpt from Wired Magazine, Animating a Blockbuster: How Pixar Built Toy Story 3, Jonah Lehrer, June 2010.

Not only are the bottlenecks reduced in cross-functional teams but also the number of ideas increase—people layer on experiences, ideas, and guffaws/mistakes in order to create the very best product.

You will encounter the ETT mind-set here and there in your career, with various people at various times. The good news is that companies are finally starting to veer away from this approach (see *Chapter 11, Scrum and the Future*), but the bad news, and I don't mean this harshly, is that it will take a generation to die off before we start to see radical innovation in organizational structure to support agility. So, expect to encounter this way of thinking in some form or fashion for a while longer.

As a ScrumMaster, you can combat this drag factor with a few tools. Running a pilot team, crunching some numbers, and helping management understand the pitfalls of ETT allocation are paramount. The trouble is that the management won't always listen. The very people who crafted the ETT model within the company are the ones to which you'll have to present a new way. In fact, expect at some point this will affect your Human Resources department's policies. This won't likely be very popular, at least at first. This is one of the top reasons why I am called in to talk with my clients' managers; sometimes it's easier to hear this news from someone outside the organization.

Bottom line: there is a cost to investing in dedicated, self-managing, and cross-functional Scrum teams, but the benefits greatly outweigh these costs. Which is smarter: investing in learning and high-performing teams, or continually seeking the short-term benefits? Fear of appearing less than 100 percent efficient keeps organizations from realizing their potential.

When managers commit on behalf of team members, those team members will eventually disassociate, or "check out"; some will use sarcasm, they may be angry and annoyed, and complain of sleepless nights and come to work visibly tired. Their family life may be suffering, and the quality of their lives is most likely reflected in a product loaded with defects and technical debt. I once met a developer named Malik. He took on the moniker of "George" whenever he was under intense pressure and stocked a personal freezer with seven types of ice cream that he ate whenever he was stressed. All Malik had to say was, "George ate a lot of ice cream yesterday." Everyone knew that Malik had pulled an all-nighter and probably wasn't in a festive mood.

What do we do about commitment issues?

Managers must realize once the organization or department says that it uses Scrum, the Scrum team now has authority to make its own commitments. A team commits to what it can do, and just as importantly, makes visible what it cannot commit to. This universal rule must be accepted in a Scrum transition or it is certain to stumble. Managers in a Scrum environment should allow teams to self-organize. Managers should remove any escalated obstacles from teams. Managers should commit to not committing to dates for the team. Finally, they should commit to at least trying the process—as is—until they discover, along with teams, what it is that needs to change.

So what's a ScrumMaster to do when managers cannot make these commitments?

- First, educate managers. Help them understand the reasons why the Scrum practices of adaptive planning, prioritization, focused team, and continuous improvement are so important. Get managers together for a presentation so that they can ask questions; engage them to help a team remove obstacles.

- Secondly, learn to recognize when your team members are stressed out. They may be afraid to tell the whole truth about what's happening when they're at their desks. Look for signs of disassociation; reluctance to attend planning or daily scrum meetings is a sure sign that something is not right. I once met a team whose members were interrupted by various stakeholders eight times in a one-week sprint! Bringing attention to this issue wasn't to point fingers or cause trouble for anyone; rather, surfacing the issue helped the ScrumMaster in this case work with the stakeholders to find a cadence of delivery that worked for everyone.

- Help teams meet their commitments by facilitating acknowledgement of their true abilities. If the team aims for a realistic level of work for the sprint, chances are they'll successfully complete it.

- Retrospectives are a key time to hold the team accountable for their commitment; if there are problems with a commitment, encourage team members to create action items and sign up for them. A sense of safety allows for confident commitments. You are the team's shield (and sword, if needed).

We will explore more examples in *Chapter 9*, *Shaping the Agile Organization*.

 Organizational drag factor #5: lack of understanding of Agile practices and values.

Scrum value #3 – Openness

I worked with a team recently whose members were concerned about the role of the business analyst on the team. One person felt that the BA should hand over a detailed specification for each user story. Another person felt that the BA should keep it high level. And another felt that there was no need for a BA at all. As we discussed this situation, I provided examples of how differently I've seen BAs integrate into teams depending on the need, and I thought I was doing a sufficient job of giving context around the "it depends" answer. But they kept pressing me. They kept asking the question in different ways. After a half hour of this banter, the truth came out. The developers much favored a spec because they had been blamed many times in the past for bad outcomes, so the fear of reprimand drove them to seek a contract, or spec, with the BA. The ScrumMaster, in trying to create an innovative, creative, self-organizing team, didn't want a BA to constrain a solution.

The CEO, who somehow was in on this discussion, felt that developers should step up and didn't see the need for a BA at all! I couldn't figure out why we had spent so much time on this conversation. It finally dawned on me: the CEO was trying to make a case for firing someone. This secrecy was driving everyone mad. Nobody could come right out and say it; they just Texas Two-Stepped around the issue. And perhaps, for legal reasons, they couldn't come out and say it, but it just goes to show you the amount of time wasted beating around the bush because nobody could come right out and say something. We see these scenarios all the time. In a culture of fear, nobody wants to step up and be courageous. Fear breeds secrecy.

Secrecy and what to do about it

Secrecy is the enemy of change. The grapevine kills. To paraphrase Gandhi: "The moment someone's motives are suspect, everything he does is questionable." If management wants to switch the organization to Agile practices but remains quiet about it, people will start to gossip and speculate. Fear breeds inertia and stagnation; on the other hand, if used to create a sense of urgency, healthy fear coupled with openness and respect can lead to great change.

It's pretty obvious when there is a culture of secrecy. People sneak off behind closed doors to have the simplest of conversations, or they always look over their shoulders to make sure nobody is listening as they say how they really feel. Non-verbal cues abound—rolling eyes, lowered heads, shrugging shoulders. Managers discuss late projects in secret status meetings and commit "resources" to work late nights and weekends in hopes of landing the project on time, rather than just reporting the truth to management, or asking the team.

[Organizational drag factor #6: lack of trust.]

What can the ScrumMaster do in this situation? First and foremost, combat secrecy with openness! Instead of following the manager into a room with a closed door, opt to have the conversation out in the main working space. If your team didn't complete any stories by the end of a sprint, be open about that! If product owners struggle with seeing the team's work, encourage involvement at the daily scrum meeting until they're in sync. If there is a perception that the team is not very productive, create and post productivity metrics. Broadcast good, bad, and ugly information. It's data—and people can make decisions if they know the truth!

[
 After Hurricane Sandy came through our area, more than two million people had no electricity. Day after day of no electricity, no water, cold temperatures, and no gasoline to run generators, people got angry and depressed. In my community, the power company told us that our power would be restored in 7 – 14 days. Well, that's a decent high-level estimate, but as each day wore on, they weren't able to give us any more detailed information than that. In other words, it would have been helpful to know where on the list my street was so that I could make decisions about my livelihood. If I knew that power wouldn't be on in my neighborhood for seven days, for example, then I could make arrangements for a hotel. Instead, I grew more frustrated by the hour because I hoped that my lights might come on any moment. It would have been wonderful for my power company to have given more detailed information so that I could have made better decisions for myself.
]

Openness exposes truth about capacity and demand

If business stakeholders do their jobs—that is, Sales people are selling, Marketing people are marketing, and CEOs are working up deals and partnerships, a business will likely realize demand that exceeds capacity. This is a good thing. Consider if you will, that all of a sudden your customers stopped asking for features—phones stopped ringing, support received no complaints, there was no news about your company in the news. This would be a very scary existence, indeed. Demand keeps companies in business. The most successful companies respond to that demand with strategic product releases, savvy marketing analysis, and of course, chasing the dollar, even choosing clients. ScrumMasters enable the business to understand the capacity of a development team (or teams) so that they can determine how best to use those teams to deliver the highest business value. ScrumMasters should make reality visible; like a stock ticker, they should broadcast real-time information so that stakeholders—particularly the product owner—can invest in the most important, valuable features for a given timeframe. Additionally, ScrumMasters attempt to create more capacity; by removing obstacles, they and the team make the development process more efficient and productive, which means they have more capacity *to spend* on important business values.

I once mentored a project that had 30 teams running in parallel. Business stakeholders had already promised a product to market; it was announced in a press release; stock prices were riding high on the news of the gadget. The stakeholders were banking on Agile to make this release happen in five months but were not willing to commit to dedicated teams, Agile development and testing practices, and so on (but were calling their process "Agile"!) It was a recipe for disaster in many ways. One such way was in release planning. Since stakeholders had already promised a release in five months, they simply took the product backlog, divided it by 30 (the number of teams), and then divided that number by five (number of sprints). Their formula was:

1,200 features/30 teams = 40 features per team/5 sprints = 8 features per team per sprint

 Organizational drag factor #7: the mind-set of, "Just add more people to the project to make it come in on time!"

Alas, they had not vetted the estimates with the teams themselves. I convinced them to do a multiteam release plan, after which the result was more like four features per team per sprint, only half of what business stakeholders needed to meet their promise to the market. Stakeholders ignored this information and requested that the teams move as quickly as possible, and that each team try to deliver eight features per sprint.

A disaster ensued. Teams and ScrumMasters felt so much pressure to deliver that they sacrificed quality. The Definition of Done flew out the window. The teams didn't "have time" to produce an integrated build every sprint. They worked weekends and late hours to *finish* stories that weren't really finished. Then they split stories, taking credit for a development story, and pushing the testing story to the next sprint (which is wrong, wrong, wrong!). After two sprints of that practice, it was impossible for the program manager to get a reliable release burndown chart. In the picture that follows, you can see the impact of such practices. Sprint 1 looks like it was a good sprint. In fact, the team demoed all seven stories and the product owner thought that the functionality was done. The team claimed 20 points of velocity. But really only three stories were complete, so the actual velocity was really only five.

The team goes into sprint 2 and must finish up testing for stories 4, 5, 6, and 7, which, by the way, they split from the original story and added story points to the testing pieces (bad, bad, bad!). In addition, the team took on stories 8, 9, 10, and 11, none of which were finished by the end of sprint 2. But they claimed 30 points of velocity in the demo, when the actual velocity was only 15 (a team should only claim story points in the sprint in which the story meets the Definition of Done). To make matters worse, they had to test stories 8, 9, 10, and 11 in sprint 3, plus they took on stories 12 and 13. They were interrupted mid-sprint by integration issues that surfaced in the code written for stories 2, 3, and 5 in sprint 1! So they had to fix these issues and, terribly, gave story points to the bugs!

So the team goes into the sprint 3 demo and claims 35 points of work, when actually the team really only completed 15 points (finishing stories 8, 9, 10, and 11). Can you see the pattern here? Because the team compromised its Definition of Done and carried defects and technical debt forward into each subsequent sprint, it became more and more difficult to take on new stories, and agility was thus compromised. Six sprints into the project, product owners couldn't figure out why velocity was so high but the amount of new features delivered seemed so low! Well, long story short, it ended up that the product was not generally available until almost a year later; by that time, the buzz had worn off, three other major competitors had already delivered a similar gadget, and the gadget my teams were working on ended up being canceled (after a brief availability for enterprise use only), stock prices in the toilet, teams demoralized. What a drag!

Sprint 1	Sprint 2	Sprint 3
1 2 3 4 5 6 7	4 5 6 7 8 9 10 11	8 9 10 11 2 5 3 12 13
7 stories "completed" "Claimed Velocity" = 20 Actual velocity = 5	8 stories "completed" "Claimed Velocity" = 30 Actual velocity = 15	9 stories "completed" "Claimed Velocity" = 35 Actual velocity = 15

The first issue with this program was that the ScrumMasters failed to provide the truth about the demand and the true capacity of the teams. In other words, they allowed their teams to cut corners, water down the Definition of Done, split stories to get partial credit for unfinished work, and they asked their people to work nights and weekends throughout the project. They cut corners instead of communicating reality. They couldn't say "no". They ran the project on hopes and dreams, not reality. Secondly, managers failed to create an environment of safety and trust. The culture at this company was so full of command and control that ScrumMasters dared not say anything other than what managers wanted to hear. The effect was that the project slipped of the rails, little by little, until one day the train was off the tracks completely, crashing into a ball of fire. The teams hated Scrum as a result. It was a dreadful and costly situation for everyone involved.

In this case, the ScrumMasters should have banded together to educate stakeholders about the trade-offs and establish realistic expectations about team capabilities and velocity. They should have related that sprints are not clown cars into which the product owner can keep stuffing more and more features; rather, sprints are taxis, and only four people are allowed in a taxi (at least, in New York City). So if you're out with five friends for a night out on the town, you must take two taxis everywhere. No ifs, ands, or buts. And as the taxi driver *will* let you know if you've broken the rules, the ScrumMaster should let the product owner or other stakeholders know when the No Clown Car Rule has been violated and *push back* on the request or demand. Opening the door for more features (or clowns in this case) just opens the door for disaster. A Scrum team only has capacity for so much work. And that's that. Period.

Keep adding more clowns and I ask: what's the quality of the ride? Fear of exposing the truth will prevent transformative ideas from taking off.

Openness exposes a need for slowing down in order to eventually speed up

Many development groups still *inspect* in quality *after* development, instead of building it in as they go. Even some so-called "Scrum" teams operate like this! This means that they are never done with the features they build each sprint, which means they face an unquantifiable amount of work before they can release features to production. When the *doneness* of a feature or sprint's deliverables is watered down, agility is compromised; no longer are the development team's sprint deliverables "potentially shippable". The Definition of Done is the forcing function that keeps teams potentially shippable during every sprint. For you, ScrumMaster, this definition is not negotiable with the team.

 Organizational drag factor #8: business alignment to skill silos instead of business value.

Yes, the quality perspective, or Definition of Done, puts a huge stress on the organization. It's a game changer. People are not accustomed to thinking in terms of quality deliverables every two to four weeks (instead, they're accustomed to throwing a large chunk of code over the wall to QA, then it's someone else's problem to deal with). Scrum teams usually realize early on that they probably don't have the right development and testing tools—or mind-set—needed to build a high-quality product increment every sprint. These issues will persist until the team resolve it. You can help them:

- A team may not have a Definition of Done in the first place; you'll have to facilitate a conversation between the product owner and delivery team members to make sure everyone shares an understanding.

- Make sure your team is staffed with members of various skill sets (development, quality assurance, database, functional analyst, and so on).

- You'll have to remind team members of the Definition of Done and that the sprint must culminate in a deliverable that includes quality assurance work, until this becomes a habit for the team. Write it on a flip chart and post it in the team's room if you need to.

- You may have to put a rule on what's "demoable" in the sprint review. In other words, the team cannot demo stories that don't meet the Definition of Done at the sprint review meeting.

- Don't allow team members to split stories along the lines of development and testing. Doing so will prevent you from getting a meaningful release burndown, which in turn means that the product owner and other business stakeholders won't have the right information in order to make good decisions.

- Make the cost of poor quality visible. Create a chart that shows the number of interruptions from production issues each sprint. Use this information when talking to the team and product owner about waste and quality initiatives. Run a cost analysis on implementing continuous integration and test automation, for example; pave the way for the right tools and practices so that the team can realize a higher quality level each and every sprint.

Scrum value #4 – Focus

Focus is the ability to give undivided attention to a problem or task, without interruption, until that problem is solved or the task is complete. It takes mental investment—eyes on the screen, fingers on the keyboard, and marker to the whiteboard—and requires conversation full of meaning and listening. Focus gives us the ability to complete a piece of work with high-quality innovation. A moment of distraction provides the possibility of a problem, a defect, a missing piece, or something gone wrong. A distraction takes our minds off of the task at hand and creates an interruption in our mental flow.

 Try this listening exercise. Pair up with someone; one of you has a story to tell, the other listens. Listener, do everything you can to appear as if you're not listening. Storyteller, continue to tell the story for a minute or two. Stop. Discuss how the lack of focus by the listener impacts the storyteller and the story itself.

It's completely impossible for the brain not to think of something; well, unless you're one of those meditative geniuses. Just try to not think about a zebra. See, one just popped in your head, didn't it? (Did yours have purple or black stripes? There you go again!) The brain has an amazing ability to focus, and a Scrum team can produce great results when they learn to harnesses that focus. But the ability to focus is both a blessing and a curse. Focus becomes a curse when we are asked to do more than one task at once. The reason is that we must actively switch our focus onto something else while taking a break on the first problem. The switch has a cost, often called a task-switching cost. For thinking about pink zebras or purple turtles, the cost is insignificant, of no consequence. Switching from working on a battery configuration for a laptop to one of a cell phone, however, is altogether different.

This focus and task-switching phenomena is so important that there are techniques for managing it. For example, many developers I know use the Pomodoro technique, which is (among other things) working in 25-minute *bursts* followed by a break. Another technique I've observed comes from my friend Lee who teaches his students to "focus, wander, and return". Acknowledge that while focusing on something, your brain will begin to wander (probably like you're doing right about now). But then decide to bring your mind back. Focus, wander, return, and with lots of practice, you can increase the speed of your return so that the wander isn't as noticeable. What's interesting is that these techniques—Pomodoro, getting things done, focus/wander/ return, ignoring distractions, and so on—are all ways that people manage their own time and brainpower. They do this based on *their* working styles or habits or best practices that they've picked up during their careers. Sometimes it's just intuition. ScrumMaster, allow team members to be the masters of their own focus. Don't allow interruptions in the sprint, no matter how seemingly small or trite.

Lack of focus and personal control = missed commitments

The moment that someone else tries to control our focus, things fall apart. While a manager might know a task that we're working on, that's all he/she knows. He/ she knows nothing about how our mind wanders to pink zebras, or our level of exhaustion, crankiness, or sickness that day. Maybe we finished one task early and are cranking out another overnight because we're hitting a slightly manic phase. At any rate, the moment the manager attempts to take *control of your focus*—all that is essential and magical about focus is then lost. And this is what the antithesis of focus does.

[Organizational drag factor #9: the mind-set that managers best manage their workers' time.]

When managers try to over-organize, over-plan, and suboptimize work, they cause problems in schedules, commitments, and the natural ways in which people focus. You see, knowledge workers are quite capable of creating their own time management techniques, personally tailored to them based on their own experiences and personalities. Nobody can describe how another person switches focus (well, unless they're under observation in a lab). So I consider it an *insult* for a mindless piece of project management software to optimize people and their thinking abilities, as well as an absolute waste of time. The opposite of focus is suboptimization and over-organization (together called micromanagement), which contributes to chaos. We discussed this at length earlier in the chapter.

In Scrum, we give teams the ability to focus on the product backlog that they've chosen and leave them alone so that they can figure out how to respond to that challenge within the sprint. Instead of optimizing and organizing at the worker and task level, Scrum allows for teams to focus and optimize their results based on customer needs while organizing themselves based on their own individual and collective team needs and abilities.

Focus implies respect. A manager shows respect for a worker by allowing the worker to focus on the problem to solve it, without the disrespect of interruption. A manager who gets Scrum or Agile principles knows and accepts that a knowledge worker can best manage himself or herself within the context of a sprint.

Focus reveals waste

When a team focuses on creating product increments in short cycles, anything that gets in the way of that is considered waste. Wait time, handoffs, defects, antiquated tools, and the like, are impediments that need resolution so that the team can reduce the lead time and increase the quality of features in every sprint. *Chapter 9, Shaping the Agile Organization*, explores some ways in which you can make this waste visible.

Focus reveals failure to understand small increments

Most people in traditional organizations are accustomed to thinking in terms of all or nothing. Product owners used to write large specs for a team to implement and show something months after working on it. This **big design up front (BDUF)** stems from traditional big-batch thinking. It is imperative that people understand the benefits of and how to write Agile requirements so that teams can work in smaller batches. This takes education, and the ScrumMaster is responsible for educating others about this topic. When stories are too big, a team can't finish them by the end of a sprint. The result is lack of visibility, which makes it impossible for the product owner to understand progress and adapt the product. You may need to educate and mentor your product owner about splitting stories and good story-writing in general; otherwise this will be a continued drag on the team's success. Additionally, you may need to talk with team members about using continuous integration practices and Agile version control to support smaller, more frequent deliveries.

Scrum value #5 – Respect

When I was a project manager at Primavera (before we did Scrum), my boss at the time was a micromanager. He would criticize my e-mails to team members all the time. "Why did you write it that way? You know, people could perceive it this way, or that way. You shouldn't have sent that." And so on. It became so bad that I got to where I wouldn't send anything at all. In fact, to this day, 13 years later, I still hesitate before hitting the Send button on my e-mail. Like an overbearing mother causes fear and uncertainty in her children, so did my boss with me. My boss didn't even respect me enough to let me learn from my mistakes. Talk about a drag with long-lasting consequences.

Respect is an admiration for a person, and more specifically the qualities, characteristics, or talents or actions of that person. "I respect his professionalism." "I really respect her ability to take control of a room." "I respect her attention to good-quality code and thinking through a broader solution." We tend to respect people for the talents, skills, and qualities that we ourselves wish we had. I once read that software developers generally don't respect a manager who isn't technical and that in fact, this can be demotivating. Why? Because developers like the challenge and stimulation of sharp minds, and they expect their boss to be smarter than they are in that regard; they want to respect their leader for his/her brilliance. I greatly respect people who put in the hard work and determination to run ultra marathons. I would never do it myself, but am in awe of those who make that kind of commitment.

When managers micromanage others, they are saying, "I don't value your skills or talents. I must therefore try to control you." I probably doesn't come across this harshly, but think about it: if the manager really respected the worker, he/she would be certain of and admire the worker's skills and talents. If the manager were certain of the worker's skills and talents, he/she would trust that the worker could get the job done without hand holding. It really is that simple. Either trust a person to do the job, or don't. It is a decision.

[A ScrumMaster may have to tell managers to back off the team.]

Power, position, and control and what to do about it

The antithesis of respect is power, position, and control. A manager has a choice: motivate someone by respecting them, or control them using power and position. A confident leader would most likely choose the first option.

A ScrumMaster will encounter power and control issues in organizations that reward good performance by promoting people. Since the promotion is the carrot, nobody wants to screw up that chance. Someone who is rewarded by promotion wants to protect that promotion at all costs so that they can then attain the next promotion. Everyone wants to climb the ladder. In order to protect their current position, they use power. They control. Heaven forbid that they show a *weakness* like respect and trust. In fact, what if they show respect to someone else and that person ends up doing a better job? This eventually builds resentment, and even contempt, among team members. I see this in situations where companies with controlling cultures micromanage under the guise of Scrum.

[Organizational drag factor #10: existing HR carrots and sticks.]

A ScrumMaster can leverage several opportunities to socialize the concepts of respect and team autonomy. The first is to close the doors to some of the team's meetings. Be very careful with this! Ultimately, we want to support the value of Openness, but in order to first get Respect, we may have to close doors. The ScrumMaster must walk the chickens and pigs tightrope. A ScrumMaster can't be afraid to squelch a manager's voice in the daily scrum. He/she can't fear asking an uninvolved stakeholder to leave the retrospective because it's only for the team. Bear in mind that the closed door policy must be done with great caution and awareness. I once consulted with a company whose ScrumMasters closed the doors to all daily scrum meetings. I reminded them that the daily scrum was for team synchronization and also for transparency of work (supporting the Openness value). They understood and acquiesced. They admitted that they were so afraid of management not allowing teams to self-manage that they closed off as many managers as possible, ultimately causing friction and suspicion.

Summary

Many people think of Scrum as something to transition to, rather than through. When you apply the values of Scrum via its framework, it will reveal all sorts of things; obstacles that get in the way of creating value for customers. Additionally, it will reveal fear and dysfunction. The organization that views Scrum as the silver bullet says, "Scrum messed everything up. We have all of these problems now that we implemented Scrum." This represents a flawed understanding of Scrum. As ScrumMaster, you must help people realize what Scrum really is—and just as importantly, help them realize what it isn't.

Many people in technology misunderstand the role of the ScrumMaster to be simply that of an iteration manager. Hopefully, you realize that the ScrumMaster role was created with the concept of *change agent* in mind. Becoming an effective change agent is a lifelong task of learning and introspection. The knowledge and experience is more than I could ever stuff into a chapter, or a book. Your teams' and customers' happiness and satisfaction depend on your taking the reins of visibility, truth, and inspiring change. The stakes are large, and should you accept this mission, you must take it seriously, practice, rely on others for insight, and most importantly, inspect and adapt. The next chapter explores everyday leadership skills you need to effectively lead a Scrum team.

Recommended reading

Here are various "waste" studies that I ran across while researching this chapter:

- http://www.scielo.cl/pdf/jotmi/v3n3/art03.pdf
- Allen, T. J. and Katz, R. (1989), *Managing Engineers and Scientists: Some New Perspectives in Human Resource Management in International Firms: Change, Globalization, Innovation*. 1989, London: Macmillan
- http://onlinelibrary.wiley.com/doi/10.1111/j.1744-6570.1997.tb01486.x/abstract
- http://onlinelibrary.wiley.com/doi/10.1111/j.1744-6570.1997.tb01486.x/abstract
- Brooks, Fred, *The Mythical Man Month*. 1975, Addison Wesley
- http://www.roberts.edu/Academics/AcademicDivisions/BusinessManagement/msl/Community/Journal/TheHighCostofLowMorale.htm
- http://blog.scottbellware.com/2009/07/relearning-productivity-problem-that-we.html
- http://cio.co.nz/cio.nsf/tech/driving-out-software-waste

8

Everyday Leadership for the ScrumMaster and Team

A couple was traveling on a long flight with their 14-week-old twins. At home before the flight, knowing that some passengers react negatively to crying babies, the couple wrote a little letter asking forgiveness from the babies' point of view and made a few dozen copies. They attached each copy of the letter to a bag of candy and handed one out to every passenger on the flight. The couple even brought enough earplugs for all passengers in case the babies decided to cry. This couple was thoughtful enough to consider those around them, preemptively identifying the potential negative reactions of the other passengers and creatively coming up with a way to soften the harshness of reaction to crying and wailing. Writing this note, as if it came from the babies, was also a great way of personalizing the situation, creating an image of little babies who just want to be nice to you. I found this story to be a great example of everyday leadership.

Everyday leadership

What is everyday leadership? It's a person's day-to-day attitude, communication style, and actions that influence others. You can lead others little by little, bit by bit—sometimes without them realizing you are leading them at all. As an everyday leader, you are in tune with yourself, calling on unique talents and traits to lead your team. Your leadership style will be different from mine, which will be different from all of our colleagues and so on. You can create your own unique ScrumMaster leadership style by practicing and focusing on self-improvement. You influence others by building great teams, and sometimes by flexing your corporate muscle.

So much has been written about the ideal leader—his characteristics, behavior, how he must imprint upon us the desire and passion for success. We hear stories about Jack Welch, Winston Churchill, Martin Luther King, Steve Jobs, and Ronald Reagan, who touch us with their words and inspire us to be better, do better, surpass, and strive to achieve great things. They can make us laugh, shed tears, and work harder. Maybe they even make us angry from time to time, but universally they've achieved great results and brilliant success by motivating people to act. Every good leader has a vision for you to behold—John F Kennedy's was that before the end of the 1960s the United States would, "land a man on the moon and return him safely to earth."

While not so galactic (although at times it may certainly feel that it is!), the ScrumMaster's mission is to build teams that deliver fast and flexibly using a simple framework that emphasizes respect, openness, courage, commitment, and focus. In carrying out our mission, we might lead our product owner by helping him understand the benefits of value-driven delivery. Or perhaps we lead our team by discussing different Agile development techniques and encouraging them to try something new. We might lead up to management by illustrating the costs of interruption in dollar signs. If you're doing the job of a ScrumMaster properly, you are also building up the leadership abilities of the people on your team. Finally, behind the scenes, every day, you are focused on leading yourself to become a better coach and facilitator.

[The ScrumMaster's mission is to foster good communication between business and technical development for successful product delivery.]

If applied properly, Scrum puts into place new boundaries that force different behaviors between team members, and between the team and the rest of the organization. This means change, both inside and outside the team. Change is difficult for humans, and the ScrumMaster's everyday leadership skills can help a team and an organization get past these difficulties. Laws of probability mean that a typical ScrumMaster probably won't be the next Walt Disney, Amelia Earhart, or Gandhi in terms of great leadership. Rather, think of the ScrumMaster as an everyday leader—a day-in, day-out, nose-to-the-grindstone, roll-up-your-sleeves kind of leader.

In *Chapter 7, Scrum Values Expose Fear, Dysfunction, and Waste*, we looked at how the Scrum values reveal fear, waste, and dysfunction. This chapter explores the necessary leadership skills a ScrumMaster must have to help a team move beyond fear and dysfunction to success. Organizations are best influenced by the stories of a successful team, so it all starts here.

First, what kind of personality do you have?

I've met people in my career I can instantly classify into a certain personality type: she's a bulldozer, he's a cloud-thinker, she's an emotional vampire, he goes for shock value, and so on. We categorize others automatically, sometimes without even knowing it as it helps shape our response and communication. Ever notice the shift in communication styles and personalities when the CEO walks into the team room; people sit up a little straighter, talk with more meaning and direction, and appear busier all of a sudden. Effective leaders recognize personality styles in others, as well as in themselves, and use this information to shape the ways in which they interact and lead.

I'm sure you've seen the Myers-Briggs and Jung, and Kiersey models that focus on some aspect of extraversion/introversion, sense/intuition, think/feel, and judge/perceive. A basic knowledge of your type can help you figure out why you may react a certain way in certain circumstances. Is there a best type? No. We're all different and can thus bring different, unique, and valuable talents and skills to the table. A style that works best in one team may not work in another, but becoming aware of our styles and tendencies is the first step in gaining control and the ability to evolve our skills and styles.

One of the best examples of a ScrumMaster style is my friend, Tobias Mayer. Those who know Tobias automatically get a picture of him in their heads: a tall, lanky, chatty Brit who tells it like it is, but who's compassionate and considerate of others' feelings. He stands by his beliefs and convictions and is not ever afraid to challenge an idea or rule. He is a deep thinker, a brilliant writer, and an organizational craftsman, and exudes that feeling of, "Wow, I'm with someone really unique and special" for others who make his acquaintance (even if they don't particularly like what he has to say sometimes). Tobias style draws people to him. He influences others by not being afraid to be who he really is.

In case you were wondering, I am what Myers-Briggs calls an **INTJ**: **Introverted**, **Intuitive**, **Thinking**, and **Judging**. Do you know what you are? Even though you have a base personality style, did you know that you can develop and even change facets of your personality? For example, I've worked for years to make myself more sociable. It's not easy for an introvert and takes constant practice and energy. Over time, I had to learn how to ask the right questions of people so that they would open up and talk about themselves. This required serious focus (and I even carried around a little cheat sheet many years ago). But now I don't have to think so much about it. It comes almost naturally. And I recognize when I'm with a team or a person who doesn't like this style; I can easily switch back to my natural introverted self. Like a seahorse that changes color when frightened or when stimulated by environmental factors, a good leader should change styles when faced with different sets of circumstances. Regardless of your base style, embrace an overarching seahorse mind-set: develop areas that need improvement so that you may switch and apply the appropriate styles for various teams or circumstances.

The first attribute that an everyday leader should possess is self-awareness. It is the seed from which incremental improvement may sprout.

Learn to look into your reflection

A person who is self-aware has the ability to look into the personality mirror and accept what they see. A person who can move the vanity to the side can do something with what they see. Until you really look closely to see yourself for who you are, you cannot change. The more you get up the nerve to look into that mirror, the more what you see simply becomes information. And you can do something with information. This is self-awareness.

So how does one become self-aware? Besides observing oneself, reflecting, journaling, and so on, a ScrumMaster may also try this little framework:

1. Go on a fact-finding mission. Get the courage to ask people at work and in your personal life their opinions of your personality style. You can ask questions such as: Have I said anything to offend you? If so, what was it? Do I engage everyone in conversation? Am I pleasant, seemingly happy? Do others seem comfortable around me? Do you? Can you talk freely and openly to me? Do you feel as if you can trust me? Is there anything that I can work on when it comes to my personality?

2. Take one (or more) of the temperament surveys. Get to know your tendencies. Cross-reference with the anecdotal feedback you received from your peers and friends.

3. Outline your strengths and weaknesses. Which do you feel are positive attributes? Which are negative? Or, which attributes help and then don't help in most situations?

4. Make a list—call this your personal improvement backlog. From this list you can form a plan of action.

5. Experiment with one thing at a time. Try new responses, new ways of behaving, new skills.

6. Identify people that you look up to for their various traits, skills, and talents. Ask them if they'd like to be on your personal board of directors to give you feedback and direction about your style, communication abilities, and how you come across to people. Seek their ideas on a recurring basis, perhaps monthly.

Personal Improvement Backlog			
Rank	Improvement	Source	Action
1	Learn better facilitation skills for meetings	team	Read Jean Tabaka's book and attend a workshop
2	I cut people off in conversations	sister	Pay closer attention to let people finish their thoughts before I jump in with mine.
3	I know nothing about what motivates teams	me	Study up on some motivation models/frameworks

Lee and I held some workshops that would help teams break down the barriers that hold back real collaboration by using techniques from theater. We created a curriculum, developed classroom exercises, thought about how the ideas were pertinent to business, and so on. When we held our first workshop, I'd never been so terrified in all my life! We had people doing silly walks, talking in strange languages, improvising situations, and so on. I felt embarrassed, self-conscious, and strange. I was on my edge, for sure. I didn't realize at the time that my *introvert* trait had reared its head. I was too 'on stage' in a way and a format that wasn't my comfortable daily routine. I intuited that the other staunch, traditionally staid business people in our workshop were finding this to be very silly, which caused me to grow ever more self-conscious by the minute. Lee and I ended up not doing many more workshops (we found that, sadly, most corporations wouldn't reserve training budget for such classes), but I learned an incredible amount from him, his techniques, and willingness to do a silly walk.

[Vanity is the feeling of self-importance, while ego is self-worth. Let go of the vanity, but always bring the ego.]

Over time—years—I learned that it was not only my introvert button that caused strife but also it was the vanity that added to my crippling self-consciousness. You see, I'm an introvert by birth and that's not going to change all that much. Yet my vanity was a product of low self-esteem and sad experiences of my childhood, which caused me to seek continuous affirmation of my self-importance. Yes, introversion played a part while vanity exacerbated my self-consciousness and fear of these workshops. After getting plugged into this concept and experimenting with putting myself out there many times, I've found that I can control vanity—some days I feel as if I've conquered it. Today, I feel as if I can connect with others more readily. I tell personal stories while I'm training and no longer worry about others judging me for my stories. I am able to create bonds with others—even if it's just for two days—by relating that I am human, open to mistakes, vulnerable to emotion, and the like. So even though I'm probably still too shy to run another of Lee's workshops, I've realized my limitations and work hard every day to improve. And, as a side note, I find it ironic that companies won't budget for classes that help people turn off the vanity (self-importance) button, which is one of the organizational drag factors we explored in *Chapter 7, Scrum Values Expose Fear, Dysfunction, and Waste*!

Throwing myself out there in a way that was uncomfortable has ultimately helped me round myself out. Actually, Meyers-Briggs says I'm pretty much right in the middle these days between introversion and extroversion. It wasn't easy, for sure. Luckily, I had a friend like Lee to coach me through the difficult days (which is why you need a good personal board of directors). But you can't take the appropriate actions until you gain awareness of the issue.

When were you last in an uncomfortable situation? What made it uncomfortable? How, exactly, did you feel? Look back. What could you have done differently in that moment? What might you do differently next time? What did you learn about your discomfort?

While I won't go into the various temperament models and such in this chapter (numerous psychologists have written books on this fascinating subject), I would like to discuss some prevalent attitudes, communication styles, and personal characteristics that you might want to study in order to hone your ScrumMaster leadership style. Doing so will create a productive team, and such a team will get others in the organization to listen.

Portrait of a leader

As a ScrumMaster, you must show that you support experimentation and learning. To do this, you must approach a team with an attitude of trust. Let the team try. Give them everything they need to be successful. Protect them from the rest of the organization so that they can experience the motivating result of finishing features in a sprint. Run interference for them in case of interruptions by someone from outside the team. Show them that you can be trusted by not causing injury—that is, protect the team and demonstrate that you are protecting them, either by removing obstacles or stopping interruption in its tracks. Say no. Speak up, especially if the team members cannot. Make the work you do to resolve issues for the team visible to the team. They will soon learn that you are in their corner.

Selfless, confident, and accountable

We've all encountered the person who immediately gets defensive and has an excuse for every bad behavior. People like this don't let others finish what they have to say before they're already firing back excuses. This creates an air of discomfort and awkwardness and eventually shuts down the other person—or worse, an entire team!

There's a big difference between ego and vanity; ego is self-worth while vanity is self-importance. The self-confidence, or ego, you exude in a touchy situation can immediately work toward your advantage; team members will observe that you are a staunch leader who stands by her convictions without blaming or going on the attack. A ScrumMaster who seems self-righteous, indignant, defensive, or sulking is most likely having a vanity attack. Always bring the ego—be confident and strong—but leave the vanity in the bathroom.

[Lose the vanity and win the ability to connect with your team members.]

Lee once said: "You are not, repeat NOT, responsible for what a person thinks about what you did. You are responsible for what you did. Big difference."

Open to feedback

ScrumMasters must be comfortable with receiving all forms of feedback – not just about obstacles and day-to-day issues, but about themselves as well. We must let the other person speak and find a way to say what he really wants to say, without fear of reprimand or negative consequence.

Stephen Covey once said that, "There is a space between a stimulus and a response. In that space, we can choose our response." Sometimes we choose to immediately act upon feedback; other times, however, it may be worth lengthening the space, pausing, reflecting back what you've heard, and taking some time to thoughtfully reply. Maybe you respond with something like, "I need to think about what you've said; let's talk tomorrow once I've had a chance to think about it. You deserve a thoughtful response." Maybe that's the T in my INTJ talking, but sometimes a delayed reaction works better than a fast one. When your face is reddened and you're ready to fire back, lengthen the space instead. The long-term benefit of giving a thoughtful response is that we encourage more feedback. And feedback is imperative for building a strong team. Over time, receiving feedback becomes as simple as reading the news.

Builds trust

One of my favorite books is Steven M.R. Covey's *The Speed of Trust*. Covey says that organizations, teams, and people move faster toward better results when they have trust. Without trust, business relationships decline to bureaucratic, contract-focused arrangements in which people check items off a list and put all the risk on the other party. Team members have trouble reaching common goals when they lack trust with each other. Without it, the team become preoccupied with hurt feelings, gossip, or speculation. This causes a team to stall out, and to some degree, we expect that a new team will experience trust issues. Keep in mind that the more trust a team has, the faster it can move to cool things such as innovating and creating great products. In the spirit of delivering the right products fast and flexibly, the ScrumMaster's quest for trust is two-fold: first, create a team whose members trust each other, then turn a dysfunctional relationship between business and development into one of trust (*Chapter 9, Shaping the Agile Organization*).

I often say to ScrumMasters, "You must model trust to build trust." In other words, if I can show my team and product owner that I inherently trust them, they will exhibit and return that trust. Trust relies on two elements: reliance and risk. Reliance is the extent to which one person permits their fate to be determined by another, and risk is the potential that the trusting party will experience negative outcomes. "Thus, risk creates the opportunity for trust." (www.stevecurrall.com/pdf/Currall_HBoT_ComplexityOrgTrust.pdf)

Think about your best friend, or someone you trust. How did you come to trust that person? Likely, you told that person something about you and over time you realized that you would not be judged, or that your secret wouldn't be told, that it was safe with your friend. In turn, she told you something about herself and that trust wasn't violated. Your friend took a risk by telling you a secret, and she relies on you to keep it a secret, otherwise damaging her livelihood. The very same trust can be created within a Scrum team and outside to the rest of the organization. If I can create an opportunity for risk—say, approach a manager about interrupting my team members—and show the team that I can give that message in a way that doesn't create a negative outcome for them, I will gain their trust. Trust is earned, little by little, day by day Establishing trust is essential to creating a good Scrum team and an Agile organization.

You can build trust by sharing something personal, facing and overcoming a common team struggle (let's work together to solve x), keeping secrets secret, and finally, by being reliable (do what you say you're going to do).

Leads with Theory Y

Theory X and Theory Y describe perceptions that managers hold about their employees. Do I think that my employees are good people, who do their best, would never cheat, and would never steal from me? If so, I have a Theory Y attitude. If I think, on the other hand, that my employees cannot be trusted, that they are lazy and must be motivated with carrots and sticks, and that they are liars, then I have a Theory X attitude. This concept, created by Douglas McGregor back in the 1960s, is a great way to think about your personal attitude toward co-workers or your team. Do you seek to blame someone for a problem or bad situation, which breaks down trust (the risk of injury—or blame—being fulfilled resulting in lowered reliance)? Or do you routinely create an environment in which team members can share responsibility, openly communicate and give feedback to one another safely, thus creating strong reliance and trust?

Theory X and Y mind-set can be subtle sometimes. I once heard a ScrumMaster say in a daily scrum meeting, "Yesterday you said that you were going to finish that task. Why didn't you report on it today?" I stopped breathing. I could hear Theory X oozing through his words. The team member immediately felt second-guessed, looked down at the floor, and turned red in the face. The ScrumMaster didn't even realize he had dampened trust and openness by asking this question in front of the rest of the team. I pulled the ScrumMaster to the side after the meeting to tell him about my observations. It was not an easy discussion.

Honest

Are you honest with your team? Do you willingly share information you've learned from the rest of the organization? Do you regularly give them updates on the progress you make on your impediment backlog? Can you openly share your opinions and beliefs with the team?

Honesty begets trust begets honesty. If I told my team that I was working with HR on new Agile performance metrics, they might not have much to say at that moment. But they'd probably think about it over the weekend or during their commute to/ from work. Perhaps a team member might speak up about it the following week and say, "You know, I was thinking about what you said about Agile performance metrics. I'm interested in helping define that; we could put together a really cool dashboard around test automation that would also give us some good performance metrics for people on the team." If I hadn't been honest about what I was up to, I might have missed that great contribution.

How to become a better ScrumMaster

I've heard from time to time that a ScrumMaster is just a facilitator, or just a coach. I disagree; rather, I feel that the ScrumMaster must have business sense, communication skills, tact, and political savvy in order to have the slightest chance at a successful transition.

> *The perfect ScrumMaster would probably have advanced degrees in engineering, business, sociology, education, and in psychology, and have worked as change agent and manager of projects with different degrees of uncertainty in different industries and sectors, and would have the energy of a teenager, the spirit of a sport champion and the wisdom of a crowd of experts.*
>
> *– Dr. Rafael E. Landaeta, Old Dominion University*

By now you understand the scope of the ScrumMasters's responsibilities as Ken and Jeff intended. This might be overwhelming, so first realize that not all changes are revolutions. You can implement change in baby steps simply by implementing the Scrum framework, escalating obstacles, and reflecting on your personal growth. It can also help to understand what else you can do to be a better ScrumMaster for your team. By doing so, you will become a better change agent.

Empower yourself and others!

It's natural for people to resist change, and folks in the "slough of despond" don't always readily seize power when it's dangled in front of them. Existing traditions, customs, beliefs, and personality traits can hold them back. It's quite easy, really, to say, "I'm empowered." Just move your lips. But to believe is a different story. The first step for a ScrumMaster is to help people realize that empowerment is there, right in front of them; all they have to do is reach up and pluck it.

Many teams fear taking chances. This fear can diminish or prevent the ability to take risks, which dampens experimentation, which ultimately means that potential may not be realized. One reason for this lack of courage is that teams feel that management doesn't trust them. For one reason or another, they've been made to feel as if they must run every little decision past a manager for approval. One way to help instill a courageous environment is to help the team make the distinction in what the team own and when the team must go outside for help. The team own the work in the sprint—they decide how it gets done. Supporting the team to make their own decisions demonstrates trust, which builds courage, empowerment, and morale. Questions such as, "What can we do about this obstacle?" or "What would you guys suggest to management that we do in this circumstance?" can help a team realize that they are indeed entitled to solve their own problems. Plan to run interference for your team to back up their decisions—encourage a "fail fast" mind-set and create the safety for the team to do so.

> After a couple of weeks with a team, I won't show up to a daily scrum meeting. I'm not doing this because I don't care; rather, I want to show the team that they can run this meeting without me. They know what to do—it's a simple meeting. Removing myself from it creates a new dynamic. Who will kick it off? Who will 'facilitate' it? Who will record obstacles? You know, I could make sure all of this is designated beforehand, but why? Don't I trust my team to self-organize and synchronize with each other? Of course I do. And the team always pulls through. Later in the day I'll stop by someone's cube and ask if there were any issues that I need to be aware of. If not, then I won't probe. There's always tomorrow's meeting, and I trust my team.

Create a culture or environment in your team in which team members feel safe to voice concerns or resistance. You want the opposing viewpoint. You want the devil's advocate so that all facets of the problem and solution are considered. Never punish someone for making her concerns or beliefs known. Rather, encourage her! Welcome the opposing viewpoint and ask the team what they would like to try next. Additionally, make the new way (Scrum) as easy as possible for people to implement. Help them understand why they might want to do things differently.

Edward de Bono, in *The Six Thinking Hats,* encourages people to think about problems from multiple perspectives. Try this in one of your team meetings: bring six hats to the meeting: white (data), red (emotion), black (cautious/risk), yellow (positive), green (creative), blue (process). Each team member gets a hat, and the color they choose depicts the thinking style with which they'll lead. They can trade hats in future meetings. Hats help team members feel free to question, support, or change an idea to fit their needs.

Empowerment comes in many forms. It might simply show up as an ability to speak one's mind, and for a person who is normally reserved, this may be a huge step. I observed one ScrumMaster who seized power by deciding to interview various stakeholders to find out what kinds of metrics and reports they need. Nobody asked the ScrumMaster to do this, she just decided to do it. Empowerment moves us from the reactive to the proactive, looking out for the next decision to make, the next understanding to glean. Empowerment squishes inertia.

What's your comfort zone? Let's face it—some of us are more courageous than others. So what do you do? Move yourself beyond your comfort zone! Set a goal that lies beyond your current abilities. Tell someone else so that it becomes more than just an idea. Maybe you're intimidated to run the Scrum of Scrums meeting, for example. Set a goal for yourself that you will volunteer to do it next month, and tell the other ScrumMasters about your goal. Prepare by reading, looking at burndown charts, observing this month's meetings, and then do it! You will learn so much by taking the leap—and you won't look back. Soon you will wonder what made you so nervous in the first place.

Help others visualize the desired state

In every class I teach, I ask participants to draw a dot in the quadrant that best represents their current process. Then I ask them to draw a second dot on where they'd like their process to be (if they could have it their way).

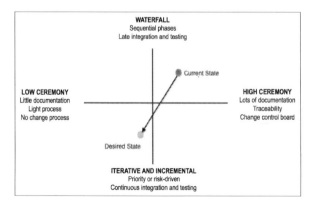

In every single case, the dots are in two different locations; that is, nobody wants to stay where they currently are. The next question I ask is, "Why? Why change? What ideas have caused you to draw a second dot in a different place? Why should your team change the way they create and deliver products?" The answers I get are pretty much the same: "We're not delivering fast enough, not delivering the right things, missing deadlines, poor quality, bad morale," and so on. Then I ask, "What prevents change?" In other words, if they knew they had these issues, why hasn't anything been done about it thus far? Almost always the answer can be distilled down to, "This is the way we've always done things." Inertia, stagnation, laziness, fear, lack of a vision, or the know-how to change. I've worked with thousands of people over the years, and they all say the exact same things regardless of the company, the country, or the business model.

Why Change?	What Blocks?
- takes so long for tangible deliverables, then, they're not right	- top-down management
- allows adaptation to late requests	- confusion of roles
- trade-offs are easier	- crawling out of past architectural decisions
- need informed, two-way planning	- pressure
- need team empowerment	- engineering mind-set
- want a better quality of life	- tools, training, and feedback mechanisms

What's interesting is that as the class or coaching session progresses, a few people argue with me. And that's fine—I encourage it in the spirit of the black hat. But I'll point back to the wall, to the reasons for change, and ask if those reasons still hold true. I'll get a weak, "Yes." remove We know from Satir's model that this is the first reaction to the foreign idea is not working well, then the team should be encouraged to try something different. And if they don't try it, how will they know it won't work? After they've tried it—and they've proven that it can't work or won't work— then argue. Half the battle is the mind-set—getting someone or a team to believe that they can make it work in the first place. Sometimes this argument can act as the first transforming idea!

Run the dots exercise with your team, or management group, or customers. Ask them to draw two dots—one for current state, one for desired state. Ask why they'd like to change and write the responses. Ask what will block them from changing and then write those responses, too. After a good discussion about empirical process, Scrum, Agile, Lean, and so on, take some action items. What would people like to try next? Post all of these artifacts in the main corridor of the office—front and center where everyone can see them. Because when Scrum begins to reveal the tough issues and obstacles, people will complain that it's difficult, that it's hard, that it's painful. Having this list, that they created, will remind them that the reasons for change came from them (not you!) and that they will have to work hard to ease the pain points. And assure them that you will do your best to help them achieve that.

Some ScrumMasters I meet say, "I could never have a discussion like this with my management team/executives/project managers!" My question is, "And why not?" Are you any less than them because you don't have a C in front of your title? Do you not have valuable information or ideas just because you're not part of the senior leadership team? Of course not! In fact, I would argue that you're more qualified because you're closer to the work!

Influence others

Information is one of the best influencers in the world. If a burn down chart indicates that a team's sprint is running off the rails, nobody can argue with that. It's reality, it's the truth, and the team can make better decisions by knowing it. It's not necessarily what people want to hear, but this is business, after all, not Utopia. Data influences. Team members are moved to action by data that shows their progress toward their goals. Management and executives are called to action by data presented in the form of dollar signs. I once had a senior level executive who kept interrupting my team for his own personal pet projects. I put together a quick cost worksheet showing the monetary impact of his interruptions on our highest priority deliverables, and the behavior stopped. People don't realize the issues their behavior causes until you put it in terms that they understand. It's not that they're bad people; they just don't understand the impact of their actions.

To find interruption costs get the hourly cost per employee and multiply this amount times the number of interruption hours in the sprint. Don't forget context-switching time! Present this number at the sprint review or other appropriate forum.

$250 dollars per hour * 20 team hours of interruption = $5,000 dollars lost to interruptions in this (two-week) sprint. At that rate, we will lose $125,000 per year for one team due to interruptions. Do I have your attention?

Another influencer is your mind-set and attitude. Adopt a "Why can't we?" attitude instead of one that whines, "Why we can't." Change the way you think about change. Model a positive attitude and you'll start to see others around you pick up on that. Anything—I mean, anything—is possible. Make up your mind that you're going to do it—and then convince others. That's all. A positive person inspires positive feelings in others. Exude an open mind-set and don't take yourself so seriously. Your team will feel as if they can approach you (because you're humble), trustworthy (because you're open), and supportive of their needs (because you listen and exhibit that you can be approached about anything).

Yet another way to influence is a simple two-letter word: "No." This word is not said enough. I once gave a presentation with my friend Michele Sliger at an Agile conference that was all about how to say no. This was one of the most well-attended workshops of the entire conference! It's amazing how powerful this word is, and yet how difficult it is for some of us to say it! Saying "no" creates boundaries that necessitate new responses. Saying no, and meaning it, asserts control and power. One way to say "no" in Scrum is when someone asks for a new feature during the middle of a sprint that's underway. One's natural inclination is to help out, but understanding that mid-sprint changes cause chaos is a good reason to say, "Put it on the product backlog and prioritize it near the top if it's that important." It's the same thing as saying 'no', but gives the person a place to put their idea so that it's not lost. This simple statement eases much tension and assures the person that their idea will be reviewed and possibly prioritized by the product owner for inclusion at some point in the future.

I once worked with a development group of 25 people who wanted to use Scrum in order to stop frequent interruptions from support representatives who were escalating production bugs—even though the group worked many late hours and weekends to fix the production issues, they were not able to get to the pile of new feature requests from customers and product managers. The group decided to split into four Scrum teams, with one of those teams dedicated to fixing support issues so that the three other teams could focus on new feature work. This made the support engineers—the people reporting the production issues—very nervous, so the manager of the support team called an emergency meeting with ScrumMasters to voice his concerns. Prior to Scrum, the support engineers enjoyed the luxury of going to any developer for any issue that came up. Now that all escalations were to be handled by one team—a subset of the overall development group—support representatives were nervous because they felt that customer responsiveness would suffer, which would make their jobs even more difficult than they already were.

The Scrum team in charge of these escalated bugs discussed this and offered to include support representatives in their planning, review, and retrospective meetings, so that they could craft the right escalation process together. Additionally, support representatives were invited to come to any and all daily standup meetings so that they could hear about the status of their escalations. Once the team opened the kimono, so to speak, support became much more comfortable with this new workflow and escalation process. Visibility and reassurance and a good old-fashioned discussion went a long way with this group. They just needed to know that their concerns were heard and that they would be included to help define the best process so that customers didn't suffer.

Roll up your sleeves and servant-lead

Robert Greenleaf coined the "servant leader" in 1970, although the concept has been around for hundreds of years. A person leads by serving by giving priority attention to serving the needs of others. A ScrumMaster can serve his team in many ways and must be comfortable with being a stagehand, not an actor. A ScrumMaster is not in the limelight and is happy when the team receives the accolades—after all, they did the work. The servant leader just cleared the path. Servant leaders (ScrumMasters) do whatever it takes to help a team be successful. They get food. They update the backlog when team members fail to do so (and gently remind them to take care of this task in the future). They fight battles with management and push for change when they know it's required. They shield the team from the fray and do everything possible to set the team up for success. Being a ScrumMaster is a thankless job—if you are looking for the spotlight and the applause, the ScrumMaster job is not the job for you. Servant leaders earn trust and the ability to influence.

Listen more than talk

Sometimes when someone comes to me to complain or to discuss a tough situation, I'll let them talk. And talk. And talk. Usually, if they keep talking, they'll end up talking themselves into an answer. At the very least, even if they can't solve the problem themselves, they will feel as if they've been heard, and I'll have a better understanding of the problem. People are too often quick to solve the problem for others, especially if they come from a management background.

I once worked with development teams in New York who had colleagues in Bangalore. The New Yorkers were complaining that the Bangalore team members just weren't up to par. Instead of jumping to conclusions and passing premature judgment, the ScrumMaster and I asked people what the issues were—on both sides—and listened to the responses. We even ran an anonymous survey to gather additional information. What we learned was fascinating. It wasn't that people had sub-par skills; rather, there were many communications issues, on both sides of the world. The feedback ranged from, "Some of the voices are not clear" (a telephony issue) to, "More than one person is talking at a time" (a facilitation issue) to, "The New Yorkers talk too fast" or the "people in Bangalore have an accent." We quickly realized that we needed some basic communications training. The ScrumMaster and I got up at 3 a.m. New York time on several occasions to hold virtual workshops with the Bangalore team members. We would actually practice simple things, like announcing your name before speaking. We held the same workshops with the New York team members. We coached the other ScrumMasters to improve their distributed team facilitation skills. We polled the teams three months later and the teams reported a 40 percent improvement in productivity, resulting from better intra-team communication.

You see, the minute we stop listening and jump to a conclusion is the moment we've closed the door to other viewpoints and solutions. In an environment in which we're trying to create empowered teams, listening is everything.

Plant seeds

You'll find that teams will struggle from time to time—some more than others. You'll plant seeds (ideas) that may grow into action at some point in the future. I've worked with a few teams that go into sprints with the waterfall mentality—they figure that they'll code for the first part of the sprint and throw it to the testers in the second part of the sprint. This is pretty common as it's the work pattern that most know and are comfortable with; they simply do not know another way in which to work. They'll quickly realize, however, that future sprints are impacted because of overflow defects, sometimes jeopardizing an entire sprint because they're unable to finish their stories according to the Definition of Done. But they still don't realize how to get out of this old behavior. So in a retrospective, or maybe at a team lunch, I'll ask the team, "Have you considered that perhaps the stories are too large"? Or, "Have you entertained the thought of pairing a developer and tester to work on the story in tandem?" Eyes glaze over, lunch chatter grows silent—maybe some eyeballs roll and perhaps nobody 'bites' on the idea. I'll continue to mention these ideas at any opportunity I get. Maybe I'll follow up by sending a link to an article about Extreme Programming practices, with a note that says, "…read this for discussion at the next retrospective." I just keep planting the seeds.

All of a sudden, when you least expect it, you'll notice a sprout from that seed that you planted. It may be in a daily scrum when a developer turns to the tester and says, "You found all those defects in my commit yesterday; can we get together after the meeting and work together to quickly resolve this? I can't seem to reproduce the issues you've found." Voila! Pairing commences! The seed has sprouted! These breakthroughs may seem minor and maybe you don't even notice them as they're happening. But they are not minor. The developer and tester work together, quickly resolve the issues, and report in the next daily meeting that all is working fine. In the retrospective they mention how well this approach worked for them, and others take notice and try it themselves. The next thing you know, the entire mind-set of the team has changed. Plant many seeds and water the heck out of them. Some will take root, eventually.

Choose to be happy, focus on the positive

Do you get out of bed each day and say, "I'm going to make this a great day, no matter what happens!" Most of us don't say it to the reflection in the bathroom mirror, but maybe we should. Positive thinking—that is a conscious choice to be happy—influences different actions and behaviors. If I'm in a bad mood one morning and I decide to dwell in that state of mind, an e-mail from my boss asking for a status report won't be well received. I'll probably grumble my way through it, loathing the entire thing, questioning why I have to do this. However, if I stop for a moment and say to myself, "I'm going to do the very best on this status report that I can," I'll find that my actions of creating the report are energized, motivated, and the outcome probably better as a result. Keep in mind that a positive attitude should not be mistaken for blind optimism; rather, it simply is telling yourself that, "I'm going to make the best out of this situation," no matter the situation. The reality may very well be that the situation is daunting, stressful, and negative, but you create a wall of positivity around you so that you don't get sucked into it.

I encourage ScrumMasters to celebrate small victories—for example, talk about how hard the team worked when you're introducing the sprint review, or bring in donuts one morning just because, or say, "thanks for all of your hard work" at the end of a daily meeting. One of the most positive exercises I've ever observed is called **appreciations**. Basically, in a retrospective each team member in the room thanks another for something that they did that sprint. I have seen people brought to tears in this meeting, simply from the positive nature and the happiness that people feel when they hear how much they're appreciated. Little things like this go a long way toward building an open, trusting, and ultimately productive team.

If we can make the most out of any situation—choose our attitude—we can go through life being happier. Happy means we have a general feeling of well being, that all is well in the world, and we are subsequently kind to others. Being happy means we are approachable, and, from a leadership perspective, we need to be approachable in order to be effective.

Know your communication style

A ScrumMaster must speak and listen effectively, and all of us have a communication style. Let's examine a few communication styles and explore the potential impact to your team.

Loud or quiet?

Are you the person in the room with the loudest mouth? You know the type: a big belly laugh or a loud "What the ?!" lets you know when you're in the middle of an overpowering, loud communicator. Everything about this person is at maximum decibels and in your face; she makes sure that you hear her. While effective in that everyone can hear what she has to say, the trouble is that not everyone knows if they're being heard in return. This can cause people to shut down and just let the loud communicator run the show.

Perhaps you're at the other extreme: the team can barely hear you in a meeting. You talk with your head down, hand covering your mouth, mumbling something. Everyone leans in to hear what you're saying. Eventually, you become invisible; the meeting runs off the rails, goals are not met, outcomes are not achieved.

I was the quiet person a long time ago. I learned this about myself when I first began training people a decade ago. In early practice training sessions, my boss really helped me out. He said, "I'll be in the back of the room watching you. When you see me tug at my earlobe, this means that I can't hear you." Do you know that Lou almost tugged his earlobe completely off the first few times I practiced my training with him? He could not hear me, at all. I actually had to practice breathing techniques to force sound from my belly instead of my throat. I had to learn to enunciate, and to stop saying "um", "y'all", and "fixin' to." I had to learn not to look down at my feet when I should have been making eye contact with the training participants.

There are times when you feel that you need to be loud and/or assertive. Perhaps nobody can make a decision. Perhaps the team members have lost their focus in the meeting. Before you get loud, however, think about how you can turn the problem to the team. Can you get them to assert themselves so that they can make decisions and keep focus? There are times when you might have to do this for them, but try to get them to step up first. Other times, quiet and subservient is the way to go. For example, the product owner may need to give the team some ideas about his business needs. I certainly don't want to railroad this conversation by asking questions that the team members themselves should ask. Think about your style in general—do you let others speak up, or do you bulldoze conversations? Or do you fade into the background because others do not hear you at all?

Direct versus passive

Sometimes it can be tough to come out with the truth in a direct, non-defensive way. Has your team ever had to claim a velocity of zero at the end of a sprint? I've had this happen a few times; it's the 'ugly' message that nobody wants to deliver, but it must be said so that appropriate actions can take place. This example also goes back to trust. Let's say that the team had a velocity of zero but they feared consequences from management, that 'zero' would be seen as a failure. While it's not the easiest thing to talk about, this risk actually provides an opportunity to create trust with my team. I want to be direct about velocity, why it was impeded, why it's not a failure, and go to bat for my team. This would not be the time to be passive and let management talk about how the team failed, ask what's wrong with them, finger-point and place blame. Nor would it be the time to cover for my team and give the appearance to management that all is on track. I must be direct in this case, especially when it comes to information about the team's status.

You may want to take the passive route, however, when two team members need to solve a problem; you might very well know the answer and you would like to 'direct' them to that answer because it seems to be the fastest way. The whole team wins, however, when team members work out the solution for themselves. You might also want to be passive when there is major conflict between two people in a meeting; it might be best to call a break and let everyone get some fresh air. Talk to both people individually during the break, and then together to see if you can help them call a truce to move forward in the meeting. I've provided a reading recommendation for conflict resolution at the end of this chapter.

By no means, however, should you choose a passive-aggressive route. Passive-aggression is when you might be angry or disappointed with someone, but you appear that everything is just fine. The trouble is that the person knows that you aren't happy, but you won't admit it; you therefore hold all control in the situation. Nothing is discussed, nothing gets resolved, and the target of your anger has lost a ton of respect for you in the process. I grew up around people who used passive-aggression, and let me tell you, it is one of the most heartbreaking, frustrating situations to be in. Don't do this to your team members; if you are disappointed or have something to say, just say it. Give them the respect at least to sort it out with you. Conflict and tough discussions are part of Tuckman's **Forming-Storming-Norming-Performing** model, so the more readily you reveal your feelings, and encourage others to do the same, the sooner everyone can get through the conflict and onto performing. Don't think for a moment that as ScrumMaster you are exempt from conflict and storming—you are a part of the team, after all! I strongly suggest taking a conflict management course once per year to sharpen your facilitation skills. A deep dive into this topic is beyond the scope of this book, and there are true experts out there who can help you become proficient in conflict resolution.

Switzerland or Supreme Court judge

It's important that a ScrumMaster does her best to communicate as an observer, not a judge. If the goal is to create a culture of trust and reliance, then it is important not to label someone for something someone says. We shouldn't permit this from other team members either; once I had a team member complain to the entire team, "Oh Bob, he's always late." I said, "Maybe Bob has a circumstance that we don't know about. Let's discuss this in the retrospective to understand if our daily scrum meeting time is optimal for everyone on the team." I directly asked the team to not judge Bob. (This is also a good example of being direct instead of passive.) If I had said, "Oh yes, Bob is always late. I mean, what is he thinking?" that would have made others think poorly of Bob, and also sends the signal that I can't be trusted to not talk behind team members' backs. This would erode trust on my team and would have created additional barriers to solving the lateness problem.

It is paramount that your communication style—the way you choose to interact with others—is appropriate to the scenario and context. Learn when to be direct or passive (but never passive-aggressive!), loud or quiet, and always speak from an observer's point of view, never from that of a judge.

Other ScrumMaster characteristics

Maybe we're very proactive, and the team knows that they can count on us. Maybe we're not very knowledgeable about a topic and thus lose credibility. Let's explore some additional attributes that will help you develop your ScrumMaster style and become a better everyday leader.

Procrastinator or proactive

Proactivity means that you think ahead in order to plan an approach or anticipate a response or set of actions. Proactivity was wonderfully displayed in the note that the twin babies on the plane wrote in order to gain sensitivity and an overall better experience for everyone. A team will know when you're proactive: maybe the sprint planning meeting was exquisitely set up so that all the team members had to do was think and do their very best at planning. Perhaps it is Pratesh's birthday next week, so you reserve a table at the restaurant down the street for the whole team. Maybe you research some Agile testing tools to bring up at the retrospective for team members to discuss and check into. Proactivity is an element of servant leadership; if you can anticipate the needs of your team members, you can forge an action plan to help them. Thinking ahead is a form of serving, of anticipating needs and creating a plan to address those needs.

Here are some examples of proactive questions that you should consider making a habit to ask:

- Is there an upcoming meeting or other team event that I could begin to plan for?
- Is the product backlog up-to-date?
- Should I talk with the customer about the contract and make sure that his/ her expectations are being met?
- Could I invite anyone else to the sprint review next week?
- Should we be thinking about another release planning session soon?

Don't fall into the trap of procrastination. You'll not only let yourself down, but your team as well.

Teacher

You probably realize by now that the ScrumMaster should have good teaching skills. He must educate people about the benefits and challenges of working in an Agile fashion, sometimes having to sell it to others. He may have to engage in heated debates with managers about the right process, moving from expert-to-task to team-to-backlog models of human staffing, and so on. The ScrumMaster must arm himself with knowledge and experience, and relate this to others in a way that is confident and with awareness of the particular challenges for the various roles within the organization. The ScrumMaster thus creates a shared understanding, a reason for transitioning to Agile, and a pointed vision of benefits that transitioning to Scrum will provide. The ScrumMaster should always seek to increase their knowledge about facilitation, planning, team dynamics, motivation theories, communicating, reporting to management, and the like. These topics should appear on the ScrumMaster's personal improvement backlog.

Student

While a ScrumMaster is in a teaching position, she also makes it a point to learn from others. I recently learned that one of my coaches was allowing his product owner to participate in story point estimation along with the development team members. I initially was appalled. I would never want the product owner to influence a team's estimates! But instead of reacting, I asked why he allowed this. He explained that the product owner thinks in terms of acceptance criteria, while a team thinks in terms of technical effort. Sometimes developers make assumptions about the feature and its acceptance criteria, which can come out in the estimates. In this scenario, the product owner raises a higher number because his assumption about the feature's behavior is that it's more involved than what the team members think. They discuss it, learn more from each other, clear up assumptions about the functionality, and assign an estimate that reflects agreement and better shared understanding.

I found this to be a very insightful way of using group estimation techniques and extending it to all team members, not just the developers. I've realized over time that opening my mind to different ways and listening to others' ideas only makes me stronger. My mind is now a database of ideas— some are mine, many are from other people—I can query them at the appropriate opportunity. Try to learn at least one thing per week from someone else at work. Write it down in your personal improvement backlog when you hear about it. Then try it yourself. The ScrumMaster is a teacher, and a student.

Scrum buddy

I can't stress enough the importance of a Scrum buddy—someone knowledgeable in Scrum (and XP, Agile, Lean) with whom you can brainstorm, vent, and exchange feedback. Can you identify someone to help you within your company? Maybe you have a friend doing Scrum at another company; get together and have lunch once a week? Maybe you could call a meeting with all the ScrumMasters at your company to talk about process and different barriers people are running into. You can even use various group discussions in **LinkedIn** to throw out questions and get thoughtful responses. The idea is to not go it alone; there are so many wonderful resources and people willing to help you if you simply reach out.

Journal/walk up a hill

Ever hiked up a steep hill? When you go 10 steps or so, you're a little out of breath but you can't see much. Walk a little farther up the hill to see a little more. The higher you go up the hill, the broader and more expansive your view. Journaling helps you do the same thing; when you're bored sometime you can pull out a journal from a year or two ago and see how far you've come in solving the problems of the day. Perhaps your old journal will give you some new insights since your experiences have grown since then. I'm a big believer in journaling. I write every day. If I hadn't done that I wouldn't have been able to write this book, nor would I be able to reflect on my progress in the larger context.

Which ScrumMaster persona are you?

I put together the following ScrumMaster personas as a way for you to think about the strengths and weaknesses of each. Maybe you can identify with one of them. Think about the advantages and disadvantages of each style; perhaps by doing so you'll find some items to add to your personal improvement backlog.

Techie Taj

Techie Taj has dual responsibilities: he is the lead Java engineer and has also been asked to play the role of the ScrumMaster. He is very smart and loves to speak his mind and give his opinion. As he is busy with technical tasks, Taj rarely gets to work on the impediment backlog for the team, which is full of organizational issues because the company is new at doing Scrum. Other managers often interrupt the team and they aren't doing too well at meeting their sprint commitments as a result. Taj tries to correct this by telling them how to implement the features and to work later hours. His aggressive, schedule-crashing ways are causing the team to disintegrate.

Taj's strengths are that he is a strong developer and has a brilliant understanding of architecture, coding standards, and approaches.

Taj's weaknesses are that he's too directive and doesn't allow the team to self-manage and come up with their own solutions. He is also afraid to say no, which is causing the team to disintegrate—and he's not getting the real ScrumMaster work done!

What would you suggest for Techie Taj's personal improvement backlog?

Bossy Betty

Bossy Betty has been a project manager for 15 years. She was recently converted to a ScrumMaster when everyone in the PMO was sent to Scrum training. She is very risk-adverse and has a Theory X attitude. The team complain that she's a 'Debbie Downer', and they feel that she's never happy or excited about anything. Because she is used to planning **work breakdown structures (WBS)** she creates tasks for the team and puts these into their Agile tool. She figures that she's being proactive and helping the team but the team feels like she's micromanaging them and that she is not very knowledgeable about technical work, as the tasks she assigns don't reflect reality. The team does not feel accountable as a group. They feel like they report to Betty, especially in the daily scrum meeting. They resent her.

Betty's strengths are that she has excellent organizational skills and that she attempts to mitigate risks.

Betty's weaknesses are that she micromanages the team and she isn't very knowledgeable about technology.

What would you suggest for Bossy Betty's personal improvement backlog?

Clammed Up Carl

Carl is very bright and sensitive to others, and he's also very reserved. He's very difficult to hear or understand in meetings. He has trouble projecting and often the team just talks over him. His ideas hardly ever get to the surface because he isn't assertive enough, which he figures is okay since he's supposed to be creating a self-organizing team. He's afraid to track simple things, like action items resulting from a meeting. As a result, meetings frequently get off track and spiral into tangents, with no real outcome.

Carl's strengths are that he's very sensitive to the needs of the team and strives to do the right thing.

Carl's weaknesses are that he's timid and quiet all the time.

What would you suggest for Clammed Up Carl's personal improvement backlog?

Thundering Thea

Thundering Thea is loud. Her team secretly call her "The Bulldozer." She is known for always getting her way and isn't afraid to go up against anybody. She even yells at people. Thea always gets things done. Management know that if there's ever a tough task, Thea is the one for the job.

Thea's strengths are that she's very results-oriented and can handle tough situations with assertiveness.

Thea's weaknesses are that she shuts the team down.

What would you suggest for Thundering Thea's personal improvement backlog?

Officer Sophie

"That's not Scrum!" Those words ring in my ears from Officer Sophie. She is the ScrumMaster and also the Scrum police. With every action or statement that might violate Scrum theory she will yellow or red flag a team. She sticks by the Scrum rules as if they are from the Bible and is often found on **LinkedIn** defending her rigid positions. She is a certified ScrumMaster and mentions this within the first two minutes when talking with someone.

Sophie's strength is that she understands Scrum and the reasons for its boundaries and rules.

Sophie's weaknesses are that she's too forceful and not open-minded.

What would you suggest for Officer Sophie's personal improvement backlog?

 Maybe you identify with Officer Sophie. Or perhaps you're a Bossy Betty. Hopefully, you're somewhere in the middle of the personas. Consider the pros and cons of each persona from the perspectives of the product owner, business, the team members, and yourself. What are you missing? What could you improve? What training or help do you need in order to improve? What can you stop doing today? What's one thing you can try tomorrow?

Summary

As ScrumMaster, you must possess self-awareness and an understanding of how others perceive you. This feedback, coupled with a relentless pursuit of improvement, will ensure that you'll find your own ScrumMaster leadership style to become an effective everyday leader.

You must have a laser-sharp focus on how you communicate, cultivate trust, and display courage and honesty. Every meeting or interaction with a team or a group of stakeholders provides an opportunity for you to grow. You first task is to create a strong team. A strong team with success stories can greatly influence the rest of the organization, as we will discuss in the next chapter.

Recommended reading

- Ben-Shahar, Tal. *Happier: Learn the Secrets to Daily Joy and Lasting Fulfillment.* 2007, McGraw-Hill.

- Bolton, Robert. *People Skills: How to Assert Yourself, Listen to Others, and Resolve Conflicts.* 1979, Simon and Schuster.

- Covey, Stephen M.R. *The Speed of Trust: The One Thing that Changes Everything.* 2006, Free Press.

- De Bono, Edward. *The Six Thinking Hats.* MICA Management Resources, Inc. 1985, 1999.

- Weeks, Dudley. *The Eight Essential Steps to Conflict Resolution.* 1992, Putnam.

- Some great leadership frameworks here: `http://www.mindtools.com`.

- Learn more about Myers-Briggs at `http://www.myersbriggs.org`.

- Difference between vanity and ego: `http://geniuscatalyst.com/tipofthedaydb_print.php`.

9
Shaping the Agile Organization

In 1955, Rosa Parks, an African-American woman, refused to give up her seat to a white person after the *white section* was filled. She later said in an interview that, "I would have to know for once and for all what rights I had as a human being and a citizen." (Charles Marsh, 2006, *The Beloved Community: How Faith Shapes Social Justice from the Civil Rights to Today*.) Her values of equality, rights, and citizenship were made clear that day when she told the bus driver to go ahead and have her arrested as she would not move from her seat. She was in fact arrested, and subsequently went to trial; her actions sparked a Women's Political Council distribution of 35,000 brochures that called for the boycotting of Montgomery buses. That boycott continued for 381 days! The courage of Parks defined a moment in the Civil Rights Movement in the United States.

When was the last time you took a stand for something? You don't have to be a president to find your voice, to lobby for what is right. Many of the ScrumMasters I've worked with lately seem to plod along, afraid to stand for anything. Sometimes I'll see a glimmer of hope, a spark of energy that might ignite into a flame, and every now and then I'll meet someone so passionate, motivated, and energized by what they're doing that it's contagious. If a ScrumMaster can take a stand, others might just follow.

Culture eats strategy for breakfast.

— Peter Drucker

You might as well know up front, right now, that you can't change a company's culture. In fact, not a single person can. You can push, pull, kick, prod, cajole, or perhaps influence it, but you can't make that horse drink! At one point in my career I heard someone talking about how stories can influence a company's culture. This made sense to me, and if this is indeed true, I think one of the best stories to influence a larger organization is that of a successful team. The news spreads through the grapevine like a snake—everyone wants to know more. How did the team do it? Did management really support it? How can we try it? How can we be that happy? *Chapter 8, Everyday Leadership for the ScrumMaster and Team,* gave you some ideas for creating the strong, successful team, while this chapter will help you take that story to the masses, as well as give you some other ideas to try. Like most complex things in life, there is no perfect way to get there. You will hit resistance at every step of the way, so creating a strong, self-directing Scrum team is the preparation for this greater journey.

I coached a development organization in Philadelphia a few years ago with a bunch of team members who really wanted to be Agile. One of the main challenges was that their VP of development came from a hardware background and was not accustomed to adaptive planning techniques; he was vehemently opposed to Agile because of ingrained behavior, misinformation, and a feared lack of visibility. So, of course, he and I butted heads every time I would come in for a visit. One day I was walking down the hallway to a daily scrum meeting, and the VP says to me, "Oh, look! There she is! The ScrumMaster superhero has her cape on and is going to save all the developers!" Basically, he chastised me in front of others, who were in the hallway. I made a wisecrack and carried on with my day, but I was seething underneath the calm exterior. I chose to be there and had a job to do; I couldn't let this jerk derail me. By golly, I was The ScrumMaster!

Will Agile cause a ripple, or a tsunami?

An executive once said to me, "We want to do Scrum so that we can get a culture." And I said, "But you already have a culture. It's there. It just may not be the one you would like to have."

Very often, the existing organizational values don't match the Scrum ones. And, well, in most cases we wouldn't expect them to, at least initially. After all, you're probably initiating Scrum (or being asked to initiate it) for a reason. Many executives and managers say, "We want to do Agile because we need to do more with less, have better quality, or deliver faster." Others unfortunately think that the Scrum framework will solve all of their problems. What they fail to understand is that teams and the greater organization must adopt the values to appropriately apply the principles. By valuing and trusting the people, and their knowledge and interactions, the organization will find the right Agile solutions through its people. It's just that management classically is trained to solve the problems, and it's very hard for them to let go of solving problems so that team members can. Keep in mind that Toyota has been *doing* the Toyota Production System (really, it's just a fancy name for their culture) for decades—even though it's taught others the system, those that learn the system don't automatically adopt the mind-set and values. Why? Because the mind-set is the difficult part!

Why is it so hard for people to live in the Scrum values? I believe it's due to the management century—the legacy of traditional management that promises process, efficiency, and productivity. Coupled with the ladder of promotion, the net sum is the lattice framework of politics, secrecy, and control. Humans, like any creature, seek the path of least resistance, so initiating and influencing change makes for an uphill battle, in the mud.

Natural culture also makes a big difference. I taught Scrum in Sweden for a few years with my dear friend Maria Thelin. Maria taught me about Swedish culture—from the food, to the architecture, to socialism—the Swedish way (or lagom). The team-based, consensus-driven nature of Swedes meant that Scrum was a natural fit, and we saw Agile methods take off in Scandinavia like wildfire. On the other hand, the United States is a territory of rugged individualism, where the person is responsible for him or herself. Scrum, with its focus on self-organizing teams and reduced or eliminated need for management, strikes fear in the heart of Americans—managers and workers alike—because the ingrained *goal* of the worker may be lost (to climb the ladder) and the ingrained *goal* for the manager (to manage and control the ladder) is seemingly forgone.

Ralph Stacey eloquently describes the conundrum. He stopped publishing his Stacey Diagram because of the ease and nonchalance with which people would just cherry-pick a management style thinking that the proper process would fix everything. He later wrote that he has moved away from thinking of organizations as systems to thinking about them as a pattern of relationships, both good and bad, between people. These patterns emerge in complex responsive processes of interaction between people, taking the form of conversation, power relationships, ideologies and social conditions, choices, and intentions. In other words, yes, Scrum is a framework that we should employ when we have a complex project or situation, yet don't think that—for one picosecond—if you pluck the right process—like picking out your socks in the morning—life will be perfect! People have to sort out their own complex interactions as they strive to succeed. Will the introduction of Agile concepts and values cause a ripple in your organization, or a tsunami?

How does your organization measure up to the Scrum values?

It's good to think of the five Scrum values and their antitheses as a scale, a continuum. Rarely will the perfect culture exist to completely embrace Scrum. So how does your organization stack up? Where does your organization measure on this continuum? Circle one number in each row and then add up the total score across all rows.

Commitment	5	4	3	2	1	Commitment by Proxy
Focus	5	4	3	2	1	Sub-optimized/Over-organized
Respect	5	4	3	2	1	Position, Power, and Control
Openness	5	4	3	2	1	Secrecy
Courage	5	4	3	2	1	Fear

The higher your score, the better. You could also use this little exercise as a survey for your team; compile the results and use this to kick off a discussion about values and ideas for improvements. Use the results to engage management in a discussion about culture and morale. Open some eyes!

What if the Scrum values score is low?

You have a lot of work to do. Answer the following questions to design a plan. Invite your team into this discussion to get alternate viewpoints:

1. Why are people not able to commit for themselves? Is it due to fear or control by management? Is it lack of knowledge? What else?

2. Why is the organization using scientific management principles to organize knowledge work? Do they not understand the waste this causes?

3. Why aren't knowledge professionals respected? Is it a fear or lack of trust on behalf of management? Is the rewards system flawed, focused on promotions? Maybe it's the cultural value of hierarchy and control?

4. Why is there secrecy in the organization? Is there a history of negative consequences to the truth? Have people been *burned* in the past?

Now you can create a plan based on the responses. For example, if people are afraid of what management might say in response to negative news, look for an opportunity to give negative news. Ask yourself: what's the worst that can happen? If the worst happens, is it worse than the current state? If not, then maybe you have a case for courage. Here's an example (the scene: you are speaking to business stakeholders): "I know that in the past we have tried to respond to every business request as soon as we receive it. We like to please the business. But this has caused us to trade quality for time's sake. And now our software needs some care, some maintenance as a result of these quick fixes. We always thought we'd get to it one day, but apparently that day will not come. We have not had the courage to speak up about it before, but we don't feel right about being silent any longer." The ensuing discussion may not be comfortable. In fact, it may be downright frightening and cause great anxiety. But it will be the catalyst for more important discussions—and resolutions—about the situation. In fact, in this example, others will now understand why there have been so many bad days and late nights supporting a shaky system. Now the discussion can turn to how to fix that problem, how to prevent people from working 10-15 hours a day, and other subsequent discussions. However, if no decisions are made, then Scrum did its job, but the people did not.

The low values score might illuminate a learning opportunity for people who are stuck in the old way of doing things. Why couldn't you organize a lunch and learn or a team lunch to talk about Scrum or other Agile ways of working? Plant the seeds of change by educating others. The current reality can change. Sometimes people take the existing reality as The Way; perhaps showing them a different way will open their minds to new possibilities. Be realistic and expect that it will take some time. Remember the planting seeds advice from Chapter 8, *Everyday Leadership for the ScrumMaster and Team*.

Culture change requires a multi-faceted approach

Because Agile is focused on people and on keeping process at a minimum, transitioning to an Agile culture requires a multi-faceted approach. An organization, working with and through its ScrumMasters, should help product managers think about incremental value and backlog management, assist Human Resources in determining new goals and measurements for employees, shift everyone's mind-set toward building in quality, use adaptive and just-in-time planning techniques in the project management office, and boost team performance. Continuous improvement surrounds all of these facets like a safety net, yet efforts across these facets should be integrated and synched on a regular basis. For example, as teams discover various tools and practices that help them do their jobs better, this information should be synchronized with Human Resources so that teams are allowed and encouraged to utilize new ways of working. Sometimes, the existing HR and performance review metrics hinder people as they try to embrace and put into practice their new transforming ideas. Let's explore hindrances to change in more detail.

Illustrating the need for and direction of change

A good leader can help others see the big picture—the need, process, direction, and plan for change. The best transitions are those led by a sponsor in a powerful position, unafraid of letting teams experiment. Or maybe you're thrust into this leadership position because you're leading the pilot team! Whatever the case, the leader must communicate the need for and path of change.

You learned the Two Dots exercise in Chapter 8, *Everyday Leadership for the ScrumMaster and Team*; that is a good exercise to align everyone on change plans and direction, as well as to get them thinking about what might be problematic during the transition. If you don't have the time to run Two Dots, you can ask a simple question, whether you're in a team or executive setting: "You all agree that we should have flexibility to respond to market needs, deliver quality solutions fast, and focus on the work at hand, right? Right! Now, let's talk about what's holding us back from those three ideas." Of course, everyone agrees and wants to be fast, flexible, and focused!

I also like to ask groups, "How will you know that these Agile efforts have been successful?" In other words, I want to know the success criteria for the transition. Maybe it's to improve quality, or increase customer satisfaction scores, and so on. Making those success factors visible provides helpful reminders to people when they're in the thick of sorting out change.

Once I have an agreement to at least try it, I like to put together an implementation timeline (generic sample shown as follows). You can use this to help managers and teams understand and discuss what's coming up next in your own Agile transition:

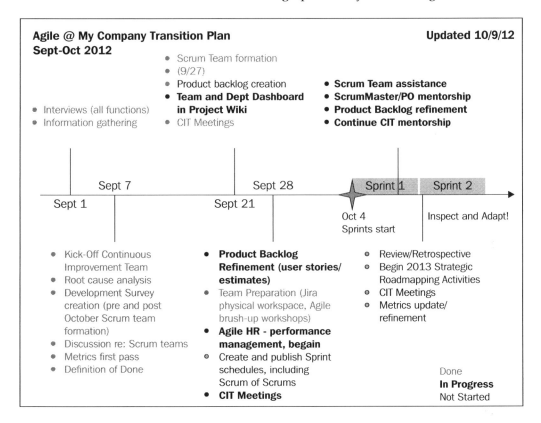

Pre-agility survey

Perhaps because I'm a consultant, I like to take a snapshot of the current state, before the team makes any changes. I'll set up an anonymous survey that asks questions like:

- Do you know whom to ask for requirements clarification?

- Do you understand the business or customer needs for the requirements that you're working on?

- How often do you receive a request for a change in scope?

- Do you feel that your input is valued?

- Do you feel that you have ownership over your estimates, tasks, and completion?

- Do you feel that you are delivering high-quality solutions?

- Are you proud of your work? Are you happy at work?

These questions (there are more) allow me to get a handle for the current state. Once Agile efforts are underway, we can repeat the survey to see if the original state of things has improved. This survey provides a baseline of data for comparison purposes in the future.

Waste score

It can be helpful to get a sense of the amount of waste in the current system. I can take the percentages from the anonymous survey and turn that into a waste score. In the following example you can see that two-thirds of team members felt as if they could not focus. Lack of focus can be driven by multi-tasking, interruptions, or lack of engagement—three of the *Seven Wastes of Lean* (*Poppendieck*). Scoring all the responses shows an **F** or failing grade in this case, which means that this group's system has a large amount of waste. The score in the left-hand column is higher for positive results, and lower for negative results, and is calculated by taking an average of all results. If we could take another poll in three to six months and show a grade of C, we'd have quite the story to tell! If waste scores and process improvements were integrated with HR's efforts, all employees might be motivated to create leaner systems. This waste scoring mechanism does not replace a Value Stream Mapping exercise, but it can help initially identify wasteful areas in which you may want to conduct a detailed Value Stream analysis. If you're interested in Value Stream maps for software, hop over to Jeff Anderson's post (http://agileconsulting.blogspot.com/2010/03/value-stream-mapping-vsm-is-lean.html).

Score	%	Question	Associated waste
50	42%	don't know whom to ask for requirements clarification	Handoff/delays
70	28%	don't understand the requirements they're asked to work	Relearning
60	33%	don't understand business need	Relearning/defect
80	14%	feel they are not delivering high quality	defects/partially done wo
40	55%	feel they write code that doesn't follow good practices/standards	defects
70	30%	feel they don't know whom to ask when they have an issue	delays
70	30%	feel they're asked to abandon work in progress	Task-switching
50	50%	have low morale	End Result
40	55%	feel they have no time to learn	Learn Constantly
30	67%	feel they cannot focus	Engage Everyone
40	57%	feel there is no process for their input on features	Engage Everyone
40	57%	feel that they do not own their own estimates and work	Engage Everyone
10	85%	feel they're disrupted	Task-switching
50 Waste Score (F)			
100 PERFECT SCORE			

Old-fashioned interviews

Talk to people! Get out there and ask questions about what would make life easier/better/more interesting at work. Listen to the unique problems of each group of people, whether they're developers, testers, or product owners. Take notes and look for patterns in feedback. See if you can tie any of the feedback to wastes or other dysfunctions.

The Agile organization chart and roles matrix

To maximize agility, the organization of people should change. Following is an over-simplified organizational chart for a matrix organization. The chain of command is over each skill silo—development, quality assurance, technical architecture, and so forth. The staff in each of these silos report up through that silo's layers of management, and staff are predominately (if not wholly) measured according to the silo's goals. QA people do QA, development people develop, and so on, and their loyalty is with their respective silos. The **project management office (PMO)** is charged with forming projects that involve the appropriate resources at the appropriate time in the various projects, following an ETT allocation model:

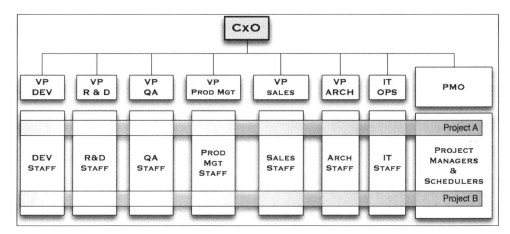

Now take a look at an Agile organization in the following diagram. The biggest difference is that people are organized based on revenue streams — or products — instead of silos. The Vice President of each product reports directly to the CEO. Scrum teams do not report to the VPs of products; rather, they make their capacity visible so that the product managers can plan accordingly. Each Scrum team is composed of 5-9 people who have cross-functional skill-sets and are dedicated to the project for as long as they wish to be. Team members self-select and self-organize within their respective teams, and each team has a ScrumMaster and a product owner. Groups like finance, IT, and architecture support all the teams within a product. Of course, there are global groups that look for economies of scale of the organization at-large, when it comes to controlling costs, IT governance, and so on, but there are times, for example, when Product A has different infrastructure needs than Product B. Having a local service group will help the individual product teams move as fast as possible. Have you ever tried to muck through a global IT ops group for permission to use an open source tool on your team, only to be denied because the rest of the organization couldn't use it? What a drag!

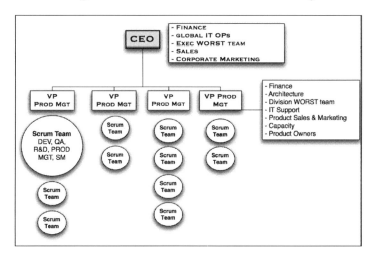

Product owners meet with the CEO on a regular basis to discuss capacity, progress, and ROI. Depending upon the need of the organization, a product group's charter may change. Let's say our cell phone company wants to move into tablets. The CEO may decide to sunset one cell phone model and put that group's teams onto tablets instead. Sure, the teams will need to learn some new skills, and perhaps bring in some people with expanded knowledge to help them. If the organization encourages its workers to expand their knowledge and skill-sets, they can work on what's most important to the organization. Otherwise, when stuck in a silo, a worker is limited to what his skill-set dictates, with no chance for growth. This idea is one of the premises of The Knowledge-Creating Company.

The traditional organization measures people at the individual and silo level, and measures projects by percent of work done and actual hours. The Agile organization measures teams' abilities, morale, quality, and success of products in the market. Agile organizations view teams as capacity that can be used for the most pressing needs. Looking at work this way frees organizations from planning overhead. Even in the flattest Agile organizational structures, there usually exists a thin layer of management focused on paving the way for technical excellence, supporting continuous learning and improvement, helping employees along their career paths, and overseeing budgets.

Traditional roles in an Agile organization

Everyone wants to know what happens to their roles when moving to an Agile way of working. It's covered in the Agile organization chart previously. What if you're a functional analyst? Well, then you probably should find a Scrum team to work with, or maybe you can support the product owner. What if you're the only architect in an organization of five teams? Well, you probably don't need to be assigned to any one team 100 percent—rather, you'd support all five teams on an as-needed basis. What happens to project managers? They become ScrumMasters, if they can make the jump. Otherwise, project managers can take on another role within a team, or provide project coordination services for large programs. What happens if we don't have enough product owners? See if there are line managers who could support teams in this capacity. Who's on the WORST team? Volunteers and ScrumMasters, line managers and product owners. Traditional roles need to find a place in the supply and demand balancing act. Are you on the product side, the delivery side, or do you support or service all teams? Those are the three categories of responsibilities in our lean organization. I don't mean to trivialize or make this sound easy, but the best Agile transitions are lead by sponsors courageous enough to change the organizational structure. Everyone else tries to keep the existing structure and pour Agile over the top of it, which is a bit like pouring grease over your waffles.

Scaling an Agile mind-set

There's plenty written about scaling Agile methods and such, but very little about scaling an Agile mind-set. How does learning happen in an Agile organization? Scrum teams learn every day about the issues and obstacles that prevent or make it difficult for them to deliver value. Agile organizations must have a tiered retrospective approach in order to effectively scale the Agile mind-set:

- Scrum teams retrospect and fix what they can. Issues that they cannot resolve are escalated to the WORST team

- WORST team resolves what it can and escalates anything it cannot to executive management
- Monthly brainstorming meetings are held across teams and departments to identify new product and process ideas to try
- Bimonthly town halls are held for teams to demo innovations in products and processes

The goal is to create opportunities for people of different levels to discuss and brainstorm new ideas. There's no perfect way to do this, just get people together!

Self-actualizing individuals create an Agile organization

Self-actualizing is the result of a person fulfilling his own individual potential. It was coined by Kurt Goldstein and utilized in the familiar *Hierarchy of Needs* by Abraham Maslow. According to Maslow, in order for an individual to self-actualize, a person's physiological, safety, love, and esteem needs must be met first.

In his studies Maslow found that *self-actualizers* had the following common traits [http://en.wikipedia.org/wiki/Self-actualization#Maslow.27s_hierarchy_ of_needs]:

- Efficient perceptions of reality — that is, the ability to judge a situation fairly and honestly. Self-actualizers can readily identify dishonesty.
- Comfortable acceptance of self, others, nature — shortcomings in self and others are accepted.
- Spontaneity — bringing creativity and energy into daily life.
- Task centering — having a problem to solve or a mission to fulfill.
- Autonomy — ability to work and solve problems independently.
- Continued freshness of appreciation — constant thanks for everything in the world; nothing taken for granted.
- Fellowship with humanity — deep identification with others.
- Profound interpersonal relationships — deep loving bonds with others.
- Comfort with solitude, being alone.
- Non-hostile sense of humor — ability to laugh at oneself and use humor that doesn't hurt others.
- Peak experiences — feeling at one with the universe, deep meaning and harmony.

It's interesting to me how these traits of self-actualizing correspond to the traits we seek in Scrum team members. We want our team members to trust and value each other, work closely together, respect the individual's need for thinking space, and thrive in a fun environment, while being creative and spontaneous. Team members need to be given the space and permission to self-actualize if the organization has any chance at all of becoming Agile.

Goals and metrics that motivate self-actualizing

Most performance review metrics and templates contain some aspect of self-actualization, but it's not the predominant focus. That should change. With some direction and ideas about the company's mission and objectives, team members should be allowed to come up with their own goals and their own rewards for meeting those goals — that is self-management after all, isn't it?

Person has a say in it

One of the best goal setting and attainment models I've observed is Google's **OKR** process — **Objectives and Key Results**. Executives initially create OKRs, and each department or team makes subsequent OKRs with more detail to support the OKRs at the level above. This OKR tree allows people at subsequent levels within the organization to see the highest level **OKR vision** and come up with ways in which they'll contribute to that vision. Since the OKR vision always has to do with the company's success, the subsequent actions are driven with success in mind as well. An executive objective might be to increase sales by 100 percent. Subsequent team OKRs might be to increase site visits by 300 percent, increase performance by 50 percent, and so on.

Objectives and goals in this model are always set at an unattainable level. They're pie-in-the-sky. The idea behind this is that it's better to attain 70 percent of a goal once thought of as impossible versus 100 percent of the mundane. If you're interested in reading more about this, Google's OKR model was introduced to the public in *The Plex, How Google Thinks, Works and Shapes our Lives*, by Steven Levy. There are several blogs and such on the Web (just Google it!).

Another model comes from Tal Ben-Shahar, Ph.D., a Harvard professor who wrote the book *Happier* and who holds regular (and very popular!) semester courses on the subject. Ben-Shahar talks about happiness in various contexts, including the workplace. He suggests that a person answer the three following questions (the MPS process: Meaning, Purpose, and Strengths):

1. What gives me meaning? In other words, what provides me with a sense of purpose?

2. What gives me pleasure? In other words, what do I enjoy doing?

3. What gives me strength? In other words, what am I really good at?

In the intersection of the answers to these questions lies an indication of what the individual probably should be doing at work in the first place and day-to-day actions that a person can take while at work.

Regardless of the model used, I feel that the most important idea is that the Human Resources department should work with people to understand their personal goals and rewards. Everyone has different goals, and a person's goals change through time; for example, this year I'd like to learn more about Java development, while next year I'd like to speak at a conference. Rewards are also personal—some are motivated by money, while others are motivated by being allowed to work on the innovative idea they have for the company's product, even though it's not in anyone's product backlog. Yet others are motivated by being given time and space to sharpen their skills.

Understanding what demotivates

I commonly use anonymous surveys to tease out what the demotivators are. One such survey recently unearthed the fact that workers perceived management to be sneaky and secretive. Because there were so many business requests (and because developers couldn't say no), the development manager would jockey around *resources* (ahem, people) and ask them to work on pet architecture projects, keep infrastructure work on the hush-hush, and so on. The result was disastrous. People worked 60-70 hours per week, they felt that they couldn't push back, engineering discipline was non-existent, and production issues plagued the teams. In this case the approach was two-fold. First, the ScrumMaster would make visible the amount of technical debt and defects as well as hours worked by the team to management in the next sprint review (and on an ongoing basis). Second, the ScrumMaster would work with the HR manager to put in review criteria like, "team member doesn't work on unsanctioned work" or, "team member regularly reports when he has enough work to fill the timeframe" or better yet, "team member does not work overtime".

Just today, Naomi Simson, the founder of Red Balloon, posted an article called *Four Things we Need to have a Good Work Day* [http://www.linkedin.com/today/post/article/20130310232250-1291685-four-things-we-need-to-have-a-good-day-at-work?trk=mp-reader-card]. She says that people need more praise, better managers, more time with friends and family, and greater trust. One may use reverse logic to quickly get a handle on what demotivates people: little or no praise or recognition, bad managers or poor management style, no work-life balance, and conflict and secrecy within the workplace. Work with HR to figure out ways to unearth and fix the demotivators within your teams.

Standardizing measurements

While it is great if team members can set personal goals as they strive for personal rewards, there is also a set of standardized measurements that should exist for the team, department, and organization.

It is important for the team to know if it's meeting commitments—and making commitments that are realistic in the first place. It is also helpful to know if the team has a velocity that is sustainable and reliably used in forecasting meetings. It is also good to know and review the team on how its members collectively stretched themselves to learn something to help the team as a whole through a seeming impasse. By no means all-inclusive or exhaustive of ideas, the following graphic aims to demonstrate that a person's performance review criteria would consist of weighted components and measurements:

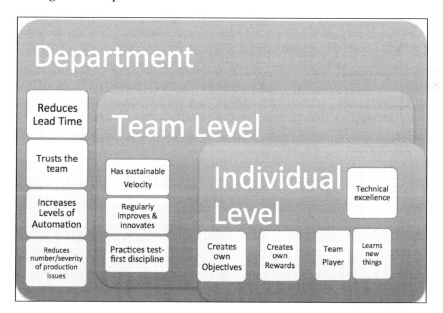

For a department it could be great to measure people on how they reduced the number and severity of production issues. It might also be interesting to set a goal for the overall department to reduce lead time—the amount of time it takes for a backlog item to be pulled from the list and pushed into production. Another great example is measuring a department on how much test automation it can put into place so that menial day-to-day tasks are not so daunting. Human Resources should work with ScrumMasters and managers to create a new or revamp an existing performance review system. Special attention should be given to creating criteria that motivates an individual toward self-actualizing traits, while creating criteria for a team and/or department that reflects alignment with strategic and organizational change goals.

I worked with a group that had frontend developers in one location and backend and database developers in another. I saw right away that one group was not talking to the other as there were numerous production issues that could have been caught with better communication. I worked with HR to set a goal for their managers for the following timeframe to align the two teams and reduce the number/severity of production issues. They challenged the managers of those two groups to bring folks together in planning meetings, by including test criteria on user stories, and involving both sides in a highly communicative fashion for the testing of features. Each of the two groups (backend and frontend developers) also had individual goals to reduce the overall number of defects and work with other groups to proactively solve problems.

Frequent, multi-perspective feedback

Give your team feedback more than once per year, in both informal and formal settings. There's nothing more aggravating than only hearing once per year what you could have done to improve! Managers, ScrumMasters, product owners, and team members should make it a habit to give feedback on an ongoing basis, from higher to lower levels, lower to higher levels, and peer-to-peer. This is commonly referred to as a 360 degree review; you can refer your HR managers to these books and articles in case you don't have this multi-perspective review process.

Jeff Sutherland created a review process that I find intriguing. You can find more information on his blog [http://scrum.jeffsutherland.com/2006/11/agile-performance-reviews.html]:

10: Trade journals are writing rave reviews about your work saying it is best in class

9: Customers are writing rave reviews about you (must be documented in writing)

8: Exceeds expectation of the company senior management

7: Exceeds expectation of the product owner and team

6: Exceeds reviewers' expectations

5: Meets reviewers' expectations

4: Does not meet reviewers' expectations

3: Does not meet development teams' expectations

2: Does not meet engineering group or company's expectations

1: Customers are complaining about you

0: You are personally roasted in PC Week

Under this system, the manager can give a 4, 5, or 6. Any other rating requires outside input from the development team, the engineering group, senior management, customers, or the press. The employee can always write a rebuttal to any review and have it attached to the review as part of the Human Resources record.

CEO scorecard

While we're at it, what's keeping the CEO from having his own review? The CEO can set the tone of the company and can in some cases single-handedly drive the culture (Steve Jobs, anyone?) The CEO must get feedback from a board of people, whom he trusts to review him on an ongoing, consistent basis. Here is a basic CEO Agile scorecard that you could use or suggest HR to use. The following points should be considered for the CEO:

- Allows for investment in tools and techniques to make development more productive
- Knowingly invests in system maintenance
- Understands the trade-off of time versus quality
- Accepts experiments that fail
- Uses both positive and negative reinforcement
- Actively creates a culture of collaboration
- Encourages new ideas, cultivates culture of openness
- Shares quarterly goals/communicates company-wide
- Shares vision on a consistent basis

- Manages for the future, not the ego
- Delegates operational details and supports management decisions
- On top of industry trends
- Customer is God
- Inspirational role model
- Flexible
- Decisive

This chapter only barely skims the surface of performance management in an Agile context. And performance management only scratches the surface of creating an Agile culture. Hopefully, this section has given you some ideas about what to do if you realize that your team may be responding to an incorrect set of measurements in your workplace.

Don't go it alone

As a ScrumMaster, you will encounter some challenging issues as you first try to create a successful team and then influence the organization. Whatever you do, don't go it alone. Meet with other ScrumMasters to discuss issues and potential solutions. Find a Scrum Buddy and create Agile learning opportunities across the organization; many larger companies hold *Agile days* in which outsiders will come to speak and talk with people. You are in such a better place than I was when I first learned Scrum—there are LinkedIn groups, blogs, twitter accounts, articles, and books galore on how to be successful with Scrum.

I once worked with a team in which everyone was so sensitive. Now, I'm a sensitive soul, myself, but they were just over the top. Every meeting you would hear at least five times sentences prefaced with, "Now, I don't mean this in the wrong way toward him," or, "I'm not being critical about this person, but," or, "Please don't take it this way…" It was ridiculous. I started to get to the point at which I was watching everything that came out of my mouth with such concern and focus that my communication effectiveness broke down. I reflected on this and had to remind myself to model courage. That means saying the things that might be uncomfortable, difficult to hear, or hard to understand in a direct, unambiguous fashion. It doesn't mean saying those things with a mean spirit, but saying them nonetheless. And sometimes, no matter how hard you might try, a person who is cautious will take everything you say—no matter how you coat it—on the defensive, concerned that your agenda is one of a hidden nature. Now multiply that concern, cautious, tip-toed-ness across a hundred, three hundred, or one thousand people. Implementing Scrum is very difficult in these situations, but you must be completely open and courageous. You may have to face at some point that Scrum values may only go so far in this particular environment.

Avoiding Scrum as a panacea

I don't know what part of the message people missed when they adopt the mind-set that, "Let's just do Scrum; it'll fix all of our problems." When people believe that Scrum is a panacea, they don't see the need to inspect and adapt. They become disgruntled over day-to-day things. One might overhear, "This Scrum process doesn't tell us anything! It's too gray. Not specific enough!" It's because the people missed the most important concepts: individuals and interactions over process and tools; courage and openness over fear and secrecy. But what happens in these Scrum-as-Utopia situations? Scrum gets the blame, because it is not an all-encompassing solution. Remember and help others remember that Scrum is a framework that exposes exactly what the organization needs to fix in order to be better at product delivery.

Why change? What blocks?

When I ask people what blocks them, their answers imply the elements of their own unhappiness at work. People want the benefits that make their lives easier, better, happier at work, and they want the obstacles removed that directly affect them. The QA person who raises his hand and says, "We want higher quality" is really saying, "I want my ideas about quality to be heard, finally." The product owner who says, "Deliver faster to customers" really wants to justify his pay, and probably wants to satisfy the customers, too. Sometimes people say, "Our managers block us"; the people are tired of their corporations, which are so steeped in command and control. Those who want a process that emphasizes visibility are probably tired of projects gone awry. People couch their own personal desires behind purported *benefits* of Agile. Don't get me wrong—I do believe that people also want their respective companies to be successful—but intertwined in there are some of their own selfish reasons. We all want to be a part of the winning team, the cool kids.

These two questions are so powerful, tug at the heartstrings of values, that I've had a couple of people grow very angry during the discussion and storm out of the room. The discussion didn't seem to match their values, or I think, worse, they felt that there was no way possible that the organization would change to accommodate their values. The trick is to wrap what personally affects people into the organization's change vision. Support for this sort of change must come from the top; people need a unifying change vision statement that helps them personally connect with the goal.

Without the five values, motivated, proactive, creative people will take their talents elsewhere because they cannot thrive. Knowledge workers are inherently motivated to do their best, and when the environment—the organization—simply won't allow them to, well, there probably is an organization that will. I further hypothesize that when value-driven people leave, they seek organizations that have similar values to their own. It's a match that they seek; the person wins in that they can thrive and have a happy, challenging life at work, while the organization benefits from the energy that's now infused. I hear it all the time when I visit companies in Silicon Valley, who may be stuck in fear and control; they get very disenchanted when presented with these values. They get the glimmer in the eye for a brief moment, and then the fire dies. They shrug and say, "Oh well, I hear Google (or Apple) is hiring. Maybe if it doesn't work out here then I'll go somewhere where I can thrive."

Immunity to change

I stumbled across this test in an old issue of Harvard Business Review (November 2001). Robert Kegan postulates that people are immune to change because they have a competing commitment that prevents personal change (`http://hbr.org/2001/11/the-real-reason-people-wont-change/ar/2`). I found this compelling and applicable. Kegan created an exercise in which he asks people to respond to the following four questions:

- What is the new commitment that is being asked of me?
- What am I doing, or not doing, that is keeping my stated commitment from being realized?
- What else have I committed to that may be competing?
- What big assumptions have I made about the new commitment?

I found this interesting because sometimes the competing commitment feels like a violation of a value of loyalty or personal dedication to another person. Other times, it can be an intrapersonal conflict—low self-esteem, self-doubt, and so on. For example, a tester on a new Scrum team, Jane, was asked to work more rapidly; that is, don't bother logging defects that could be resolved right away. She responded that her competing commitment was that she had an upcoming performance review and wanted to meet the criteria on that review, one of which was to find lots of bugs. This prevented her from talking directly with developers to fix simpler defects on the spot rather than logging them into the defect management system; this, in turn, held the team back. Her assumptions were that she would be negatively viewed if her defect numbers were low. What's interesting is that her big assumptions are great fodder for the ScrumMaster's Impediment Backlog. In this case, the backlog item would be: "Talk to Jane's manager to see what can be done about performance reviews, so we consider Jane's performance from a team angle."

Face it, Scrum might not be for your organization

Your job as a ScrumMaster is to take a stand. Be courageous. Laugh in the face of fear. Your mission is much bigger than to be an iteration manager or to create a burndown chart. You are attempting to change things for the better, enrich people's lives, and make work a better place to be.

I do not, for one moment, feel that it's fair to put all the responsibility on one person, the ScrumMaster, to incite and sustain change in an organization. But it must start somewhere. And if we wait on the perfect combination of events or people, change will never happen. However, you might feel overwhelmed after reading this chapter. Maybe you didn't know that this is what a ScrumMaster is chartered to do. Maybe you knew but hoped you didn't need to know! ScrumMaster as change agent was the ultimate vision that Ken Schwaber had in mind when he created the role. All of this gets lost in translation, when the practices override the mind-set.

At some point, you may have to give up on your organization. You may need to find another employer, whose values align more closely with yours. This is a personal decision about which I cannot give any solid advice, other than if you get up every morning and dread going to work, it's probably time for a change. Not every company is going to be an Agile company, or will espouse values that are modern or forward thinking. Sometimes you just have to cut your losses.

Summary

Creating a successful team is be tough, but shaping an Agile organization may be your career's most challenging task. The existing culture, openness to change, and a myriad of factors will influence your ability to bring change to your organization. Remember to create a shared understanding of the need for change, and to lead with values. Since Agile and Scrum teams are all about strong, self-actualizing people, you need to work with management and HR within your company to give people a chance to self-actualize. Band together with others and create learning opportunities within your organization. The inroads you make will also help in programs of scale, which we'll talk about in *Chapter 10, Scrum – Large and Small*.

Recommended reading

- *The Goal: A Process of Ongoing Improvement 1984-2004, Eliyahu Goldratt, North River Press*
- *A Sense of Urgency, 2008, John Kotter, Harvard Business School Publishing*
- *Leading Change, 1996, John Kotter, Harvard Business Review Press*
- *Fostering Organizational Learning: The Impact of Work Design on Workarounds, Errors, and Speaking Up About Internal Supply Chain Problems, Anita Tucker,* http://hbswk.hbs.edu/item/7156.html

10

Scrum – Large and Small

Let's say that you've been training for the past few months for your first 10 kilometer race. You've studied some training schedules, started out slowly, and built up mileage over time. As you've hit a new threshold of fitness, you've begun throwing in tempo and interval runs to build speed. You've learned about hill work from a fellow runner and incorporated that into your training as well. You also learned that you run fastest if you have a bagel two hours prior to your run, but you only found that out after some misadventures with lasagna. You're ready for the big day; you know your fitness abilities, nutritional requirements, and body better than ever before.

Word of your success has leaked out and a running team of 12 has asked you to help them prepare for their first 10 kilometer! Now you have to understand each runner's fitness level, weaknesses, pain threshold, old injuries (and new ones, too!); you must make weekly adjustments to 12 training plans based on 12 weekly reports. Multiply the level of effort that you put into your own training plan by 100! Kiss your free nights and weekends goodbye! That is, unless you can get them to manage their own training plan.

The basic framework for 10k training is the same, whether you're planning your own race or teaching a team of 12 people to run their first races. However, information emerges as people get into their training programs, which means that people need to inspect and adapt. You can't inspect and adapt for all of your trainees; imagine how cumbersome it would be to manage diets, weekly mileage, injury rehab, RICE therapy, mental state, and training gear for 12 other folks! Your trainees need a base level of information so that they can take accountability for all aspects of their training, week in and week out. Like a running training framework, in the technology world, whether creating a simple website for the mom-and-pop hamburger stand in town, or the newest whiz-bang consumer gadget, the Scrum framework does not change.

Scrum works the same way for one team, 20 teams, or 100 teams; and for people to get the most out of it, they must practice the mechanics as well as the mind-set. In this chapter, we'll explore small and large Scrum implementations and provide you with some pointers from the oval track. People with the knowledge utilize Scrum's framework to help them realize when the finish line has moved, and how best to respond to that knowledge.

Scrum stops the resource shell game

Walk down any street in NYC and you're likely to see someone taking people's money in the shell game—a quick-handed guy (called a **thimblerig**) moves shells around while a poor guy has to guess which shell the ball is under. The sucker will never be right, because the shell game is a fraudulent game—it tricks players into feeling confident so that the thimblerig can take their money. I see ETT resourcing as such fraud!

When project crunch time is near, managers respond by shuffling around people. This shuffling gives the appearance of efficiency, and since money is exchanged—in the form of wages and budgets—this is fraud. The resource shell game hides the real problem, which is that the company is trying to do too much with too few people. The ScrumMaster's job is to make the gross imbalance between demand and supply visible, and put an end to the thimblerigging. One place to begin is by helping the business identify its strategy and prioritize its initiatives (we lightly discussed this in *Chapter 2, Release Planning – Tuning Product Development*, and *Chapter 5, The End? Improving Product and Process One Bite at a Time*). Everything isn't of equal importance.

I once worked with a team that had four project managers—for eight developers! And the project managers each had two or three projects for which they fought over the same eight developers. The answer for the team (and others in similar situations) was to create one team, with one ScrumMaster. So, one out of the four project managers volunteered to become the ScrumMaster, two project managers became product managers, and the fourth was let go. The two new product managers worked with business stakeholders of all types in order to prioritize the product backlog items. Now this caused a lot of infighting among the business stakeholders. Everyone wanted their own items at the top of the list. It was so bad that the CEO, who happens to be a U.S. television personality, had to come to one of the team's meetings to give a rundown of the vision and strategic objectives for the company. This made the prioritization of the product backlog crystal clear. There was nothing more to fight about; some of the stakeholders' items were not important for now, but hearing the message from the CEO assured the stakeholders that focusing on others' priorities was the right thing to do. Now the product owners were able to prioritize a backlog with clarity, and the one team of eight developers pulled items from the top of the list and chaos was greatly reduced.

When programs get large, managers want to layer on additional management. Keep management small; that is, let teams own as much as they can, and make their results visible so that the product owner can make important product decisions, while management removes obstacles.

Small Scrum

The first Scrum team was at a Boston company called Easel Corporation in 1993. Under the advice of Jeff Sutherland, this team created a modern development framework that included a dynamic object-oriented programming language, among many other cutting-edge components. The team was cross-functional, collocated, and never exceeded eight people in size.

This is small Scrum. By now you probably have a good grip on how to do small Scrum. When it's one team to one backlog, that's a pretty easy existence, one called simple, or small. As long as the product backlog is kept in a ready state, teams can pull the next item. Small Scrum can also be described as the basic Scrum framework applied in its pure form with no modifications. However, I bet that even Easel made modifications, because, as we'll explore later in this chapter, they simply were Agile, not just doing Agile. Modifications come easily, naturally, and sensibly to those who live the mantra of *inspect and adapt*.

The smallest Scrum team I have ever worked with was in a mobile gaming startup in Silicon Valley. One person played all three roles in Scrum: ScrumMaster, product owner, and he also worked on team tasks from time to time! Heresy, you say! Actually, the entire company was only five people. People had to assume different roles in order to move fast and flexibly. Darren understood the benefits of iterative development and got the rest of the team up and running using a very light form of Scrum. He played all three roles at the appropriate points in time. Since these folks worked together in a small office space, they did not meet every day in a daily scrum. They worked so closely together, and talked all the time, that a daily scrum would have been redundant. So were they doing Scrum? Yes, but in a way that suited them. They were able to show value every two weeks to their investors. They worked from a product backlog. The team was comfortable telling their product owner/ScrumMaster when he needed to back off. When the company grew, this small original team dispersed and became product owners of the new teams, providing guidance along the way. This is organic scaling.

Big programs, small Scrum

When the business can prioritize its initiatives and features within product backlogs, the Scrum teams can get down to the business of building products in small increments. Small teams can work effectively if they are given the goal and left alone to self-manage. Even when programs get big, with upward of 40 teams, the basic Scrum team construct should be left alone. Self-directed Scrum teams don't need to be told how to work day to day in large programs; instead, they need:

- An understanding of the big picture: Teams need insight into the program's goals and why the organization is investing in the effort. They need to feel aligned to this effort.

- Encouragement and support to build quality into each sprint's deliverables.

- Knowledge and tools to integrate early and frequently, so that issues may be resolved as soon as they're created.

- Help communicating with other teams.

- Fast and efficient resolution to their obstacles.

- Space to create innovative solutions to everyday problems.

I worked with a company in Amsterdam whose five teams started off with two-week sprints. They all pulled from one product backlog, and they got darn good with Scrum. They learned, however, after a few sprints, that the time-box was slowing them down. They asked, "If we have completed features two days into a two-week sprint, then why would we wait until the end of the sprint to push to production? Why wouldn't we push as soon as the features are ready?"

They wanted to get new functionality into the hands of the users as soon as possible. In fact, what was really interesting about this company is that the features were not even thoroughly acceptance tested by the product owner. Rather, the product owner gave a general idea of what she wanted, and then the team would build and deploy. There were several LCD monitors bolted to the wall in the teams' war room that broadcasted various metrics. One of the metrics was the number of conversions, or a measurement of how many times customers bought something; if this number increased, then they could determine that the released functionality was successful. If the number decreased, then they could determine something in the release was causing a problem—sometimes this meant that they would roll back the released functionality. Through the use of Extreme Programming practices and effective version control and roll back strategies, the teams got so fast that they were releasing to production several times per week. Effectively employing a *Scrumban* system, this company continues to be very successful today.

Teams can move this fast if they are given a clear sense of priority and are empowered to experiment with new practices. Courage, willingness, and a *what's possible* attitude is what the Scrum mind-set is all about. A typical organization that gets practices and not mind-set would have placated themselves with two-week sprints, figuring that it's good enough. If this typical organization were a competitor to my Amsterdam client, they would have fallen behind in market share and revenue. Teams that get practices and values transcend mediocrity. Ensure that your Agile program has space and time built-in for process innovation; it's just as important to business as product innovation.

When Scrum gets big—dysfunction or constraint?

While I still prefer an Agile method such as Scrum over a traditional methodology for large projects/programs, the fact of the matter is that any effort that has 20 or more people poses a significant communications challenge. In a program with 35 Scrum teams, all of which will use Scrum the same way, a program of this size of, say, 300 people, takes a tremendous amount of coordination, communication, and organization among teams and stakeholders.

As I mentioned in a previous chapter, I once worked with a company that was creating a new gadget. The program plan called for roughly 35 teams whose focus ran the gamut from firmware, software and tablet apps, integration with conferencing systems, and so on. It was a huge initiative and unfortunately ended up not being very successful in the consumer market.

I was one of the Agile mentors for the program and was limited to 10-15 hours per week to help guide the program. I worked with the ScrumMasters, product owners, and program managers to ensure that the teams built features in every iteration, and that they were inspecting and adapting. I will introduce the challenges and failure modes of scaling Scrum teams through telling the story of the gadget program in this next section. These issues universally apply to any large Scrum program running in a traditional enterprise; if teams stray too far from the basics, problems will quickly get out of hand. In large programs, ScrumMasters should work together to figure out if the teams' issues are truly constraints or dysfunctions.

Challenge 1: Fearful ScrumMasters

The gadget company had a command and control culture. People take orders from their bosses, and they don't question those orders. Bosses dole out promotions as rewards; therefore, it is not likely that a worker will challenge a boss: too much is personally at stake. You can imagine, then, that the ScrumMasters for these teams really didn't push back when it came to challenging situations. They were afraid to say no, afraid to surface obstacles, and afraid to challenge management in their assumptions about velocity or estimates. The result was development *foie gras*. That is, management just kept stuffing features into teams, without regard for the true capacity of the team, defined by how fast a team can deliver high-quality features while maintaining a sustainable pace. This caused bad code to be released upon bad code, iteration by iteration. Enhancements and fixes became more difficult and more costly to implement or resolve. This is difficult enough to manage with one team, but imagine the muddy waters caused by 35 teams that aren't proving a clear picture of their true capacity.

What can be done about fearful ScrumMasters? Well, first, understand that they are not doing the job. So do we fire them? Well, maybe, but perhaps we can try to coach a fearful ScrumMaster, and work with him through good mentorship to identify an action plan and resolution. But at the end of the day, either that person is going to take a stand, or he won't. At the very least, management expectations should be set as to what to expect from a ScrumMaster, else any mentorship efforts will fall flat. The bottom line is this: if the ScrumMaster can't exude courage, then who will? One of the recruiting criteria for a ScrumMaster should be that the person exudes "c-c-c-courage"! Remember, I came from the **KSSSHK (Ken Schwaber Scrum School of Hard Knocks)** — I don't let things like this go on for very long, and I have little patience for them. This is serious business.

Management should create a sense of safety so that ScrumMasters and team members are free to reveal the truth and speak about issues without the fear of reprimand.

Challenge 2: Late integration

While hardware integration certainly poses its own unique set of challenges, the gadget teams were not keen on integrating anything — even the application software that several teams wrote in parallel. Even worse, the teams made no effort to integrate with hardware as drops of new prototypes were delivered. This caused delays in discovering where the big technical gotchas were. Just like cancer in which a patient hopes that it has been found in its early stages, a large program should seek out issues as they are introduced; issues are exponentially more costly and damaging the longer they lie around unresolved.

The gadget team is not alone in their fear of integration. Henrik Kniberg, in his *Agile Version Control* article (`http://www.infoq.com/articles/agile-version-control`), describes *mergophobia* — teams worry about the issues that merging will expose. In fact, I see this in 60-70 percent of Scrum transitions with which I am recruited to help. What can be done about it? I feel that the best first thing to do is to quantify the waste associated with late integration. This surfaces in the form of defects and re-learning, and in many cases, interruptions due to production issues. One way to get a sense of this number is to ask team members the following:

- Approximately how much time per week/month do you spend resolving conflicts caused by integrating with other team's/developer's code branches?

- How many hours does the branch/merge process take to end up with one integrated branch of all developers' code?

- Approximately how much time do you spend per week/month fixing production issues?

- Approximately how much time do you spend per week/month waiting on your code to be tested and/or a bug that you fixed to be verified?

Now I know that these questions are a non-scientific way of gathering data for a baseline, but we must start somewhere. True measurements of this nature are very difficult, if not impossible, to quantify in a complex system as there are too many dependencies and variables to truly decouple the measurements. But I've found that this is a reliable baseline, after which you can create metrics to measure improvements.

So let's say the team came back with numbers that represented 30 percent waste due to interruptions, production issues, and wait time for code testing or bug verification. This means that out of 10 assumed productive hours of a developer, three are devoted to clean-up and fixing things that should have been right the first time. If you were to envision the manufacturing equivalent of this, the **Rework Bin** would be full. The goal of the ScrumMaster is to reduce the amount of time spent working on items in the Rework Bin and, even more importantly, reduce the amount of stuff that makes it to the Rework Bin in the first place. This means pulling integration up earlier in the process, and doing it frequently to discover issues lurking beneath the surface. In the beginning, doing so may mean that the team find a bunch of issues, and that's the point. Teams can resolve these issues and clean up code as they go so that over time, they create fewer issues. Another way the ScrumMaster can help this situation is to encourage teams to pair and use test-driven practices; in fact, it might be a good time for an Extreme Programming tutorial altogether! Extreme Programming is a set of principles and practices that help developers build high-quality code the first time around. It's like the programmer's version of Deming's Total Quality Management. Extreme Programming practices, while they affect the individual team member, can help multiple teams reach a point of flow in feature delivery.

[Extreme Programming practices help large Agile programs to scale.]

Challenge 3: Communication across multiple teams

In addition to all the automated ways to understand code conflicts, rework, defects, and so on, it's also good to have an old-fashioned discussion. While the daily Scrum is for a team to solve its own issues, the Scrum of Scrums is a discussion among team members with the purpose of resolving cross-team issues and obstacles. Usually, a developer-tester pair from each team attends the Scrum of Scrums. Each team representative will discuss code they checked in since the last Scrum of Scrums, tests that are failing, defects that have been found, what they plan to do by the next meeting, as well as bring up any obstacles. The goal is to remove any technical obstacles that get in the way of *Done*. Additionally, each team must set aside time each sprint in case there are issues that need resolution (this goes back to the buffering concept from *Chapter 2, Release Planning – Tuning Product Development* and *Chapter 3, Sprint Planning – Fine-tune the Sprint Commitment*).

Team members are the best attendees of the Scrum of Scrums meeting.

I see groups make the mistake of sending ScrumMasters as the primary communicators in this meeting. I am certainly fine with ScrumMasters attending and even facilitating this meeting, but the technical team members need to be the "pigs" as they are the ones coming up with the solutions to the problems. It may be difficult to keep the Scrum of Scrums, because of its problem-solving intent, to only 15 minutes. However, the same rules apply as in a regular daily scrum—once the team have identified the problem, they can take the discussion offline. The Scrum of Scrums may not require a daily cadence. Teams that have achieved flow, with automated ways of depicting system status, may meet once per week to discuss high-level status and such. However, until this flow is achieved, the Scrum of Scrums team should meet as often as required to solve technical issues among teams in a large Agile/Scrum program and to escalate blockers to management.

Challenge 4: Big picture metrics

Let's get back to our gadget teams. I discovered that team performance wasn't measured based on team metrics. People were still managed as individuals in this Agile program, with individual performance metrics. Team members weren't really team members; rather, their loyalty remained with their line managers and their skill peers. I talked with a tester on one of the teams and he mentioned that he received a bonus if he found lots of bugs, so he made sure that he found lots of them, and would even invent some to ensure that he exceeded his bug quota! This reminded me of a Dilbert cartoon I saw once! The tester wasn't really a part of the team, though, because testing lagged behind development by a sprint or two.

Imagine the developers with whom he worked—they would get bug reports and issues kicked back to them all the time, and it was probably very hard if not impossible to discern the root cause of the issues, causing all sorts of waste. A team metric that measures all team members' contributions is a more useful way to create the desired behavior. If you measure **lines of code** (**LOC**), and hold developers accountable for lines of code, you will get lots of lines of code! If you measure number of defects and hold QA people accountable for finding lots of defects, then you get an issue-tracking system full of defects! To what end? At the end of the day, we want few (ideally zero) defects and well-written code. So how does a large program achieve that? Instill a team mind-set in the Scrum teams and change the metrics!

Kicking off a new Agile team or program affords a great opportunity to revisit and revise performance metrics. The Definition of Done provides many team-level metrics, but you may wish to consider introducing a larger set—metrics that *measure the whole*, in Lean speak. Since both team and big-picture metrics are important, I've provided examples of both as follows. As teams progress through sprints, you can measure some or all of these items. We'll look to see, for example, if the number of bugs identified in production or reported by end users has decreased over time. That should be the long-term trend. We may also see a decrease in sprint velocity when a good Definition of Done is first instituted. The numbers would show that teams are slowing down in order to go faster. I'd bet that your team has some good ideas for measurements as well!

Metric	Description
Sprint Velocity	Story Points Awarded for sprint (requires a standard Definition of Done)
Cumulative Project Velocity	Total Story Points Awarded for project
Percent Complete for Sprint	Story points awarded for sprint/story points planned for sprint
Average team velocity	Total Completed Story Points/# Completed Sprints
Bugs/Sprint in QA Environment	How many bugs were found in the QA environment?
Bugs/Sprint fixed in QA Environment	How many bugs were fixed in the QA environment?
Bugs/Sprint identified in PROD	How many bugs found in production?
Bugs/Sprint fixed in PROD	How many production bugs fixed during sprint?
Bugs/sprint reported by users	How many bugs were reported by end users/customers?
Percent test cases automated	# automated test cases/total test cases
Percent code coverage by test cases	
Test cases pass/fail	
Present sprint:	Backlog updates completed and on time for all team members
Project to date:	Is team productivity improving?
	Productivity = (# of story points per sprint for good parts/total hours available to team for present sprint)

Metric	Description
	Compare to average of same calculation over previous three sprints
Project to date:	Quantity of running tested features as measured over time
Present sprint:	Increase in running, tested features* achieved during sprint
Present sprint/project to date:	Acceptance rate of stories per sprint/customer satisfaction

*Running means that the features successfully integrate into a single functional product

*Tested means that the features are continuously passing the tests provided by the correlated acceptance tests

Features? Meaning real end user features, pieces of the requirement given by the product owner, not technical tasks such as install the database or get web server running

The following figure represents a balanced scorecard for the big picture; team and programs at large can measure various things under each of the main headings such as quality, customer happiness, and so on. Measurements need balance, and they need to be revisited from time to time so that ScrumMasters and managers can correct any imbalances. For example, if a program manager measures quality, but not the **Time to Market (TTM)**, it could be problematic. The teams could make the best possible product but miss important market timeframes. Another interesting comparison is that of TTM and employee morale. If TTM is super-fast and morale is low, a development *foie gras* situation may exist—that is, the company is trying to do too much too fast, stuffing as much down the developers' gullets as possible. This may appear tasty to businesses at first, but the *goose* dies.

This balanced scorecard approach has been around for a long time, and many still consider it quite useful. Following are some examples of metrics that could underlie each of the four main headings:

Customer happiness

- Good user experience
- Customers want to spend money; higher sales call volume
- High net promoter score
- High social impact (likes, trending, and so on)
- Positive usability test results
- High customer satisfaction scores
- Decreased customer support call volume

Time to Market

- How long does a request take to go from idea to implementation?
- How many non-value added activities such as fixing defects, wait time, and so forth happen along the way? Can we reduce the amount of non-value added time?
- How many stories have requested rework by the product owner?
- What is the teams' productivity? Is velocity trending up over time, while defects and issues are trending down?

Quality

- Number of defects introduced in each sprint
- Number of production issues and support escalations per month
- Number of test cases passed/failed
- Number of daily issues as a result of integration

Employee morale

- Percentage of employees who are happy at work
- Percentage of employees who feel they have a good work-life balance
- Percentage of employees who take pride in the products they build
- Percentage of employees who understand the business problems they're solving

Scrum doesn't prescribe metrics. These ideas come from Lean, Extreme Programming, Customer Relationship Management, and Risk Management. Some metrics are diagnostic in nature while others represent information that we want to gather to understand long-term trends. A good ScrumMaster expands his/her skill set to pull in whatever metrics and techniques are necessary to help teams identify and fix problems. In programs with multiple teams, this is especially important. Just like helping the running team prepare for their first 10 kilometer by providing them with mileage split times, nutritional intake, and so on, coordinating multiple Scrum teams presents the challenges of ensuring that everyone has a common understanding when it comes to cross-team visibility and sharing adaptations across teams.

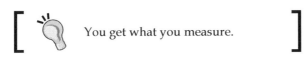

[You get what you measure.]

The greatest lever for change is awareness.

Challenge 5: Not done – the root of all evil

The handheld teams were cross-functional in that they had a tester on the team with developers. However, the teams were effectively doing waterfall inside and across sprints. In some teams, developers had a "code freeze" date toward the end of the sprint and then it was up to the testers to test the code and report defects. Naturally, defects would carry over to the next sprint, or in some cases, the testers wouldn't get to the testing at all as there was simply not enough time. In other teams, testing was an afterthought a sprint or two behind development. So what did the teams do? Did they invoke the Scrum value of commitment and finish the stories together as a team? Not quite. Because they were super-concerned with scoring points and looking good to management, they instead split the stories along the development/testing tasks. So a story would have a development sub-story and a QA sub-story. That way, if the story could not be completed to the sprint's Definition of Done, the team could take partial credit. Well, this looked good on paper, but caused a complete disaster when it came to tracking and understanding the status of the project. Trying to create the release burndown chart was like trying to put toothpaste back in a tube.

How can a team or ScrumMaster enforce the Definition of Done? Loathe as I am to point to a document (how un-Agile of me!), a good Definition of Done checklist can work wonders. Remember the lens magnifications from *Chapter 6, The Criticality of Real-time Information*? The following sample checklist clearly shows how one Definition of Done is a subset—or deeper magnification—of another. In other words, a sprint Definition of Done is at a more granular level than a release Definition of Done. In the ideal world, we try to collapse all of these containers and attempt to be Release Done at the end of every sprint, or even better, with every story; in the example of the Amsterdam company earlier in the chapter, the External Release Definition of Done was, in fact, equal to the User Story Definition of Done. No containers, no subsets. You should attempt to reduce the levels of Done through time in order to increase teams' agility. Remember: a good working Definition of Done results from ongoing discussions between the product owner and the team(s) and should evolve over time.

External Release DoD
Last Sprint of Internal Release DoD
Sprint DoD -Scrum Team
User Story DoD - Scrum team
Design, Code and Unit Test complete for the user story
Code review complete (peer coding is suitable substitute)
Code builds with zero errors and committed
Unit Integration Tests completed
Feature Test complete
Backward compatibility tests complete as applicable
Zero Outstanding severity 1-3 defects against the User Story - exceptions approved by product owner. Resolved defects verified.
Any necessary user doc for the user story is complete, reviewed and verified as applicable
User Story Accepted By Product Owner and Status Updated In [tool/whiteboard]
Automation of Unit Tests/Unit Integration Tests
Automation of Functional Acceptance Tests
Sprint User stories Accepted By Product Owner
Static Analysis Complete (Zero warnings in New Code)
Demo from integrated team branch; Retrospective Held
Regression test the user stories completed in previous sprints
Zero Outstanding s1-3 Defects Against The Sprint (regressions) - exceptions approved by PO
Update release backlog with any unfinished items (do not assign story points to unfinished work, unless a vertical story "slice" is identified)
Incremental updates to Test Plans complete, test results published to team's wiki page
Create working, installable build for new feature developed
Continuous integration is highly desirable
SDK and end user doc is complete at end of each iteration, reviewed and verified
Team branch collapse criteria need to be met as per merge readiness criteria doc
Remaining severity 1-3 defects approved by release readiness team
Release demo slides prepared for features ready for other internal teams and product approval committee
All documentation complete
Solution readiness criteria passed per document xxx and per senior product management approval
Change control created for production team; code pushed per their protocols

In the sample Definition of Done, you can see that a team needs to integrate its work with other teams in order to release the product; however, you can tell that inter-team continuous integration does not exist (late integration!) In this example, teams can run continuous integration to their own team branch for the sprint, and then all branches must be merged for a release. It's not the ideal situation, but enable inter-team continuous integration should be an item on the ScrumMasters' and the *WORST* team's impediment backlog (some teams may simply not be able to get there due to their technologies or hardware/software dependencies, and so on.) A company dedicated to continuous improvement would do its best to resolve this impediment over time.

Create a consistent Definition of Done and hold teams accountable to it.

Challenge 6: Too few product owners

The first rule of scaling is *don't*. Start small—in other words, let a small group of people build up some knowledge and then ramp up additional teams organically. That way the original team seeds knowledge to new teams as they onboard.

If your management chooses the big bang approach by kicking off multiple teams at once, ensure that you have a good product owner team in place, with designated proxies for each team. People in large Scrum programs quickly realize that there just aren't enough product owners to go around.

In the case of the handheld teams, I think we had only five product managers—for 35 teams! What were we to do? We had to find product owner proxies. Conveniently, we had an awful lot of perplexed line managers running around asking, "Oh! Now that Scrum teams are self-managing, whatever am I to do?" (cue the Macaulay Culkin face in Home Alone). Well, the line managers had vast knowledge about the various technologies with which the teams were working. In many cases, line managers made an excellent fit for product owner proxies from a technical perspective. In other cases, line managers made a terrible fit because, remember, team members were accustomed to doing whatever the boss said; coupled with weak ScrumMasters this made a bad scenario. Product owner proxies could wreak havoc on teams! And in some cases, they did! *Foie gras* with plum sauce, anyone?

Every team needs to hear the voice of the customer.

For the gadget project, product marketing already had a chief product owner team that was made up of executive product managers; the tricky part was finding subsequent area-level and Scrum team-level product owners (see following figure). This was a massive undertaking, replace with "especially in coordinating and preparing product backlog items for sprints." The most important thing we did was initiate a Product Owner Forum, where product owners came together to share experiences, address cross-team issues, review burndowns and progress, make sure they were aligned and up-to-date on customer requirements and product backlog preparation, and to get support for the most pressing issues.

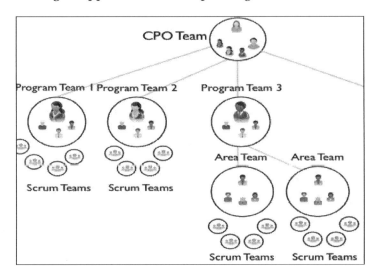

Challenge 7: Scaling too much, too fast

Don't look at a large program as simply a numbers game: "Well, we have seven man months of work, so we must need seven people to get it done in one month." Ha! I've seen this faulty logic applied in much larger scenarios—19 teams, 27 teams, 37 teams! It simply doesn't work like that. Rather, think of starting your large effort off with a Phase 1 called "Keep it Small." Recruit a team to work on a prototype, flesh out a product backlog, and estimate the effort at a high level. Have them recruit and teach others, and grow the teams organically. The user interface may be pretty simple, and only require a few people to do it, while the logic and backend systems may be quite complex.

Whatever the situation, let the original team figure out what's needed, recruit new teams, and then act as product owner proxies to those teams. That way the original knowledge is being passed along to (and allowed to evolve with) other teams over time. The small team of experts can move very quickly; seven or so people can work together much more effectively than a group of 70. As Bas Vodde and Craig Larman, authors of *Scaling Lean and Agile Development: Thinking and Organizational Tools for Large-Scale Scrum* have said: "Start with a small group of great people, and only grow when it starts to hurt. That rarely happens." If you're interested in reading more about scaling Scrum, I highly recommend that you pick up a copy of Vodde and Larman's book.

[Don't scale if you can help it. Start small, then adapt based on emergent needs.]

Challenge 8: Wrong team structure

If you find yourself or other ScrumMasters and product owners drowning in dependency management within a larger program, you may want to consider the possibility that the team structure is wrong. The original intent of a Scrum team is that it's staffed cross-functionally so that it can start and finish an item of value for the customer. If teams are organized by component, that means there will be lots of dependency management in the product backlog, as items of user value are broken down into component stories that must be tracked and whose integration must be monitored. If the program is large, I'd much rather approach combining team members from adjacent components; for example, have people who can perform data extraction, transformation, and loading all on one team to complete an ETL transaction, rather than on separate teams whose dependencies and interactions have to be managed. This results in much less overhead and management, and usually ends in a better result. If you think about it, aren't component-based Scrum teams really doing waterfall?

[Create cross-functional teams when you can. Component teams open the door for ETT resourcing.]

Challenge 9: Distributed teams

I highly suggest you check out the writings of Martin Fowler (www.martinfowler. com is a good start). He goes into great detail about distributed teams—from setup to sprint lengths to technical considerations—and I'm not going to rewrite all of that good work. What is important to remember, however, is that ScrumMasters and their teams have much tougher communication issues to solve when teams are distributed. Agile practices actually better facilitate team distribution than do other processes or frameworks. But there will be many issues for you and team members to contend with: culture and language barriers, greater chance for requirements mistranslations and defects, longer trip time for responses to questions, more difficulties in attaining high-performing team status—it's difficult to trust people you can't see and can barely understand (and that goes both ways!). There's no silver bullet for distributed teams; team members must deal with differences in time zones, language, and culture day after day, with no face-to-face time to make headway on these issues. I've included a few things to think about if you have distributed teams:

- Make all the team members' work visible to the entire team. Can you point a webcam to the physical taskboard? Should you investigate an online tool? What does the team think is the best way to go?

- Set core hours. During core hours or overlap time, see if team members can agree to use richer forms of communication, such as Skype, conference call, and the like.

- Help team members put a face with a name. Can you fly in a couple of remote team members to work with the onsite folks for a week or two? Would team members be willing to put a picture on the wiki, or in their profile?

- Encourage good communication skills. Can you hold communication workshops with team members to help them through some of the most common communication obstacles?

- Keep sprints short. If team members get off track, other team members will likely catch it in a daily scrum; worst case, the team catch it at the end of the sprint. If the sprint is short then the team won't get too far off track.

- Is the team able to know the impact to the system when one developer checks in code? If your team do not continuously integrate work and does not have test automation, this may be something you want to look into immediately.

Face to face is the most effective way for people to work together. Expect higher communication costs when team members are spread across the world.

A real need for a project Grand Poobah

Yes, I'll say it, in a book for the whole world to see: in a large program, with matrix organization, there may be a need for skills that we might dub project coordination. Imagine a program of 300 plus people. replace with "Who is responsible to facilitate the creation of teams?" For organizing teams cross-functionally? Who is responsible for communicating with vendors to plan and track deliverables? Who works with HR and finance to budget for and procure resources? Who facilitates the Scrum of Scrums meeting? In other words, when the group is larger than three teams, someone should be in charge of keeping all the dogs pulling the sled in the same direction. Not responsible for the product's success in the market (I believe that responsibility lies with the product owner no matter the size of the program) but responsible for coordination, for getting the whole thing rolling to some cadence, some sort of schedule, and promoting and allowing for change while helping teams carry out a vision.

There are some other books/articles out there that say that this is the role of the product owner, too, yet I cannot imagine how a product owner can do all the day to day responsibilities and also coordinate a program of super scale. I've just been in the thick of it too often to think that one person can do it all. A project manager who has an Agile mind-set can be a huge asset to a large program.

A good project manager can help facilitate communication at all levels. He/she can take information from all the Scrum teams and present this information so that it facilitates good communication between executives and other stakeholders, as well as suppliers and downstream dependent groups. A good project manager can get the status of the Agile program without creating a detailed project plan, without bugging people day to day, or without managing a work breakdown structure and having team members enter actuals into a timesheet. A good agile project manager knows how to work with the ScrumMasters to understand the release plan and objectives, velocity, and the unfolding of the release plan sprint after sprint.

The following table is a simple status mechanism that an Agile project manager can easily pull together by working with the ScrumMasters of the teams. In the gadget team program, the program manager held a weekly status meeting with ScrumMasters and senior stakeholders. It was only 30 minutes long, and all the red and yellow teams went first. That way if they ran out of time, they at least discussed and addressed all the risky issues first.

Team	Status	Impediments/Action Item
A	RED	Team ran into trouble with the reset feature; 5 stories had to be dropped; impacts release plan
B	GREEN	All stories appear to be on time.
C	GREEN	Team is slightly ahead. They will see if they can help out Team A.
D	YELLOW	Team slightly behind. May have to drop a story; they have alerted the product owner.
E	YELLOW	Same as above.
F	GREEN	Team appears to be meeting commitments.
G	GREEN	Team is way ahead; will see if they can help out Team A also.

People can get in their own way. Instead of organizing projects for success, with motivated people, many management groups think of projects as mere number games. I mean, they are numbers games, and they're also so much more than that. Every project holds the potential for innovation. Large Scrum programs can be made less complex by starting small, and then creating cross-functional teams as needed that manage their own dependencies. Scrum of Scrums meetings should be comprised of technical team members who solve problems and who employ infrastructure and policies built for flexibility and the delivery of high-quality, integrated product in every single iteration. Teams should be involved in planning so that the business problem is understood and that a good plan can be formulated. And if the program is risky, or especially time-sensitive, by George, bring people together to work at least in the same time zone! If the project is late and you've missed the market opportunity due to the financial savings of outsourcing, well, you didn't really save that much by outsourcing after all, did you?

It's almost as if when people have a large initiative they automatically put on their Frederick Taylor beanies and start planning away. Note that I said I support a project manager/Grand Poobah in a matrix organization. What if the organization isn't matrix? Well, that's the next chapter!

More tips for large Scrums

- Initiate a Scrum Master Forum to focus on resolving cross team issues and finding new ways to help teams be their best

- Meet with development and test managers to discuss implications of Agile on their roles, have a candid discussion around expectations for managers, and work toward alignment of vision

- Start up and/or facilitate a *WORST* team to ensure that teams' most critical roadblocks are removed

- Continue to gather feedback from Scrum teams to ensure awareness of and resolution of the most difficult technical implementation and quality assurance issues

Agile DNA

I believe that the biggest issue with many traditional organizations seeking to use Scrum on programs big or small is that they want to do Scrum or transition to Scrum—the emphasis mistakenly on doing Agile instead of being Agile. Big difference. While Toyota invites its competitors to learn the **Toyota Production System (TPS)**, TPS is not really in the other car manufacturers' DNA. That is, they can learn the practices, how to do Kanban, kaizen, and so on, but if continuous improvement and human first/product second mind-sets are not in the mix, they won't be as successful. The same for agile. Two companies can do exactly the same Agile practices, but the one that gets the mind-set and the values will be more successful.

Likewise, if we look at the most successful tech companies as of the writing of this book—Apple, Google, Adobe, and others—they are regularly cited by employees as having collaborative environments, small teams, work-life balance, open environments, and the like. In fact, Apple is known to be relatively flat in management and operates like a collection of startups, rather than a big company. So are these companies Agile or not? Well, yes, even though they may not be using Agile! What?

You see, the difference in the traditional waterfall enterprise and the Apples of the world is that the traditional enterprise is trying to use Agile to get more with less, with better quality, and faster, and other such buzz phrases! Whereas, Apple simply embodies an Agile spirit: it may not call it Agile, may not use sprints or the like but it is Agile in mind-set, delivering fast, flexibly, and with focus! And it just so happens that companies with these mind-sets and attitudes toward development are incredibly successful. In a recent article citing the best places to work in 2012, employees of top companies shared the same comments that indicate the values that underlie their respective companies:

- From **LinkedIn**: "Big ideas are welcome, and it's easy to get leadership support for projects/ideas."

- From **Facebook**: "[I like] the ability to take an idea and turn it into a reality without the need for level after level of approval."

- From **Guidewire**: "The company truly values all contributors."

I can tell you that of the traditional enterprises that I've helped transition to Scrum, *NONE* had these mind-sets. They were (and are) very much the command and control, competitive culture. We'll discuss this at length in *Chapter 11, Scrum and the Future*, but I believe the relevance here is that an organization must attempt to create and preserve an Agile mind-set—not just practices—in its projects. This is increasingly difficult the more teams and projects an organization has.

Summary

Scrum has been used in implementations small and large, in just about every corner of the earth with just about every technology! It is simple enough to start today, yet humans can greatly complicate things. Sometimes teams can be too small; look at ways of grouping people so that five different projects aren't competing for the same resources, causing people to multitask and to lose precious productive hours as a result.

When scaling Scrum, start small if you can, and grow teams as needed. Regardless of the number of teams, focus on creating an environment in which people thrive and get things done. The resulting team motivation will help people outperform any other way of management. Recruit an Agile project coordinator in the largest of programs to help keep everything moving and everyone on the same page. In *Chapter 11, Scrum and the Future*, we will discuss how Scrum will change the organization and operation modes of businesses in the future.

Recommended reading

- Jeffries, Ron. Anderson, Ann and Hendrickson, Chet. *Extreme Programming Installed.* 2000, Addison Wesley.

- Vodde, Bas and Larman, Craig. *Scaling Lean and Agile Development: Thinking and Organizational Tools for Large-Scale Scrum.* 2009, Pearson Education.

11
Scrum and the Future

Imagine showing up to work whenever you felt like it. You know what to work on because you signed up for the project. Your day-to-day work results from brainstorming sessions with your team, and you work hard to accomplish great things together. You feel proud of your work; you understand how that work contributes to the company's mission. You work your hardest but you have a life outside of work. You understand the market and how it moves. And yet you are free—if you hear of another cool initiative from your friends at lunch, you are free to join it. Anytime! Your colleagues work with you in the same building. Everyone on a team sits next to each other. When you move to a different team, someone moves all your stuff overnight and rebuilds your workstation in that new team's area. You don't have to think about it. In some cases, you have no CEO. In these cases, everyone works together and shares the wealth. A back-office staff pays the bills, keeps the books, and so on. You're reliable, you generate smart ideas, you innovate, and of course you work hard. You are not a cog in the wheel; rather, the company values you for your talents and smarts that you bring to the table. You are free to observe other teams and learn from them. Performance is measured in terms of how the company is doing. You are not micromanaged to these crazy performance reviews that you heard so much about from the past. You cannot imagine being constrained in such a way.

After bogging through the swamps of organizational change, fraught with bottomless pits of mud (career ladders), lurking alligators (politics), and water moccasins (angry managers), I'd like nothing more than to see the organization and management of companies change to something like I've described previously. No longer solely focused on cutting costs every quarter to keep the shareholders happy, but companies whose people react quickly, together, aligned in vision and purpose. I believe there is no greater thrill than knowing that the actions you take today will have a big impact on others at some point in the future.

You see, Ken and Jeff had a vision much greater than that of this little empirical process called Scrum. I believe that they are the craftsmen of this new era of knowledge work. Maybe they didn't know it at the time. Or, perhaps it was their little secret—this "ta-da" moment of which we can all begin to glimpse on the horizon. While Scrum is about transparency, the interesting thing is that there is a surprise after all. This new era, the new organization, is the best surprise, the best gift of all. Who could have possibly seen that coming 10 years ago? Even five years ago? While Drucker, Deming, Pinchot, and others had some wonderful ideas, ideas that are valid, I believe that Ken and Jeff brought a tangible process to the world that realized these ideas. Ken and Jeff provided a gateway. Only now are we realizing the tremendous possibilities; and I think it'll be another 10 to 20 years before it's fully realized, but that's fine. It will happen.

We've discussed coaching, facilitation, and psychological tips and tricks so far. Things you should be aware of in your current use of Scrum. But where can Scrum take us in future organizations? It's fun, thinking of the possibilities, and what's even more fun is that we're starting to see a glimpse of this future in companies right now, today.

In this chapter, we'll look at what's possible. It's a theoretical glimpse of what we're beginning to see in practice. We'll do this by cutting out part of the Agile Manifesto; stripping it down to its leanest. We'll look at the organization through the Scrum lens; through the principles and values that it espouses. We'll also look at the importance of a prioritized list of work, as well as space for discovery and innovation. Regular demos are critical for inspecting and adapting, and we'll discuss how this complements the modern organization. Finally, we'll look at the modern Scrum organization structure, roles, and ideals.

A leaner Agile Manifesto

Here's the Agile Manifesto, again—the statement that started the Agile movement back in 2001:

Individuals and interactions ~~over process and tools~~
Working software ~~over comprehensive documentation~~
Customer collaboration ~~over contract negotiation~~
Responding to change ~~over following a plan~~
~~That is, while there is value in the items on the right, we value the items on the left more.~~

Notice that I've struck the items on the right, and the final value statement. Now it becomes a mantra.

I believe we can drop the stuff on the right, along with its final statement. Forget it—we're moving past that now. Focus on people, great products, the customer, and change. The other stuff will bog down the organization and corrupt people's mind-set. The items on the right are mainstays of the 80s and 90s—process was led by those ideas. Well, those decades are long gone. Even though the emphasis is this over that, even mentioning the *that* keeps it fresh in our minds. Know that process, tools, documents, and contracts will live in the background—they're back office and business essential; however, they should *NOT* dictate the way that a creative process happens in your organization. In fact, that's quite the oxymoron. Time to move on. Let's leave these stale items in the past and think about our work and engagement with other humans in the day-to-day work of projects.

Redefining the role of the organization

As I'm writing this chapter, we're a few weeks from a big presidential election. On the right, we have a conservative who believes in the spirit of the individual—capitalism, American dream, and small, limited government. On the left, we have a liberal who believes in redistributing wealth—that everyone deserves a fair share, even if that means taking from others. It's an extreme example of the battle of small or large government, to put it simply. I lean toward keeping government small. It should come as no surprise, then, that I feel the same way about management in organizations.

The knowledge worker has his talents and skills inside his brain. He takes his brain with him from job to job, from employer to employer. He wants to know that he contributes and that his team and his organization value him. He does his best work when he's surrounded by smart people who challenge him. He wants to be left alone at times in order to focus, yet needs interaction with others to brainstorm and create.

I believe that the role of the organization is to facilitate people working together to achieve something greater than what just one person can do. Like the conservative approach in state governments, organizational 'governance' should not be trickle-down; rather, it should exist merely to enable workers and teams of workers, provide infrastructure, and other basic needs. It should merely provide a space—and sometimes a vision—in which and through which all work happens.

Gifford Pinchot coined the term **intrapreneurs** in the 1980s to describe teams that work for a company to carry out the company's vision, yet they manage everything else about how that work gets done. Traditional organizations rely on big management to create, assign, manage, and report on tasks. The intrapreneur does this for himself. Newer organizations have increasingly conservative management styles that echo Pinchot's ideas. When I travel to Silicon Valley, I always catch the buzz about which company is the one to work for. Lately it's been **Google**, **Apple**, **Facebook**, **Instagram**, **LinkedIn**. Just the mention of these companies in casual conversations causes eyes to light up and lots of flurry in discussion. People are excited by exciting products and autonomy of work!

Self-managing teams – the inmates run the asylum!

Scrum can help us realize not just the self-organizing team, but teams that self-manage. What's the difference? Self-organization is the way a team responds to a goal and a time-box. It's reflected in the way that team members agree to work together, how they handle things such as documentation, testing, and any artifact that they need to create during a sprint. Self-organizing team members come up with their own work tasks and then choose the work they'd like to work on.

Self-managing teams take it a step further. They make their performance and results visible. They are responsible to make innovative, creative decisions. They give each other critical feedback and thrive in openness. They are responsible for their own professional development and for their own learning. Quality is never an issue—they consider themselves craftsmen of fine quality work. I've worked at a couple of companies in which employees set their own goals. In one such company the executives asked for people to set goals that were so high that they'd probably not reach all of them; the point was *reach for the stars*. The teams weren't rewarded for meeting all of their goals; they were rewarded on how happy the products made the customers. Goals were a means to an end. Sometimes the end couldn't be defined in advance; it emerged.

An unhealthy patient is a good analogy of this idea. A self-organizing patient takes orders—takes two pills and calls the doctor in the morning. A self-managing patient challenges the doctor and becomes a willing participant, researcher, and experimenter in his own health.

A self-managed team is made up of self-managed workers. This means that in the modern organization, self-managing workers take charge of their career paths, their work, learning, getting feedback, and helping others. They answer to a higher calling—creatively solving problems to fulfill the needs of the customer. Ideas can come from all levels, not just from the creative or marketing person. As organizations are complex, success cannot be attributed to one person's contributions. Rather, it's the amalgamation of lots of people, their ideas, feedback, and so on, that spells success. Success, then, and the reward for it, must be measured at a higher level. I believe that the balanced scorecard in *Chapter 10, Scrum – Large and Small*, is one such way of measurement.

Career paths

What about the traditional career path, then? As far as I'm concerned, advancement and promotion carry over from Tayloristic thinking—that is, if I'm good enough I can be a manager and I'll get more pay and have less work and get to tell others what to do. While I think that advancement should still have a place in knowledge workers' lives, I think it should happen differently. People should select their leaders as leadership emerges. A leader's job is to challenge, teach, and support others. I believe this happens organically in organizations already. That is, even though Howard is the manager, the team really respects Andrew because he's super-smart and super-laid-back about things. The team secretly despises Howard. In our modern organization, Lisa might step up as a leader on one project because she knows a lot about or is very passionate about the subject, but in the next project, Carl steps up because he feels finally ready to do so. Career advancement would happen based on the employee's motivation and inspiration. Or could one simply say, "I'm ready to be a team lead now; therefore, I am!" What about pay increases? Well, let the team decide!

Since the organization would carry out projects in which people are motivated to work, leadership would more readily advance. Leadership would be a skill for one to develop, not a title to achieve. Since people in this scenario would thus be rewarded by the happiness of the customer, the success of the business, and so on, is advancement vis-à-vis a role or title necessary any longer? In other words, is having the title of "manager" only enticing because that's been the reward structure to date? Give people different stars to shoot for and they'll change direction.

In our modern organization, workers manage themselves. They work on projects in which they're interested. They can freely move to other projects without having to get the boss to allow them, while they may need the new team's OK on the matter. A list is posted in the corridor, or on a wiki/intranet that lists all the initiatives various teams have going so that anyone at any time can change teams. Everything is visible, all of the time.

The main purpose of our modern management team, then, is to create a vision and set a strategy. Teams can then self-organize around the vision, and workers self-manage every aspect of their work. They make their work and progress visible so that company executives may make good decisions around release dates, marketing, partnerships, and so on. There is no interference by executives into how the work gets done. Teams make commitments for themselves. It's up to the team if they'd like to appoint a representative team member to interface with the executives.

I guess it boils down to this question: if I'm doing what I love, working with interesting people on challenging projects, and making good money, then do I really need a career path? Can't I show—should I ever have to search for a job—that I performed management and leadership functions, even if I didn't have the exact title?

True visibility

In our modern organization, forced by the degree of openness that Scrum values, everything is out in the open—profits, losses, bonuses, salaries, budgets, performance, and the like. This exposure of the truth sets everyone free. Politics are squelched. There are no secrets.

The courage that results from this openness enables an organization. Fear and distrust of management hinders performance. Without visibility, trust cannot exist. Without trust, an organization and its teams cannot achieve full potential. It becomes paralyzed, limb by limb. An organization that is fearless has at least the possibility of becoming high performing.

Transparency enables agility. Change becomes welcomed, expected, and something to look forward to, rather than something that inspires fear and loathing in teams that have been burned many times before.

Capacity, not projects

In the modern organization, people think of demand and capacity. There is a list of things to do, try, or research or explore. Sometimes there's an idea that just needs some experimentation. Regardless of the nature of the work, teams have a certain capacity—a pace of work that they can sustain and that the business can rely on. Projects in our modern organization are not really projects any longer—rather, they become a continuous balancing act of supply and demand. This moving away from a project mind-set into a capacity mind-set is something that Mary Poppendieck stated very eloquently: "A predictable organization does not guess about the future and call it a plan; it develops the capacity to rapidly respond to the future as it unfolds." The outcome of this just-in-time mind-set, coupled with self-managing workers and teams, is an exciting future to consider!

The CEO of Me

I believe that Gifford Pinchot's **The Intrapreneur's Ten Commandments** succinctly and accurately sum up the modern knowledge worker's self-managing responsibilities (`http://www.pinchot.com/`):

1. Come to work each day willing to be fired.

2. Circumvent any orders aimed at stopping your dream.

3. Do any job needed to make your project work, regardless of your job description.

4. Find people to help you.

5. Follow your intuition about the people you choose, and work only with the best.

6. Work underground as long as you can — publicity triggers the corporate immune system.

7. Never bet on a race unless you are running in it.

8. Remember, it is easier to ask for forgiveness than for permission.

9. Be true to your goals, but be realistic about the ways to achieve them.

10. Honor your sponsors.

How does a ScrumMaster help create the self-managed knowledge worker? By helping each person live by those 10 commandments; by standing ground and upholding the five Scrum values. The moment a ScrumMaster relents — people and organization revert to form. They go back to what's been comfortable. Problem is, what was comfortable will not allow for the maximum flexibility and fast response that these modern times require.

> *Knowledge work requires a high level of freedom, trust and responsibility ... an informed, ethical and willing population that believes in the system they are part of.*
>
> — *Gifford Pinchot*

Customer collaboration via prioritized product backlog

I've seen product backlogs do wonders for dysfunctional companies. At the very least, it gets all the work into one list that all product owners and managers can review together. It requires people to be up front about the work in progress and ideas for future work. Nothing is hidden any longer, and that visibility alone can be a changing force in an organization in which it was difficult to *see* anything at all.

While at one level, I think it's important for a company to have a list of projects, and within each of those projects a backlog of work to be done. A modern organization knows the importance of allowing blank spaces in its product backlog. What do I mean by this?

Don't squeeze innovation out of the product backlog

Many organizations focus so much on product backlog creation that they miss the opportunity to collaborate, to invent, to innovate. Many teams unfortunately end up taking all of their orders—including technical 'how' orders—from product management. Of the myriad reasons for this, most boil down to lack of management support or lack of team knowledge of 'how to' become innovative. This is wrong, and dangerous to a business.

How modern organizations make space for innovation

An innovation results from the creative process, and often as the result of creative collaboration. The result is a new product, service, or idea—sometimes immediately recognizable as valuable, other times tossed to the side as interesting but not worth the pursuit for now. Sometimes an innovation is an idea that's been vetted; a product backlog is created from that idea which encapsulates steps that will realize the innovation and give it life. For many important reasons such as ROI, a new thing—an innovation—must create value if the business will invest in it. However, for a myriad of reasons, many good ideas don't get to the table. Why is this? Well, the difficulty that a business faces is that many ideas require additional investmentto explore and test the idea. This is risky. This means that as a business owner, I may pour some dollars into an idea that may not make it. It's a gamble because that one thing I decide isn't worth the risk is actually worth every bit of the risk; it could change my business in positive ways. An innovation breaks with the past, takes us into new territory, and we won't know about that new territory until we've landed there.

There are two types of innovations—sustaining and disruptive (Bower, Joseph L., and Christensen, Clayton. (1995) *Disruptive Technologies: Catching the Wave* Harvard Business Review, Jan-Feb 1995). Adding new ringtones to a mobile phone is a sustaining innovation as it provides more value (personalization) for mobile phone users. The iPhone, on the other hand, was a disruptive innovation for a couple of important reasons. Firstly, the iPhone was the result of Steve Jobs taking over control of its design from the carrier; until then phones were designed by a committee often driven by the carrier, not the vendor.

Additionally, the iPhone gave us the touchscreen that has forever changed the way humans interact with devices. There are several other disruptive and sustaining innovations provided by the iPhone; if Steve Jobs had said to his team, "Here's a list of features on a product backlog; go build it," the iPhone might never have been born (or at least as we know it). In other words, Jobs had a vision, a *BIG* idea that would change the landscape, and did not back off. I'm sure that many of his ideas could not be expressed in a product backlog; they emerged as the result of collaboration, and trial and error, toward the bigger goal. In other words, if we try to perfect the writing and preparation of our user stories, we might miss out. There is a thin line between preparation and devaluation. Over-preparedness of product backlog items could squeeze out ideas for ways to do them better. Yet, consistent under-preparedness could yield chaos. Yes, this is a gamble, Yes, this is a gamble, and a balancing act, and no, there is no perfect solution. no, there is no perfect solution.

The crux is that a business wants confidence in that what teams work on will provide value, or ROI. A business wants to associate a profit, contract, and dollar amount with each team's expended effort so that it may justify the effort. Businesses like certainty. Problem is, if an outcome is truly new, the business can't yet value it very well, so the marketing department must guess a lot and customers simply won't know in advance that they'll like something they haven't yet seen. Yet delivering the unseen—the mystery, the surprise—is innovation. And innovation is absolutely business-critical in this age of viral **YouTube** videos and 3D printing—new markets and gadgets are produced every day!

Accommodating this reality of modern technology and markets takes a huge conceptual leap for the traditionally-minded business—it changes the way work is conjured up, carried out, and outcomes measured. Many times, new business-transforming ideas are discredited as weird (the idea was from that developer!), rejected as not within current portfolio budgets or strategic plans, or, worst case, ignored altogether or never bubbles up! The unknown nature of an innovation's value means that traditional ways of making a thing, service, or idea need rethinking; a business must allow for exploration of better ways of creating the thing, and that can itself translate into innovations in internal process. For example, a team realizes that its product's quality is a differentiator in the market; therefore, the team introduces new tools and quality standards for itself each sprint. The innovation here is an astute internal quality process as well as a response to the market's finicky tastes. Something new requires new ways of making, new attitudes toward making, and new ways to enable makers. Beyond that we can say only two things for sure. First, if we truly collaborate, we will make something new. Secondly, we can't immediately tell if the new thing will have value right away, in the future, or ever. So the modern organization needs to have an inborn attitude of acceptance and comfort for the ambiguities and iterative nature of creativity and discovery.

The creative culture

To innovate effectively, we need to learn how to create and operate in a new environment: let's call it a **creative culture**. To help us think about such a culture, I propose a set of considerations to help management and leadership think creatively and respond productively to the creative thinking of each other. The first step to realizing innovations is to accept that there is no such thing as failure in an innovative process. The only failure is not being receptive to new ideas.

Management can help innovations bubble up to the top by seeking, identifying, and budgeting space in which they may happen. Here are some opportunities within an Agile framework that management can leverage in order to set the creative stage:

- **Work ethic**: Does your company call a person working 20 hours overtime per week a hero? Do you get a bonus because you put in lots of extra time on a project to bring it in on time? If you're caught twiddling your thumbs or surfing the Internet, are you considered a slacker? If your organization's attitude is to increase team and individual velocity–that is, do more product backlog items each and every sprint—it's doubtful that teams find the time to be creative. The modern organization values creativity and discovery just as much as completing bona-fide product backlog items or tasks. The modern organization realizes that slack time or downtime is an absolute essential for creative thinking and sometimes, innovation. In fact, a study by the **University of Singapore** showed that employees who have freedom to surf the Internet at work are more productive (`http://www.pcmag.com/article2/0,2817,2391622,00.asp`). What does this mean for management? Allow slack time. Don't expect that every task is accounted for and that every hour results in 60 minutes of writing code. In fact, realize that a human's time at the water cooler, a visit to big-map-blog, or other seemingly "nonsensical" activities could actually yield a new idea beneficial to business. Stress the word "could"—yes, it is a gamble, but would you rather gamble on mentally fresh workers bringing their very best to work every day or maximum hours worked?

- **Research and development**: So many developers long to be one of the chosen few for the research and development team. Why is it that companies consider research and development—really, innovation work—as reserved for the special few? Modern businesses should recognize that innovation knows no limits or boundaries; empower and enourage everyone to think creatively. Provide a place to capture random ideas; call it the *Innovation Backlog*, or just allow any employee to add an idea to the product backlog. Give employees the chance to make business cases; this is not only a great way to discover innovations but also helps develop a well-rounded technical employee by building his sense for business. Encourage creative thinking even in the mundane, planned backlog items; I consistently observe higher energy in teams that work on the new technology, the new widget, or gadget. This is because there is a level of research and development involved here, and the entire team contributes, shares discoveries, and builds on those discoveries. As we discussed in previous chapters, people who perceive that they're solving problems in a new way tend to be happier. Happier people produce better products. Allow every worker to engage in research and development; innovation will result.

- **Iteration planning and execution**: Agile teams plan for and commit to a reasonable amount of work from the product backlog each sprint. By doing so in a prioritized fashion, this ensures that the iteration is stuffed with work that the customer has pre-defined as highest value. While this is a great way to execute projects, be careful of looming deadlines that squeeze out or inhibit fresh thinking. Allow each team to reserve a percentage of their time for true creative and discovery work, to dream up new ideas, or chase ideas from the *Innovation Backlog*. This is similar to Google's 20 percent allowance in which every employee gets a day per week to innovate. Additionally, modern organizations coach their people to inspire creative approaches even in the mundane predetermined work.

- **Day-to-day interaction**: Do team members have time for pairing? Or does the company see this as a waste? Does the ETT style of resourcing exist, in which the expert resource sticks to his/her area of expertise and specialization in order to move faster? Modern organizations pooh-pooh the notion of 100 percent efficiency; rather, they encourage everyone to get involved and share expertise. Individuals learn more in the long run giving the organization more flexibility and innovation. Check out Tom Demarco's *Slack* for amazing ideas about this concept.

- **Funding innovation**: Modern organizations can balance structure and risk by adopting a venture capital model to fund innovation. The funding board can invest in a new idea, making time and money available for development. As the work proceeds, the board can establish benchmarks; when they're met, and the idea still has legs, it can invest more resources. Think about how excited your developers would be to present a case to the innovation board and gain time to work on their new idea; it would be the software development equivalent of Shark Tank. Developers would show incremental progress and continued validation of the idea - how they've spend their awarded innovation time. Such a construct would send a strong message to everyone that *this management team values creative thinking*.

- **Hiring talent**: Instead of asking a potential hire, "What certifications and degrees do you have?" ask, "What's the most creative use of technology that you've implemented?" Modern organizations get a sense for the person's ability to think in creative ways, to chase ideas past reasonable limits. Modern organizations ask, "Can you feel a passion and excitement for making new things, or is this simply a job that your college advisor told you pays well? Help us understand what new ideas you can bring to the table." Think beyond the certification, degree, or other seemingly important piece of paper to creative talent and fresh thinking. "It's important for the entire company to be innovative, and not just (one group) designated a 'Department of Innovation.'" (http://www.huffingtonpost.com/robert-f-brands/innovation-training-coaching_b_1835869.html).

- **Creative contracts**: Customers need to be educated about the need for the technical team's experimentation. Remind them that creativity can take calendar time. Will your customers go to the cheapest bid or to the company/team that can produce unusual (and unusually useful) results? How can your company use an emphasis on creativity and collaboration as a market differentiator; how can you turn this intangible into something that clients want to pay for? Remember, the modern Agile Manifesto is about customer collaboration, so do that!

- **Categorize initiatives**: Put current initiatives into the following buckets: *Run the business*, *Grow the business*, and *Transform the business*. How do your initiatives stack up? Modern organizations allow at least 25 percent for research in the Transform category. Here's why: not every innovation is *THE* innovation, so we need to allow for more iteration, more discovery, and sometimes a wholesale change of mind. One example is Ronald Mannaks' Ninja Master toy that, through creative thinking, iteration, and inviting children in to share their ideas, morphed into an air drum (read his story here: `http://newsle.com/article/0/5560736/`). In six months' time, Mannak and his team created eight iterations of the product, testing and confirming (and discarding) many hypotheses along the way by getting real feedback from real users. Had they not been able to re-categorize and re-conceive the initiative altogether, the Ninja Master would have never morphed into V-Beat Drumsticks (`http://newsle.com/article/0/5560736/`).

Regular product reviews or demos

Modern organizations embrace iterations as experiments—after all, that's what they are. They apply the scientific method of building a hypothesis and an approach to the solution (iteration planning), testing it out (iteration work), and concluding with "Was it right?" or "Was it wrong?" (iteration acceptance).

Each iteration for each of your teams holds within it some new discovery. The modern organization properly sets the stage so that teams can chase ideas. The organization also provides a mechanism for discoveries to percolate through the organizational froth. Modern organizations view their people—and their brains—as their number one asset! Modern organizations provide mechanisms for new ideas to surface and provide space for those ideas to be chased. By doing so, these modern organizations are successful not by cutting costs every quarter to increase the stock price, but by bringing cool products and releases to market to entice customers. Some of these organizations have a cult-like following!

We are all ScrumMasters

In the modern organization, we *all* become ScrumMasters—keepers of lean thinking, craftsmen of fine products, liaison to customers. As a ScrumMaster, make your organization the very best it can be, and don't stop trying until you know in your heart that you've done all that you could. You are a change agent, after all, the way Ken and Jeff intended.

Peter Drucker stated this idea so eloquently so long ago, and I consider it a fine way to end this book. I hope you have found some inspiration as you work your way toward becoming a Professional ScrumMaster:

> *Once the individual understands the system of profound knowledge, he will apply its principles in every kind of relationship with other people. He will have a basis for judgment of his own decisions and for transformation of the organizations that he belongs to. The individual, once transformed, will:*
>
> *Set an example;*
>
> *Be a good listener, but will not compromise;*
>
> *Continually teach other people; and*
>
> *Help people to pull away from their current practices and beliefs and move into the new philosophy without a feeling of guilt about the past.*

Carry on, Scrum Maestro!

The ScrumMaster's Responsibilities

Most of the Scrum literature only scratches the surface when it comes to the responsibilities of this role. This appendix will expand the role definitions so that you fully understand your responsibilities as a professional ScrumMaster; it may also help in hiring or career path development situations.

The ScrumMaster's role

As ScrumMaster you must have a deep understanding of the Scrum framework. Your job is to help the customer and team work very closely together so that the team completes the customer's most important requests first; incremental features allow the customer to give feedback and thus shape the product with the team's help. You facilitate the team members to reflect upon ways that they can improve their day-to-day communications and processes—and you inspire them to take appropriate actions. You help customers organize their thoughts about features and importance based upon the functionality demonstrated at the end of every sprint. Ultimately, by supporting team members who can self-manage and be empowered to make decisions for themselves, you are creating an environment in which people and creativity will flourish. Finally, through an unrelenting focus on and effort toward improvement, you help the organization at large find ways of stopping activities that are wasteful in order to put more resources on value-added activities.

Core knowledge

The ScrumMaster understands the Scrum foundational concepts. In other words, you can easily vocalize why certain game rules exist to those who may struggle with Scrum:

- Ralph Stacey's diagram and further thoughts on human behavioral dynamics and organizations as complex adaptive systems

- Takeuchi and Nonaka's *The New New Product Development Game* (Harvard Business Review, January 1986)

- Ken Schwaber and Mike Beedle's *Agile Software Development with Scrum* (Prentice Hall, 2001)

- Jeff Sutherland's contributions toward Scrum and organizational success (various blog and White Paper Publications — see `http://scrum.jeffsutherland.com/`)

- Difference in scientific management and self-management (various sources; read up on Frederick Winslow Taylor and contrast with Peter Drucker's knowledge worker)

- The myth of *multi-tasking* and its impact on human productivity (one of my favorite sources is *Slack* by Tom DeMarco (Crown Business, 2002)

- Team dynamics, Tuckman's stages (see `http://en.wikipedia.org/wiki/Forming-storming-norming-performing` as a start)

- Social psychology frameworks such as Maslow's hierarchy of needs, Mayo

- Lean systems thinking by Toyota Production System: Beyond Large Scale Production, Taiichi Ohno, Productivity Press, 1988 and Mary Poppendieck's *Leading Lean Software Development* (Addison-Wesley Professional, 2009)

Responsibilities

From running the sprint to helping the product owner to working obstacles, a ScrumMaster's responsibilities are varied and numerous. As discussed earlier in the book, your duties can sometimes be overwhelming and can feel like it's more than what one person can do.

Running the sprint

As ScrumMaster, running the sprint will feel like the mechanical set of things to do; in fact, I consider this the *easy* list. Keep in mind that it is through short cycle times with focus on delivering value that the team discovers everything that gets in the way of delivering value. Running the sprint will inevitably surface obstacles—from the exciting to the mundane—that you will have to remove with unrelenting courage and tenacity. Remember that the ScrumMaster shepherds the Scrum process in order to provide visibility into the resulting *potentially shippable product increment* at the end of every sprint; in doing so, the team and product owner achieve the ability to inspect and adapt both product and process. While seemingly simple to do, the sprint's yield is the critical input to improvement; that is, the resulting set of features shown at the sprint review is not only the end state of that sprint, but also the input into the next.

In running the sprint the ScrumMaster:

- Schedules the scrum meetings and invites appropriate stakeholders:
    - Proactively identifies people who might be interested in the sprint's outcome.
    - Sends invitations via calendar or other means well ahead of time, so that interested persons may elect to attend.
    - Realizes that some flexibility may be in order. If the product owner, for example, is traveling abroad and cannot attend the sprint review, the ScrumMaster may decide with the team to push the meeting out by a day or engage the product owner throughout the sprint to accept features as they are ready.
- Helps the team deliver high-quality features by facilitating actions toward improved communication, a focus on quality, updated tools, and creative practices
- Works with the team and product owner so that they are prepared for sprint planning
- Handles logistics for meetings (meeting rooms, food, supplies, and so on)
- Follows up on parking lot and action items after meetings; works to improve facilitation for next time
- Establishes common goals for meetings and encourages participatory decision making and team consensus
- Removes obstacles that prevent the team from achieving their sprint goals

Assisting the product owner

The ScrumMaster knows that the product owner's team participation and preparation of the product backlog will contribute to team success. Thus, the ScrumMaster:

- Ensures that the product owner is maintaining the product backlog—knows where to keep it, the appropriate frequency, and depth of updates

- Helps the product owner write product backlog items and acceptance criteria if needed (that is, holds a story-writing workshop for product owners to learn the user story format)

- Reminds the product owner of the value of grooming sessions and offers to schedule and facilitate these discussions

- At any chance, brings the product owner together to directly discuss implementation issues and ideas with the team; refuses to be the *go-between* between the product owner and team members at all costs

- Influences the product owner to test/accept the team's sprint features as soon as they're complete, not waiting until the end of the sprint to see new functionality

- Includes the product owner in all Scrum meetings

- Asks that the product owner share important business collateral with the team (product vision, roadmaps, and so on) and assists the product owner in preparation if needed

- Encourages a visible product backlog to which everyone may contribute

- Reminds the product owner to prepare the backlog for the next sprint cycle (decompose backlog items, write acceptance criteria, get estimate from the team if needed)

- Regularly checks in and offers assistance to the product owner

Creating a high-performing Scrum team

A ScrumMaster knows that a high-performing Scrum team will create products that customers love. In order to create such a team, the ScrumMaster:

- Removes obstacles, and then encourages team members to remove their own obstacles

- Blocks and handles interruption from any source, protecting the team members from the distraction

- Protects the team construct: cross-functional, dedicated, empowered team

- Does not allow team members to be *taken* from the team

- Recruits missing skill members for the team upon the team's advice (or enables and encourages existing team members to learn new skills)
- Helps them discover new ways of working (for example, helps the team adopt Extreme Programming practices)
- Encourages investigation into tools and infrastructure that supports the lean concept of *building quality in*
- Supports pairing and learning within the team
- Supports learning across teams; challenges the organization to build in learning opportunities for teams
- Educates team members on the benefits of test-first mind-set
- Empowers team members; encourages risk-taking; delegates
- Inspires the team to realize greater potential
- Applies adaptive leadership styles appropriately
- Utilizes open, collaborative, and honest communication style
- Allows the team to self-organize whenever possible, eventually leading to team self-management
- Helps the team develop good problem-solving skills
- Displays a positive, trusting attitude
- Helps the team plan realistically
- Encourages shared roles and responsibilities toward an over-arching team goal; makes such goals visible
- Helps the team to increase efficiency and reduce time spent in meetings—get in, get out

Making progress visible

A ScrumMaster needs to perform the following tasks to make the progress visible:

- Work with the team so that they know and understand their velocity for effective planning, commitment, and delivery
- Ensure that the team is making its sprint status visible
- Help the product owner gather data in order to understand and publish release status
- Escalate obstacles in a timely fashion so that they're quickly resolved
- Keep track of obstacles that haven't been resolved; revisit at a later, perhaps more appropriate time

- Alert management to the costs of lingering obstacles, when possible
- Work with the team and product owners (possibly collaborate with additional teams) to devise a release plan that is workable, flexible, and amenable to the business:
  - ○ Create baseline for a number of sprints
  - ○ Reports on release and release burndown

Supporting and living the Scrum core values

In every class I teach or every team I coach, people consistently say how they've discovered a newfound respect and understanding for the ScrumMaster role. This is especially so when discussing the courage a ScrumMaster must have to live the Scrum values when the rest of the organization does not. A ScrumMaster:

- Displays openness with every action. No hidden agendas. Good, bad, and ugly news is treated equally.
- Is respectful of others, even in questionable situations.
- Has courage, not afraid to speak up for the team, the project, and the customer; respects people but is not intimidated by them.
- Meets commitments—does what he or she says he/she will do
- Understands the importance of focus so that the team may finish sprint goals

Educating others

The ScrumMaster educates others about Scrum and the deficiencies in the old way of doing things. He must contend with entrenched thinking, fear, and anger until people begin to understand new possibilities as potential realities. The ScrumMaster:

- Realizes that he is first and foremost a *change agent*—someone who is not afraid to challenge the old ways for the sake of improving process, influencing better outcomes, and enriching people's lives.
- Schedules training for various people—team training, product owner training, manager training—so that everyone in the organization is aware of what Scrum is and knowledgeable of how to support teams.

- Finds additional teaching opportunities via running the sprint—every meeting, every backlog session, and so on. Sees the opportunity to teach others about Agile practices and mind-set.

- May find himself challenging traditional human resources practices to align them with a newer, more agile way of working.

- Regularly challenges the team and the organization to find its own solutions rather than provide the solutions himself/herself.

Improving personal skills and characteristics

A ScrumMaster must be intelligent, technology-minded, tactful, resourceful, and creative. He/she must be able to take in and respond to criticism and feedback, continually working to improve skills and enhance personal characteristics. The ScrumMaster is self-critical and vanity less, comfortable with not taking the credit for a team's success, but willingly takes the blame for a team's failures. The ScrumMaster knows that a happy team and happy customer are the two best measurements of his or her effectiveness and works hard to achieve this in every team scenario.

B

ScrumMaster's Workshop

This Appendix should be used as a companion as you read the book. As you go through each chapter, refer this section for additional questions and exercises to help you discover areas for future focus or improvement. You may also download this as a PDF at `packtpub.com`.

Chapter 1: Scrum – A Brief Review of the Basics (and a Few Interesting Tidbits)

1. Explain the four pillars of Scrum and how they are interrelated.

2. Describe an empirical process. How do the Scrum meetings, artifacts, and roles support empiricism?

3. What happens when a Scrum meeting is dropped? What are the consequences or impacts when an artifact like the sprint backlog is missing?

4. What makes your organization, your project, and your team complex?

5. Which of the five Scrum core values (commitment, openness, respect, focus, courage) will be most challenging for you to personally adopt? Why?

6. Which Scrum core value will your team be particularly challenged by? Why?

7. Which Scrum core value will your organization be particularly challenged by? Why?

8. Why should a sprint length, once determined, never be changed?

9. Why is it so important that team members are not interrupted during a sprint?

10. Is your team ready for Scrum? Why or why not?

Chapter 2: Release Planning – Tuning Product Development

1. Congratulations! Last weekend, you and your significant other decided to get married and agreed upon a date two years from now, which gives you plenty of time to plan (and save some money!). What level of planning would you engage in today? Conceptual, like maybe a *Star Wars theme* or *which venue should we visit*, or detailed, like *the bride should wear pink toenail polish and her hair in braids*. Consider your initial planning approach, followed by more detailed levels of planning that you'd engage in as the wedding approaches. What information emerges through time? How does this affect your plan? Is the word "plan" more usefully thought of as a noun or a verb? Why?

2. Think back to a recent *surprise* on a project that you were involved with. Was it preventable? Would thinking longer and harder about the problem have unearthed the issue sooner? Are all surprises avoidable? How does Agile say that teams should deal with surprises, via avoidance or embracement?

3. Your senior architect is not very fond of moving to an Agile way of working. He balks and verbally resists Scrum in every meeting. He is concerned that attention to good architecture will be traded in for *cowboy* coding and hacks. How do you involve him in the team's discussions, yet not let his all-or-nothing approach hinder progress?

4. How do story points and hours differ? How would you explain using both to a reluctant team? (This will happen, so please don't skip this question!)

5. **General tip**: For all meetings, create scripts and agendas that keep things moving, ideally with as much team involvement as possible. Prior to the meeting, construct a storyboard of the meeting and identify what the *actors* will do in each scene, along with the necessary inputs and expected outcomes of each action. These scenes in your meeting storyboard provide an excellent start to your agenda and help you visualize your meeting as a movie ahead of time; this is a great use of your imagination to help you create a tangible, workable agenda!

Chapter 3: Sprint Planning – Fine-tune the Sprint Commitment

1. The project manager and the marketing manager are arguing in front of the technical team about the importance and order of product backlog items. They've decided to combine their most important needs and have stated that they have 50 *critical* items among which the team may choose which to deliver in the upcoming sprint. What is wrong with this picture? How might you handle the situation?

2. What tool does your product owner utilize for backlog management? Is the product backlog visible? Can anyone contribute to it? Does everyone know who the product owner is and what his/her responsibilities are? If the answer is no to any of these questions, please put an item on your Impediment Backlog to discuss and resolve this impediment.

3. Let's say that your team suggested that instead of tasking stories out during sprint planning, they would rather individually send you their tasks before the sprint planning meeting in order to save time. This way you can just total up the tasks and hours for the team and let them know in the meeting if they are over or under capacity. They are excited about the time savings of this approach, but you have reservations about this. What do you tell the team?

4. Please see the Sprint Planning Checklist in *Chapter 3, Sprint Planning – Fine-tune the Sprint Commitment*. What steps would you expect that you could alleviate over time, given that your team remains the same sprint after sprint? What general ideas do you have to keep meetings light, focused, and efficient?

5. During sprint planning, one of the team members wants to reprioritize stories because of some logical technical dependencies. What should the team do?

6. You are interested to know if the team have reached consensus on the plan, so you ask the team their opinions. All the team members feel confident except for John, who is concerned as he feels the team has selected an amount of work that might turn out to be too much for the sprint time box. What can you do to help John feel comfortable about the proposed sprint commitment?

7. While the team is tasking out the work, you overhear a lead developer assume that the feature should function a certain way, and then instructs everyone in the team accordingly. What is wrong with this situation, and how might you fix it on the spot?

8. Are you a good facilitator? A good facilitator:
   - Understands the team, its lingo and jargon, behaviors, and history.
   - Creates a sense of safety; that is, everyone is free to speak his/her mind in a space that will kindly receive it. "Together, with everyone's participation, we can come up with an outcome better than what one person could create. Nobody will be talked down to, and there will be no condescending behavior."
   - Is like the Switzerland of the meeting, remaining neutral but not afraid to stop bad behavior or layer on knowledge. This does not mean to choose sides, but rather to make information and data available that might help the team reach a conclusion.
   - Spends adequate time preparing for the meeting, creating scripts, agendas, games, ice breakers — anything necessary to help the team meet the goal.
   - Has an arsenal of tricks and skills to pull on at any given moment should the meeting's attendees need a perk or conflict resolution.
   - Is skilled in conflict resolution.
   - Creates tools to help team members remember action items (clean up).
   - Does not cut off people as they are speaking, or finish others' sentences, or make decisions on behalf of the team.

9. See Jean Tabaka's *Collaboration Explained* for more wonderful tips, tricks, agendas, and ideas.

Chapter 4: Sprint! Valuable, Collaborative, and Meaningful Work

1. Are your team members dedicated to the team sprint after sprint? If not, add an item to your **impediments backlog (IBL)**.

2. Is the team made up of multiple disciplines so that they may deliver a set of fully tested features by the end of each sprint? If not, add an item to your IBL.

3. Is your Scrum team Scrummerfalling, or doing some other weird form of Scrum? If so, add this item to your IBL and think about the discussion you'd like to have with the team in the next retrospective. Specifically, are they doing a Scrum hybrid due to a true constraint or an organizational dysfunction? Is a broader discussion necessary with management? How will you prepare for that discussion?

4. Do you manage or direct the daily scrum meetings? What can you do to stop this? Are the team members getting into deep enough detail to truly synchronize? If not, how can you help? Are they going into too much detail? If so, how do you help them? Are they making obstacles known, or are they too shy? What can you do about this if you suspect they're not forthcoming with issues? Are team members willing to help each other solve their issues/impediments? If not, how can you encourage this behavior?

5. Let's say that your organization does not have a trusting culture. How might you utilize the Scrum meetings to build such a culture? Are there any action items that you can come up with after thinking about this?

6. Which of the four corporate culture adjectives— Collaborative, Creative, Competitive, Controlling—best describe your organization?

7. If the organization does not value openness, respect, commitment, focus, and courage, how might this impact your team? What will you do about this? How will you tangibly know that you've made an impact on the organization's values?

8. To what degree can you influence your peers, your team, your product owner, your manager, your VP, and your CEO? Which style might you choose to influence each type of co-worker (consider: demand, demonstrate, request, persuade, avoid).

9. Which of the four legs of Scrum—self-managing, dedicated teams; time-boxing (sprints); prioritized product backlog; or inspect/adapt—will be most difficult to implement in your organization? Why?

Chapter 5: The End? Improving Product and Process One Bite at a Time

1. Discuss with your team: what do they need to do in order to prepare for the sprint review? Would they like a practice run? Do they know who's demonstrating what? What were the big issues in the sprint that might be worth mentioning? What does your script look like?

2. How would you go about preparing your product owner for the sprint review? What if he/she is not available to attend?

3. What do you feel is the single most important metric to give at the sprint review? Why?

4. You notice that your team is unhappy because stakeholders asked for changes in the functionality as a result of the sprint review. You, on the other hand, are quite happy about this. Why is there a disconnect between you and the team? What do you feel they're most concerned about?

5. What observations did you make about the team during the sprint? When do you feel would be the right time to bring up your observations? Put yourself in the shoes of the team member as you consider the answer to this question.

6. What if part of your team is offshore and follows a command-and-control culture; therefore, they are terrified of speaking up in the retrospective? What can you do to help them feel safe to speak up?

7. After a few retrospectives with your team, you've noticed that one team member is especially profound with his ideas for change. That is, he has some great ideas, but most of them probably won't pass muster with the rest of the organization. How do you keep him engaged and speaking up even though most of his ideas are too *progressive* for everyone else? You certainly don't want to shut him down!

Chapter 6: The Criticality of Real-time Information

1. A vision exercise. I like Geoffrey Moore's vision statement from *Crossing the Chasm*. One way to make sure everyone on the project team gets the Level 1 magnification is to hand them each a blank sheet of paper and ask them to write the vision statement; it's fine for team members to pair up or work in small teamlets of three. After 15 minutes have each pair/teamlet read its version of the vision statement. Responses that are similar reflect a good communication and understanding; vastly different responses signify that the vision should be revisited. What natural opportunities are there for restating the project vision throughout the Scrum project? When might the vision need to change? What happens when there is no vision statement? (Note, if you do not currently have a vision statement for your team's project, please add this to your impediment backlog as something that should be resolved with the product owner as soon as possible. If you do not have a product owner, that's another item for your list with an action to find a proxy at least for the short term.)

2. How can you ensure that the product vision stays visible and fresh in every team member's mind?

3. What do you do if the product owner does not have a vision statement? To whom might this issue need to be escalated? What specific actions can be taken to ensure that the team has a well-stated vision?

4. Referring to the Gantt chart view in this chapter, would this be necessary for every team and every project? In which situations would it not be applicable? Is this a view you would want to provide?

5. The team wants to add tasks to the product backlog. What's wrong with this idea?

6. The product owner is frustrated that the team says, "We only do release planning for three months into the future because we're Agile." The product owner needs a forecast for eight months in order to win a contract. What can you do? What are the pros and cons of planning so far ahead and basing a monetary exchange off of this plan?

7. When might a team not need a sprint burndown chart?

8. Let's say that your team likes the idea of a 55" LED monitor in the team room to project their sprint metrics and your manager approved budget for it. But the team is worrying too much about the *perfect* set of metrics causing them to stall out on making anything visible at all. Which one or two bits of information would you encourage them to start with? How would you ensure that the job gets done?

9. Scrum focuses more on real-time broadcasting versus distributing reports; however, which reports (the static kind) might be helpful in your environment?

10. How might you kick off the Management Scrum or WORST (Waste and Obstacle Removal Scrum Team)?

Chapter 7: Scrum Values Expose Fear, Dysfunction, and Waste

1. How does the Definition of Done incite organizational change? Cross-functional, dedicated teams? Product backlog? The role of the ScrumMaster?

2. Are you a ScrumMaster by mistake, choice, or design? Did you realize just how important the role of the ScrumMaster is? Do you think you can carry out the responsibilities of this role?

3. What are your personal strengths that will aid you in the role of ScrumMaster?

4. What are your weaknesses? Can you add these to your impediment backlog in the personal category so that you can work on them? How will you know that you've successfully conquered these weaknesses?

5. What personal convictions do you repeatedly compromise at work? Why? How does this make you feel? What is the ultimate consequence of this compromise? What can you do about it?

6. Run a *waste* exercise with your managers; if you're unsure about this, practice it with the team. Use the waste worksheet from this chapter to quantify the wastes in traditional software development as a template. Put dollar signs to the final numbers. Shoot holes in it. Is this something you might feel comfortable presenting to management? If you're really feeling courageous, give the department a waste score (from *Chapter 9, Shaping the Agile Organization*)

7. What is initially costly about moving to a dedicated, cross-functional team model? What are the benefits gained from these costs?

8. Do you have a "personal board of directors"—people whom you trust to give advice that will help you reach your goals? If not, put a list together. Approach each person with why you'd like their mentorship, the goals that you have for yourself, along with your initial plans to get there. Ask if they can agree to check in with you once a month to give feedback, criticism, and suggested next steps

9. Tell your story and suggest that team members do the same. As you begin to make progress and see a shining light at the end of the tunnel, ask the team if anyone would be interested to present their story at an Agile conference. There are many smaller groups (as well as international events!) both in person and virtual that love to hear success stories. This can be very motivating for teams!

10. When's the last time you said "no"? When is the next time you might be able to? Can you commit to saying it?

11. When is the next time you can serve your team? Maybe it's by bringing snacks to the next meeting, standing up and facilitating, helping the team drive to a resolution. Identify the next opportunity, put it in your calendar, and commit to do it.

Have you self-actualized? Review the checklist in *Chapter 9, Shaping the Agile Organization*. Answer each on a scale of 1 to 5 (1: barely satisfies; 5: completely satisfies). If your total is between 44-55, you are in the self-actualizing zone. If your total is around 11-20, you have some work to do today. Highlight the lowest-scoring attributes and pick one to start on today. Write them all in your impediment backlog in the personal category and seek opportunities to practice these characteristics. Sometimes the best way to create permanent and lasting change is to fake it until you make it!

12. When you feel comfortable, have a heart-to-heart talk with your team about your department's performance review process. What works well? What hinders people? What suggestions do you have for improvement? Then, talk to other ScrumMasters. Put together a formal proposal for managers and HR for changes in the performance review system that would enable higher performance and risk-taking in individuals and teams. Start from the ground up.

Chapter 8: Everyday Leadership for the ScrumMaster and Team

1. What's your personality style? Go out and take the Meyers-Briggs assessment if you haven't already. Which traits will help you as a ScrumMaster? Which traits might hinder you?

2. Talk with others. Get feedback about your performance during meetings with respect to your verbal and written styles, effectiveness of communication. See if you can tease out criticism and areas for improvement. Don't forget to celebrate the things that you do well.

3. Set up a bi-weekly leadership meeting with fellow ScrumMasters. Identify books to read, blogs to follow, things to try. Report back to each other, critique each other, help each other improve.

4. When you feel threatened, what makes you feel this way? Is it a person? A communication style? A situation that brings out feelings of inadequacy? Once you've identified the trigger for your feeling, try to pinpoint why you feel this way. Are you afraid of losing? Appearing dumb? What reasons do you have for feeling intimidated in certain situations? Are these reasons legitimate? Even if they are, there must be one thing you can do to start to change the situation. Maybe it's your reaction. Identify and practice it.

5. Pay attention to what you say for one week. Write down every statement that you make that has a negative twist. Evaluate this at the end of one week; did you have many? Did these tend to fall within the same categories?

6. Do you have a Scrum buddy? Get one if not?

Chapter 9: Shaping the Agile Organization

1. Where does your loyalty lie? Are you dedicated to your team and team members' happiness or are you too worried about what your manager thinks?

2. How can you get management to accept that a Scrum team makes its own rules and essentially governs itself? What if management cannot accept this?

3. Are your team members able to focus? Or are they being pulled in too many directions?

4. Are you completely focused on your team? Laptops closed, mobile phone off? Undivided attention? Observe yourself. Give your team your full attention; ask them to respect each other and do the same. If the meetings are taking too long, discuss ways of shortening.

5. When is the next opportunity for you to share something with your team that they may not expect? Maybe it's something you learned from a management meeting that you feel your team might be interested to know. Perhaps the product owner keeps stopping by your desk to discuss user stories and you feel the team might like to be pulled into that conversation. Start breaking down barriers to visibility and free communication. Identify these small opportunities that make large strides in openness and trust.

Chapter 10: Scrum – Large and Small

1. Do you feel that if you're truly performing the role of the ScrumMaster that you would have time for more than one team? Under what circumstances might you?

2. Let's say you have a team of 13 people, each with a very narrow specialty. Scrum is causing difficulty as the team seems too large. What other alternatives are there?

3. How does a product owner ensure that quality is good when there are multiple teams involved in developing one product? What's the ScrumMaster's role in this?

4. Who attends your Scrum of Scrum meeting? Based on what you've learned in *Chapter 9, Shaping the Agile Organization*, is this the right set of attendees?

5. Does your team or teams have a Definition of Done? If not, please find the next immediate time to discuss this

Index

Symbols

1x magnification 146, 147
2x magnification 147, 148
4x magnification
  about 149
  baseline, with updates 151, 152
  burndown baseline 150
  Gantt chart, in agile project 153
  team velocity chart 152, 153
8x magnification
  about 154
  user, requisites 154, 155
16x magnification
  about 155
  acceptance criteria 156
  user stories, in sprint planning 155
32x magnification
  about 158
  burns 163
  daily broadcasts 158
  daily scrums 158, 159
  sprint backlogs 159, 160
  sprint burndown chart 160, 162
64x magnification 164

A

action items
  assigning 132
  prioritizing 132
actual velocity 152
Adkins, Lyssa
  URL 109
agenda 65

Agile 232, 233
Agile Acceptance 178
Agile, culture change
  Agile mind-set, scaling 241
  Agile organization chart 239, 240
  Agile organization, traditional roles 241
  multi-faceted approach, need for 236
  need for 236, 237
  pre-agility survey 237, 238
  roles matrix 239, 240
  waste score 238
Agile Manifesto
  about 278, 279
  URL 175
Agile method 8, 9
Agile organization
  Scrum values 234, 235
  shaping 231, 308
  traditional roles 241
Agile organization chart 239, 240
agreeableness, five big factors 104
Alhazen
  URL 10
anyone task 75
appreciations 220
Atari 11
ATDD 97

B

barstool 14, 15
big scrum 257
Bossy Betty 227
broadcasts 144
Brooks, Fred 202

Bruce M. Tharp
  URL 106
Bruce Tuckmans model
  URL 109

C

calendars 76
capacity planning worksheet 70-73
Carl 227
Carolyn Snyder
  website, URL 55
commitment, Scrum values
  about 182-184
  Expert-to-Task (ETT model) 185-187
  issues 190, 191
  Team-to-Backlog (TTB model) 187-189
communication
  about 143
  broadcasts 144
  Face-to-face 144
  reports 144
conscientiousness, five big factors 102
continuous adaptation 30
continuous flow frameworks
  sprint reviews for 124
control 142
corporate culture
  about 106
  empowerment, fear 107
  team, assumptions about management 107
courage, Scrum values 181
creative culture 286-289
crystal-balling 30
customer collaboration
  via prioritized product backlog 283

D

daily scrum
  about 146
  meeting 21, 92, 94
  meeting, permission for attending 98
  meeting, questions 94-98
done
  defining 51, 157

E

E flat 32
epics 61
Estimatable 61
estimated velocity 152
Evan Robinson
  URL 73
everyday leadership 203, 204
expert tasks 74
Expert-to-Task (ETT model) 185-187
extroversion, five big factors 103

F

Face-to-face 144
five big factors
  agreeableness 104
  conscientiousness 102
  extroversion 103
  neuroticism 104
  openness 101
Five Factor Model (FFM) 101
five personality test
  URL 104
focus, Scrum values 197-199
foie gras 258
Food and Drug Administration (FDA) 26

G

Gantt chart
  in agile project 153
Gut method 48

H

Henrik Kniberg
  URL 259

I

IKIWISI (I know it when I see it) 123
impediments backlog (IBL) 302, 303
Independent 60

Independent, Negotiable, Valuable,
  Estimatable, Small, and Testable.
    See **INVEST**
INTJ 206
intrapreneurs 280
Intrapreneur's Ten Commandments 283
INVEST 48, 60, 61

J

Jeff Anderson's post
  URL 238
Jeff Sutherland
  blog, URL 246
Jeff Sutherland's Scrum Handbook
  URL 28

K

Kanban
  URL 109
Kanban board 91
KSSSHK (Ken Schwaber Scrum School of
  Hard Knocks) 258

L

Ladas, Corey
  URL 109
large Scrum 273
leader
  features 209
  feedback, receiving 210
  honesty, with team 212
  portrait 209
  Theory X 211
  Theory Y 211
  trust, building 210, 211
leadership frameworks
  URL 229
LEAN meeting 117
Legacy Scrum 57
lines of code (LOC) 261

M

Martin Fowler
  URL 270

Myers-Briggs
  URL 229

N

Negotiable 60
neuroticism, five big factors 104
New Product Blog item 38
Nintendo Entertainment System (NES) 11
norming phase 105

O

Objectives and Key Results (OKR) 243
obstacle
  removal 169-173
Officer Sophie 228
openness, five big factors 101
openness, Scrum values 191-196
organization
  capacity 282
  career paths 281
  innovations, space for 284, 285
  role, defining 279
  teams, self managing 280
  true visibility 282

P

personality
  self-awareness 206-208
  traits 205, 206
physical
  taskboards 167
physical space 62
Plan-Do-Check-Act (PDCA) 9
planned velocity 152
Prezi
  URL 118
product
  adapting 113, 114
  demos 289
  inspecting 113, 114
  reviews 289
product backlog
  about 23, 32, 33
  on user 34

on value 34
project portfolio backlog, example 37, 38
team, early engagement 36, 37
product backlog items (PBIs) 35
product owner
about 18, 19
acceptance 114
contacting to 61, 62
need for 115
project Grand Poobah 271, 272
project management office (PMO) 239

R

REAL action items 132, 133
Real-Time Information 304, 305
release planning
about 22, 39, 300
agenda 47, 48
and releases timing 39
buffers, making visible 41-43
event, conducting 44, 46
Gut method 48
Independent, Negotiable, Valuable,
    Estimatable, Small, and Testable
    (INVEST) 48
meeting, facilitating 46
output 51-54
participants 46
physical space 49, 50
summary 54, 55
reports
about 144
creating 168
distributing 168
research and development 287
respect, Scrum values 200, 201
retrospective
and review 136-138
future, visualizing 134
team cave art 135
techniques 133
yoga/meditation 136
Rework Bin 260
roles matrix 239, 240

S

scenery
changing 134
scratchpad 65
script 65
Scrum
about 10, 58, 299
artifacts 22
avoiding 249
challenges 257-270
core values 15, 16
elements, checklist 27
large 308
microscope 145
product owner 19
roles 18
small 308
team 18, 255, 256
team, working 84
values 178-180, 305, 306
values, low scoring 235
values, of organization 234
SCRUM 127, 128
Scrum artifacts
product backlog 23
sprint backlog and burn down 24, 25
Scrumban system 257
Scrum-ban write-up
URL 109
Scrum barstool. *See* **barstool**
Scrum framework
about 20
daily scrum, meeting 21
release planning 22
sprint backlog 20
sprint, retrospective 22
sprint review, meeting 21
ScrumMaster
about 7, 19, 58, 83, 108
core knowledge 292
core values, supporting 296
desired state, visualizing 214-216
educating others 296, 297
empowerment 213, 214

features 212
high-performing scrum team,
  creating 294, 295
influencing others 216, 217
personal skills and characteristics,
  improving 297
product owner, assisting 294
progress visibility, creating 295, 296
responsibilities 292
role 291
sprint, running 293
ScrumMaster, characteristics
about 224
journal/walk up a hill 226
procrastinator or proactive 224
scrum buddy 226
student 225
teacher 225
ScrumMaster, communication style
direct versus passive 222, 223
loud or quiet 221, 222
Switzerland or Supreme Court judge 223
ScrumMaster, Persona
Bossy Betty 227
Carl 227
Officer Sophie 228
Techie Taj 226
Thundering Thea 228
ScrumMasters 289, 290
Scrum microscope
about 145, 146
Level 1x magnification 146, 147
Level 2x magnification 147, 148
Level 4x magnification 149
Level 8x magnification 154
Level 16x magnification 155
Level 32x magnification 158
Level 64x magnification 164
summary 165-167
Scrum, roles
product owner 18
ScrumMaster 18
Scrum team 18
Scrum team 18
Scrum, values
about 178-180
commitment 182-184

courage 181
focus 197, 198
openness 191-196
respect 200, 201
Scrum village 100
Scrum website
URL 12
self-actualizing
about 242
CEO scorecard 247
common traits, by Maslow 242, 243
measurements, standardizing 245, 246
motivating 243
motivating, reasons finding 244
multi-perspective feedback 246, 247
**Serious Crud Required by Upper
  Management.** *See* **SCRUM**
Small 61
small scrum 255, 256
sprint
about 86, 87, 111
backlogs 159, 160
burndown chart 160-163
definiton of done 69
goals 157
planning 32
product backlog item 99
retrospective 22, 126, 127
reviews 158
working in 85
sprint backlog 20
sprint buffering 76
sprint events 130
sprint planning
about 57, 59, 301, 302
improving 81
meetings 59
preparing for 60
sample checklist 78, 79
sprint planning meeting
agenda 65
High-octane stories 60, 61
physical space 62
product owner, preparing for 61, 62
scratchpad 65
script 65
visualizing 63, 64

sprint planning meeting, running
  about 67
  anyone task 75
  calendars 76
  capacity planning worksheet 70-72
  committing 80, 81
  expert tasks 74
  How 70
  sprint buffering 76
  sprint tasks, identifying 73
  stories, types 69, 70
  team members interaction 77
  What and Why 67, 68
sprint retrospective 22
sprint review
  about 117
  context, setting 118
  for continuous flow frameworks 124
  meeting 21
  outcomes 123, 124
  prior to 115-117
  stories, keeping straight 119, 120
  time for collaboration and trust 125, 126
  visual, giving 118
Stacey Matrix 12
Stacia Viscardi's Scrum website
  URL 28
stakeholders 168
state of evolution 177
string 31

T

Team-to-Backlog (TTB model) 187-189
Techie Taj 226
Testable 61
Theory X 211
Theory Y 211
thimblerig 254
Thundering Thea 228
Time to Market (TTM) 263
Toyota Production System (TPS) 273, 274
traditional project
  metrics 29

U

user stories 61
UXPins
  URL 36

V

Valuable 61
vanity and ego
  differences, URL 229
VARK 93
velocity 152
Visual-Aural-Read/Write-Kinesthetic.
    See **VARK**
VPN 96

W

waste
  removal 169-173
waterfall model 88
Weight Watchers 58
work
  estimating 89, 90
work breakdown structures (WBS) 227

X

Xavier Quesada Allue's Visual
    Management Blog
  URL 82

Thank you for buying
The Professional ScrumMaster's Handbook

About Packt Publishing

Packt, pronounced 'packed', published its first book "Mastering phpMyAdmin for Effective MySQL Management" in April 2004 and subsequently continued to specialize in publishing highly focused books on specific technologies and solutions.

Our books and publications share the experiences of your fellow IT professionals in adapting and customizing today's systems, applications, and frameworks. Our solution based books give you the knowledge and power to customize the software and technologies you're using to get the job done. Packt books are more specific and less general than the IT books you have seen in the past. Our unique business model allows us to bring you more focused information, giving you more of what you need to know, and less of what you don't.

Packt is a modern, yet unique publishing company, which focuses on producing quality, cutting-edge books for communities of developers, administrators, and newbies alike. For more information, please visit our website: www.packtpub.com.

About Packt Enterprise

In 2010, Packt launched two new brands, Packt Enterprise and Packt Open Source, in order to continue its focus on specialization. This book is part of the Packt Enterprise brand, home to books published on enterprise software – software created by major vendors, including (but not limited to) IBM, Microsoft and Oracle, often for use in other corporations. Its titles will offer information relevant to a range of users of this software, including administrators, developers, architects, and end users.

Writing for Packt

We welcome all inquiries from people who are interested in authoring. Book proposals should be sent to author@packtpub.com. If your book idea is still at an early stage and you would like to discuss it first before writing a formal book proposal, contact us; one of our commissioning editors will get in touch with you.

We're not just looking for published authors; if you have strong technical skills but no writing experience, our experienced editors can help you develop a writing career, or simply get some additional reward for your expertise.

Ext JS 4 Web Application Development Cookbook

ISBN: 978-1-84951-686-0   Paperback: 488 pages

Over 110 easy-to-follow recipes backed up with real-life example, walking you through basic Ext JS features to advanced application design using sencha's Ext JS

1. Learn how to build Rich Internet Applications with the latest version of the Ext JS framework in a cookbook style

2. From creating forms to theming your interface, you will learn the building blocks for developing the perfect web application

3. Easy to follow recipes step through practical and detailed examples which are all fully backed up with code, illustrations, and tips

Appcelerator Titanium: Patterns and Best Practices

ISBN: 978-1-84969-348-6   Paperback: 110 pages

Take your Titanium development experience to the next level, and build your Titanium knowledge on CommonJS sturcturing, MVC model implementation, memory management, and much more

1. Full step-by-step approach to help structure your apps in an MVC style that will make them more maintainable, easier to code and more stable

2. Learn best practices and optimizations both related directly to JavaScript and Titanium itself

3. Learn solutions to create cross-compatible layouts that work across both Android and the iPhone

Please check **www.PacktPub.com** for information on our titles

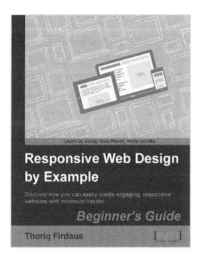

Responsive Web Design by Example

ISBN: 978-1-84969-542-8   Paperback: 338 pages

Discover how you can easily create engaging, responsive websites with minimum hassle!

1. Rapidly develop and prototype responsive websites by utilizing powerful open source frameworks

2. Focus less on the theory and more on results, with clear step-by-step instructions, previews, and examples to help you along the way

3. Learn how you can utilize three of the most powerful responsive frameworks available today: Bootstrap, Skeleton, and Zurb Foundation

ElasticSearch Server

ISBN: 978-1-84951-844-4   Paperback: 318 pages

Create a fast, scalable, and flexible, and search solution with the emerging open source search server, ElasticSearch

1. Learn the basics of ElasticSearch like data indexing, analysis, and dynamic mapping

2. Query and filter ElasticSearch for more accurate and precise search results

3. Learn how to monitor and manage ElasticSearch clusters and troubleshoot any problems that arise

Please check **www.PacktPub.com** for information on our titles

62364253R00187

Made in the USA
Lexington, KY
05 April 2017